Roots *of our* FAITH

Chuck & Karen Cohen

"...I worship the God of my fathers, believing all things
which are written in the Law and in the Prophets."
Acts 24:14

CFI Jerusalem
PUBLISHING

Published by CFI Jerusalem Publishing

ISBN: 965-90458-0-8

Printed in Israel by AHVA Printers, Jerusalem, Israel

Poem page ii by Karen Cohen
Cover design by Norma Megson & Karen Cohen

How to Order

Copies may be ordered from Christian Friends of Israel
P.O. Box 1813 Jerusalem 91015, ISRAEL
Tel: 972-2-6264172 • Fax: 972-2-6264955
e-mail: cfi@cfijerusalem.org

Visit us at: www.cfijerusalem.org

בשבילו

Acknowledgements

We praise God for the influence of His priceless grace and mercy in our lives, initially through the prayers of the Graziano family, when our eyes were opened to the call and claim of Yeshua. Their love for us and their open arms provoked us to jealousy.

Our former congregation in the USA, *Temple Aron haKodesh*, pastored for many years by Yosef and Marty Koelner, friends we don't see often enough, has been faithfully supportive in many ways. In the same category are Neil and Jamie Lash, and all the *Jewish Jewels*, who have personally stood with us and helped us with their time, energy, and resources - a real *mishpacha*! And we certainly thank our present congregation, *King of Kings Assembly*, Pastor Wayne Hilsden, his wife Ann and family, and the faithful staff for their love, encouragement, and prayers.

Many thanks to *Christian Friends of Israel's* Ray and Sharon Sanders for having the vision with us for *Roots*, for making our books possible, and for delicately balancing their desire to redeem the time with their patience. Thanks also to their faithful co-laborers, especially Norma Megson, who "got it all together." We are grateful to Marita Brokenshaw for her availability to share her expertise and experience gained from the first time around. We have not forgotten Liz Baxter, who, with Marita, did so much work on our first book. Thanks also to Coral Mings for much proof-reading. There are others we appreciate for their contribution in other ways - like Walter C. Kaiser Jr. whose teaching and books became an influential part of this book – in fact spurred us on to look more deeply at the importance of solid theology.

We love and appreciate our two sons, Michael and Jedidiah who had to live with us while we worked on this book. Reparations aside, they deserve a huge thanks for continuing to love, pray for, and support us though the process.

Finally, thank You, Yeshua, precious Messiah and Lord, for bringing us to your holy city and putting in our hearts and the hearts of all of these friends and family the desire to provoke our people to jealousy.

Foreword

Little Hebraic influence remains in the Church today because of replacement theology. Many gentile believers think of Christianity as a replacement for Judaism and that "Jewish roots" are unimportant. On the contrary, everything the Church possesses today has come through the Jewish people.

The Cohens' *Roots of our Faith* will help us recover the spiritual connection between the Church and Israel by restoring knowledge of Christianity's *biblical* roots. Theologically sound, *Roots of our Faith* will help believers who want to build a solid and more mature Messiah-centered life. We know that believers who read it will be challenged to deepen their relationship with the God of Israel.

In the Bible, Ruth is a portrait showing what our relationship with Israel should be. God forbid that the Church follows the way of Orpah, who parted from Naomi (Israel). Like Ruth we must cling to Naomi (Israel and our biblical roots) or forfeit many spiritual blessings in our lives and in the life of the Church worldwide.

As you read and study this book, know that around the world many others also will be rediscovering and reclaiming their biblical foundations. One of the greatest moves of the Holy Spirit in the Church now is a preparation for the restoration of all things - a preparation for restoring a biblical understanding of the foundations of our faith.

Ray and Sharon Sanders, Directors
Christian Friends of Israel - Jerusalem

Messianic terms used:

Messiah = Christ
Yeshua = Jesus
Tanach = Old Testament

Unless otherwise noted, all scripture quotations are from the Authorized King James Version of the Bible.

Some words and phrases within quoted scriptures have been bolded for emphasis. Bracketed words within quoted scriptures are the authors'.

Contents

Introduction

Chuck was on a plane heading for an Israel conference at Christ For the Nations Institute in Dallas, Texas. The Lord said something like this to him, "When you have finished teaching, someone will ask you where you studied, what seminary you went to, and what books you have read to be able to see the Scriptures in the way that you do. Here is what you are to say."

After Chuck's first teaching session, a young man did approach him, asking those very questions. Chuck replied, "You're the one God told me about. Here is what He said I should answer you: I simply read the Bible from the beginning!"

Many believers covertly think that their Bibles start with Matthew. They may give lip service to the fact that the Old Testament is part of the Word of God, but if they really believed in its validity for today, the major deception known as "replacement theology"[1] would not be rampant in the Church. In the second century the Church officially cut herself off from anything Jewish. Since then a dangerous mixture of truth and error has ruled over its theology.

We look at Scriptures differently from many believers. Chuck is Jewish. After Yeshua revealed Himself to him, he needed assurance that what he now believed about the Messiah of Israel lined up with the Scriptures of Israel, the *Tanach*. Many believers

---

[1]Replacement theology results from the pride about which Paul warned gentile believers in Romans 11. Its adherents believe that national Israel has been replaced by the Church which now inherits all blessings as the people of God, while Israel inherits the curses. Under this thought the only way that a Jew could have any relationship with the God of (spiritual) Israel, that is, with the God of the Church, would be if he or she becomes a Christian and foregoes every Jewish tradition.

have been taught to interpret the Old Testament through the filter of the New. But we interpret the New Testament through the filter of the Old. This is what Yeshua, His disciples, Paul and the first century Body of Messiah did. They had no choice – all they had was the *Tanach* to prove that what they were saying was of God.

After making *aliyah* (immigrating to Israel) and living in a restored Jerusalem in the resurrected nation of Israel, we trust in the God of Israel's Word from Genesis onward. Our theological stance is holistic. We are not New Testament believers – we are Bible believers. Our Bible starts at Genesis and goes to the end of the book of Revelation.

Yet we do recognize the truth of progressive revelation. Often, what God reveals later in the Scriptures, especially in the New Testament, throws more light on the *Tanach*. But it does not conflict with it. God does not change or decide that "Plan A" won't work. The Lord is omniscient and knows everything in advance. His plan is prepared from beginning to end - He doesn't have to change. In fact He states this in the *Tanach: "For I am the LORD, I change not; therefore ye sons of Jacob are not consumed"* (Mal 3:6).

The New Testament brings clarity to certain things which were declared beforehand. Chuck saw a wonderful analogy of this while sitting outside on a partly cloudy day. He was looking at a faint shadow cast by a tree. Then the sun broke through and the shadow of the tree became so sharp that he could distinguish even the outlines of individual leaves.

Parts of the Old Testament (especially the rituals and feasts of the Law) were shadows of the good things that were to come (Col 2:17; Heb 8:5; 10:1). But when Messiah Yeshua appeared and finished what His Father assigned to Him, the shadows didn't disappear – in fact, they became clearer, understandable, and edifying.

Our desire as you study this book is that you will become a "Bible" believer and have such deep *Tanach* roots in the Word of God that the various winds of doctrines blowing through the Church in the last days will not be able to uproot you.

"Blessed is the man that walketh not in the counsel of the ungodly, nor standeth in the way of sinners, nor sitteth in the seat of the scornful. But his delight is in the law of the LORD; and in his law doth he meditate day and night. And he shall be like a tree planted by the rivers of water, that bringeth forth his fruit in his season; his leaf also shall not wither; and whatsoever he doeth shall prosper" (Psa 1:1-3).

Prologue

The ancient Israelites were not famed seafarers like their questing neighbors. Unlike the Phoenicians, Greeks, Egyptians, and Romans, who navigated, explored, and settled frontiers on three continents, the Israelites had already entered their Promised Land.

Thousands of years after Noah, the gentiles, busy conquering the earth and paganizing the world, would hear a call from that Promised Land. This call would lead them on a spiritual journey back to the source of eternal life in the One true God. In the last two thousand years many of them have heeded that call.

We have written this book to encourage and guide all travelers on their way back home. Their journey can be compared to a sea voyage - an appropriate illustration for those ancient mariners' countless offspring, those peoples whose strange-looking craft sail today between planets.

Here is the illustration - something like a parable - based on Psalm 107:23-31.

God did not create man and then leave him like a shipwrecked sailor, clinging to floating debris on an evil sea. He comes alongside and offers to all a berth and provision in His "ark" of safety – the Messiah, who is both ship and Captain.

Although Noah's ark had no rudder or sails, Messiah's ship has both. To fill the sails He has sent His breath – the Holy Spirit. And to steer the ship He has placed in it a crew. But this is no pleasure cruise. No paying passengers wander the decks at their leisure. Everyone who has accepted Messiah's offer to come onboard becomes a member of the crew.

But where is this ship sailing and why? To answer these questions God has safely stowed onboard His maps and compass – the Scriptures. The "+" on the map marks the Tree of Life in the Promised Land. The Captain Himself marked the route in blood-red.

1

As His crew, we are on the most important and demanding quest of all time. The Golden Fleece, the Fountain of Youth, the Holy Grail, the Home Planet – all of them phantoms and shadows. We set course instead for reality, truth, and the eternal. God desires to share these with us.

Because He knows what's good for us, we should take Him seriously, studying the Scriptures to navigate well, obeying the Captain, and learning the ways of the ship. And one day, because of His faithfulness, we will step out into a glorious land and behold in its fulness the Tree of Life everlasting.

However, during our voyage, we only make progress toward that goal by correctly applying what we have learned from our studying the navigational charts and tackling without complaint our sometimes tedious tasks onboard. One of our primary duties, easily crowded out by other things, is to guard the integrity of our ship, making sure it remains water-tight and seaworthy.

This duty is foundational and requires familiarity with the very unique properties of the wood from which our ship is made. We soon discover that the same type of tree which provided the material used to build our ship also provided the material used to make our navigational charts! Would it surprise us also to know that this wood came from the Tree of Life itself? It seems that our means and our goal are one and the same!

So let's begin "learning the ropes" by examining this tree on which our whole quest depends. It is an ancient olive tree, ever green...

PART ONE

Teachings

As members of the Body of Messiah we have a covenant obligation to become established in our faith. Every major teaching of the New Testament has roots deep in the *Tanach*. For a full understanding of these teachings we must dig into their Hebraic soil. Only well nourished by God's complete Word will we stand through the storm.

CHAPTER 1

Is the Old Testament Still the Word of God Today?

In Romans 11[1] the Apostle Paul compared believers in Yeshua to part of an olive tree. Since a tree needs deep roots to withstand strong winds, our community of faith also needs "deep roots". The Holy Scriptures contain warnings of many last days deceptions and "winds" of false doctrines that would blow against the congregation of Yeshua.[2] We need God's complete revelation to strengthen the roots of our faith, in our daily walk as well as our theology, *"that we henceforth be no more children, tossed to and fro, and carried about with every wind of doctrine, by the sleight* [deception] *of men, and cunning craftiness, whereby they lie in wait to deceive"* (Eph 4:14).

If we view ourselves as part of that Romans 11 Olive Tree, then the Spirit of God is the life-bearing sap which brings nourishment and water from our roots in the *Tanach* (Hebrew for the Old Testament) to the fruit-filled branches of believers. A partly uprooted tree is cut off from much of its strength. Sadly, roots without soil mirror the state of much of the organized Church during its history. Many old and resurgent heresies, such as Gnosticism and Replacement "theology" come from a misunderstanding or a misuse of the Word of God in the *Tanach*. Therefore, recognizing the validity of the Old Testament for our walk with God *today* is of the greatest importance to make us scripturally mature – our first line of defense against endtime deception.

Consider that when our Messiah walked the earth, there was no New Testament. When Peter preached to his fellow Jews on the day of Pentecost (*Shavuot*), he preached from the *Tanach*. When Yeshua resisted Satan in the wilderness, He

5

quoted from the "Law of Moses" (Deuteronomy) three times, and the Devil withdrew![3] Paul preaching to the gentiles, used only the *Tanach*. In fact, to validate "New Testament" doctrines in the book of Romans alone, Paul uses or refers to Old Testament verses as his proof texts about *sixty* times. This indicates that the basis for Paul's doctrine, as well as the prophetic credentials for identifying the Messiah, were to be found in the *Tanach*.

Questions and Answers

Here are some vital questions for which believers must know the biblical answers.

Do we trust in, and verify our faith by, the same scriptures that Yeshua, the apostles, and the early believers did?

If the *Tanach* was the Word of God then, is it still the Word of God today?

Is it as much the Word of God for us today as is the New Testament?

To understand the total revelation of Himself that God has given us, the answers to these questions need to be settled in our minds and hearts. How often have you heard someone say, or maybe said yourself, "I'm a New Testament believer"? Personally, we prefer not to imply that we are cut off from our roots. We are Bible believers. We recognize that the written revelation of God begins at Genesis 1:1 and goes to the end of the book of Revelation. In fact, if Genesis 1:1 is not the foundation of our faith, that is, faith in God who is the Creator, then everything else we believe is built on sand.

Historically The New Testament uses the term "scripture" to refer only to the Old Testament. Keep that in mind as we look at the following verses:

John 10:35 *"...the **scripture** cannot be broken..."* [4]

John 5:39 *"Search the **scriptures**; for in them ye think ye have eternal life: and they are they which testify* [bear witness] *of me."*

The following passage is so important that we explore it in depth later on:

2 Tim 3:16-17 *"All **scripture** is given by inspiration of God, and is profitable for doctrine, for reproof, for correction, for instruction in righteousness: That the man of God may be perfect, thoroughly furnished unto all good works."* The New Testament is saying this about the Old Testament.

If the *Tanach* is still God's Word for us today, we should be able to find convincing answers to the questions, "What is the New Testament view of the *Tanach*?" and "How did Yeshua view the *Tanach*?"

What is the New Testament view of the Tanach?

According to Walter Kaiser Jr., in his excellent book *The Uses of the Old Testament in the New,*[5] the New Testament contains approximately 300 directly quoted verses, 200 unacknowledged quotes, and 1,100 re-worded or paraphrased verses from the *Tanach*. The New Testament uses these 1,600 Old Testament verses for proof that Yeshua is the promised Messiah, for doctrine and teaching, for encouraging and warning.

Kaiser points out other facts that demonstrate how the New Testament authors viewed their Bible, the *Tanach*. For instance, often the New Testament does not make a distinction between what God says and what the *Tanach* says. If the *Tanach* states something, the New Testament writers assume that it is God who states it, even if it is not directly credited to Him. Here are a couple of examples.

In Acts 4:24b-25 the apostles are praying, *"Lord, thou art **God**, which hast made heaven, and earth, and the sea, and all that in them is: **Who** by the mouth of thy servant David **hast said**, Why did the heathen rage* [behave arrogantly]*, and the people imagine* [devise, plot] *vain things?"*. The apostles are quoting from Psalm 2 which was written by David, but they correctly assume that it was God who said it through David (see bolded words).

Paul, in Galatians 3:8 states, *"And the **scripture** [Tanach], foreseeing that God would justify* [declare righteous] *the heathen* [gentiles] *through faith, **preached** before the gospel unto Abraham, saying, In thee shall all nations[6] be blessed."* Paul claims that the scripture says this when, in the original account, God is speaking (see Gen 12:1-3).[7]

We have already mentioned 2 Timothy 3:16-17, the pre-eminent New Testament statement on the relevance of the *Tanach* for believers. Do we grasp what God's Spirit is saying in this passage about the benefits of the Old Testament? Let's examine the passage in detail.

2 Timothy 3:16-17

"All scripture is given by inspiration of God, and is profitable for doctrine, for reproof, for correction, for instruction in righteousness: That the man of God may be perfect, throughly furnished unto all good works."

"All scripture..." today includes the Old and the New Testaments, but in its historical context Paul can only be referring to the *Tanach*.

"All scripture is given by inspiration of God..." By using the word "inspiration", Paul declares that the *Tanach* is God-breathed by the Holy Spirit and just as accurate as if God used the pen. Peter affirms such a high view of the *Tanach*. When speaking concerning *Tanach* prophecy he says, *"Knowing this first, that no prophecy of the scripture is of* [came into existence by] *any private interpretation. For the prophecy*

came not in old time by the will [or desire; pleasure] *of man: but holy men of God spake as they were moved* [carried along] *by the Holy Ghost"* (2 Pet 1:20-21).

"All scripture...is profitable for doctrine..." "Profitable" means useful, advantageous; "doctrine" means teaching. Under the direct inspiration of God's Spirit, the Apostle Paul is encouraging the Church to study the *Tanach* to get her doctrine and teaching material. He knew that we cannot have solid doctrine without the foundational part of God's Word. For example, how can we fully understand salvation and what occurred at the Cross without understanding Leviticus 16 (*Yom Kippur*, the Day of Atonement), Isaiah 53 (the Suffering Servant), and the many other pictures in the *Tanach* that fully reveal what happened at Calvary?[8]

"...profitable for...reproof [rebuke]*..."* Reproof or rebuke is an act of mercy on God's part. For example, *"Turn* [repent] *you at my reproof: behold, I will pour out my spirit unto you, I will make known my words unto you"* (Prov 1:23; see also 3:11-12). Has God's Spirit ever rebuked you using the *Tanach?*

"...profitable for...correction..." "Correction" literally means being restored to an upright position or right state, setting straight that which has become bent or twisted. The *Tanach* can often be used as a tool in the hand of God to restore us to Himself after we have sinned.

"...profitable for...instruction in righteousness..." This phrase pictures the submission of a disciple to the rules of instruction given by his teacher. It implies growth from childhood to maturity, from weakness to strength. Note also that such righteousness is by faith. The New Testament constantly uses Old Testament saints and/or verses to prove that *"the just shall live by his faith,"* a verse originally found in Habakkuk 2:4b.[9] In fact, in Romans 10:6-8, Paul uses Deuteronomy 30:12-14 to describe *"...the righteousness which is of faith..."*. We shall look at this in more detail in a later chapter.[10]

"That the man of God may be perfect [complete, mature]*, thoroughly furnished unto all good works."* To one who is born of the Holy Spirit, spiritual maturity requires understanding the *Tanach*. It is spiritual arrogance to think that we can know God and His will and yet not read, study, and believe more than 75% of the revelation of Himself that He has given us. It can lead to a misunderstanding of who God is, and that is a sure path to deception's door.

Previous to these verses, in 2 Timothy 3:14-15, Paul had encouraged Timothy to *"continue thou in* [do not depart from] *the things which thou hast learned..."* This specifically includes *"the holy scriptures* [The Holy Spirit's name for the Old Testament] *which are able* [have the power] *to make thee wise unto salvation through faith which is in Messiah Yeshua."*

People can, and do, get saved by reading or hearing God's Word in the *Tanach* and seeing that Yeshua is the promised Messiah. We should be able to preach the Gospel out of the Old Testament just like Peter did on the Day of Pentecost. Can you, using only the *Tanach*, present the gospel message of Yeshua the Messiah? It is amazing how many Jewish people will listen to scriptures from "their" Bible. *"And when they had appointed him* [Paul] *a day, there came many to him...to whom he expounded and testified the kingdom of God, **persuading them concerning Yeshua, both out of the law of Moses, and out of the prophets**, from morning till evening"* (Acts 28:23).

How Did Messiah Yeshua View the Tanach?

Yeshua saw the *Tanach* as the Word of God. In Matthew 5:17-18, He warns us against even thinking that He has come to do away with it, stating that it will stand as God's Word until all has been fulfilled, which means until there is a new heaven and earth (Isa 65:17). *"Think not that I am come to destroy* [or overthrow, render vain] *the law, or the prophets: I am not come to destroy, but to fulfil* [cause to abound, cause to be completed]. *For verily I say unto you, Till heaven and earth pass, one jot or one tittle* [smallest parts of letters of the Hebrew alphabet] *shall in no wise pass from the law, till all be fulfilled."*

In Mark 7:1-13 Yeshua pointed to a serious problem with the Pharisees' attitude toward God's Word. In verses 7-13 He accused them of worshipping God in vain because they taught man's tradition as the basis of their doctrines and not *"the commandment of God."* In effect, they had rejected God's Word, because the end result was making *"the Word of God of none effect."*[11] Before we look down on the Pharisees too much, it would be worthwhile to consider in what ways we in the Body may be guilty of the same thing.

Here is a sampling of other verses where Yeshua states that the *Tanach* is still God's Word:

Mark 12:24 *"And Yeshua answering said unto them, Do ye not therefore err* [roam from the truth; become deceived], *because ye know not the scriptures* [the *Tanach*], *neither the power of God?"*

Mark 12:36 *"For David himself said by the Holy Ghost..."*

Luke 16:29,31 *"Abraham saith unto him, They have Moses and the prophets; let them hear them...If they hear not Moses and the prophets, neither will they be persuaded, though one rose from the dead."*

John 10:35 *"...and the scripture* [the *Tanach*] *cannot be broken..."*[12]

Yeshua also used the *Tanach* to settle arguments. In Matthew 12:1-7, when some Pharisees accused His disciples of breaking the Sabbath law by plucking heads of grain to eat, Yeshua responded by telling how David had used the Tabernacle showbread to feed his hungry men and also pointed out that the priests in the temple worked on the Sabbath.

Another time Yeshua quoted from Psalm 8:2 in the *Tanach* in defense of children giving him praise. *"And Yeshua saith unto them* [the priests], *Yea; have ye never read* [read and understood, or acknowledged that], *Out of the mouth of babes and sucklings thou hast perfected* [completed, repaired] *praise?"* (Matt 21:16b).[13]

Yeshua had absolute faith in the power of God's Word as found in the *Tanach*. When tested in the wilderness, He resisted Satan by quoting three times from the book of Deuteronomy. Yes, Yeshua used "the Law of Moses" as a sword to defeat the Enemy (see Luke 4:1-13)!

His teaching used direct and indirect *Tanach* quotes frequently. For example, His teaching on His return (Matthew 24:29-31) is taken from many *Tanach* scriptures (referenced in brackets). *"Immediately after the tribulation of those days shall the sun be darkened, and the moon shall not give her light, and the stars shall fall from heaven, and the powers of the heavens shall be shaken* [from Isa 13:10; 34:4]: *And then shall appear the sign of the Son of man in heaven: and then shall all the tribes of the earth mourn* [from Zech 12:10-12], *and they shall see the Son of man coming in the clouds of heaven with power and great glory* [from Dan 7:13-14]. *And he shall send his angels with a great sound of a trumpet* [from Isa 27:12-13], *and they shall gather together his elect from the four winds, from one end of heaven to the other* [from Deut 30:4; Zech 2:6]. *"*

Even His ethical teachings are rooted in the same soil. Here are two classic examples:

*"Therefore all things whatsoever ye would that men should do to you, do ye even so to them: for this is **the law and the prophets**"* (Matt 7:12).

*"And, behold, one came and said unto him, Good Master, what good thing shall I do, that I may have eternal life? And he said unto him, Why callest thou me good? there is none good but one, that is, God: but if thou wilt enter into life, keep **the commandments**. He saith unto him, Which? Yeshua said, Thou shalt do no murder, Thou shalt not commit adultery, Thou shalt not steal, Thou shalt not bear false witness, Honour thy father and thy mother: and, Thou shalt love thy neighbour as thyself"* (Matt 19:16-19).

Finally, consider that the whole basis of His own role as the Messiah depended entirely on His conviction that He must fulfill the *Tanach*. There are many verses in the gospels to support this but we will cite only three and list a few others in the endnotes.

To answer John the Baptizer's question of whether He, Yeshua, was the one prophesied to come, Yeshua says "yes" by telling John's disciples to report what works they see Him do – works listed in several prophecies from Isaiah: 29:18-19 and 35:4-6, *"The blind receive their sight, and the lame walk, the lepers are cleansed, and the deaf hear, the dead are raised up, and the poor have the gospel preached to them"* (Matt 11:5).

In a synagogue in Nazareth, when Yeshua first proclaimed who He was, He quoted Isaiah 61:1-2a, *"The Spirit of the Lord is upon me, because he hath anointed me to preach the gospel to the poor; he hath sent me to heal the brokenhearted, to preach deliverance* [release from bondage] *to the captives, and recovering of sight to the blind, to set at liberty them that are bruised* [broken, shattered], *To preach* [proclaim publicly] *the acceptable year of the Lord"* (Luke 4:18-19). Then He said, *"This day is **this scripture** fulfilled in your ears"* (Luke 4:21b).

And in John 5:39 Yeshua declares that we need to *"Search **the scriptures*** [the Old Testament]; *for in them ye think ye have eternal life: and they are they which testify of me."* The Old Testament is where He directs us for proof of His Messiahship.[14]

Conclusion

There is no doubt that the New Testament authors viewed the *Tanach*, the Old Testament, not only as the Word of God, but as still valid for them in their walk with the Lord. There is not one sermon or teaching in the New Testament lacking a solid doctrinal foundation in the *Tanach*.

In the following chapters we will explore the roots of the Gospel and of much of the New Testament's doctrinal teachings. We will see how all of it is grounded in God's Word as found in the *Tanach*. That is where the seeds were planted, the tree watered and weeded, pruned back and watched, until the fullness of time. Then the fruit was ripe, and our Messiah appeared,

"A light to lighten the Gentiles, and the glory of thy people Israel"
(Luke 2:32).

---

1   Romans 11:16-24.

2   Matt 24:4-5,11,24; Rom 16:17-18; 2 Thes 2:2-4.

3   All three were from the same book – Deuteronomy: Matt 4:4 from Deut 8:3b; Matt 4:7 from Deut 6:16; and Matt 4:10 from Deut 6:13a and/or 10:20a.

4   This could be translated, "there is no power or authority which can annul, subvert, dissolve, destroy, overthrow, deprive of its authority or declare unlawful the Old Testament…"!

5   Walter Kaiser Jr., *The Uses of the Old Testament in the New*, Moody Press, Chicago, 1985, pp 2-3.

6   This is the same Greek word that was translated "heathen" previously in this verse.

7   Here are some other examples: Matt 19:4-5 with Gen 1:27; 2:23-24; Rom 9:17 with Ex 9:16.

8   See Chapters 10, 11, and 12, "The Cross in the *Tanach*" for a study on this theme.

9   See Rom 1:16-17; Gal 3:11; Heb 10:38; also Rom 4:3 and 10:5-6.

10 See "Salvation by Faith in the *Tanach*" in Chapter 4, and "Saved by Faith" in Chapter 9.

11 Mark 7:7-13 "*Howbeit **in vain*** [unsuccessfully] ***do they worship me, teaching for doctrines the commandments of men***. *For **laying aside*** [used of a man divorcing his wife; also disregarding, omitting, neglecting] ***the commandment of God, ye hold*** [seize; retain] ***the tradition of men***, *as the washing of pots and cups: and many other such like things ye do...**Full well*** [With great skill] ***ye reject*** [nullify or violate] ***the commandment of God, that ye may keep*** [guard carefully] ***your own tradition.*** *For Moses said, Honour thy father and thy mother; and, Whoso curseth father or mother, let him die the death: But ye say, If a man shall say to his father or mother, It is Corban, that is to say, a* [sacred] *gift, by whatsoever thou mightest be profited by me; he shall be free. And ye suffer* [allow] *him no more to do ought* [anything] *for his father or his mother; **Making the word of God of none effect*** [depriving it of force and authority] ***through your tradition***, *which ye have delivered: and many such like things do ye.*"

12 See Endnote #4 above.

13 Some other examples, see Matthew 22:29-46 and John 5:39,45-47.

14 Here are a few of many other examples: Matt 22:41ff; 23:37-39; 26:24; 27:46; Luke 12:49-53; 18:31-34; 22:22,37; 24:25-27, 44-49.

CHAPTER 2

The Nature of God
in the Old Testament

Many doctrines which believers in Yeshua consider essential to the Gospel have their roots in the *Tanach*. The truth of "progressive revelation," the idea that God gave more revelation to His people in the course of completing the Holy Scriptures, does not change the fact that certain concepts were revealed early in history.[1] Malachi 3:6a states, *"For I am the LORD, I change not..."* If this is true then the revelation of His nature and person through His Son, Yeshua,[2] and through the New Testament *must* have deep roots in the *Tanach*.

Already in the second century certain "Christian" sects, Marcionism and Gnosticism, were identified as heresies. Among other errors, they alleged that the God of the *Tanach* was inferior to the God of the New Testament. Unfortunately people today, especially those unfamiliar with the *Tanach,* can be vulnerable to the same false teaching. As we will soon discover, God is the same in both Testaments.

God is Love

*"He that loveth not knoweth not God; for **God is love** "* (1 John 4:8); *"And we have known and believed* [been persuaded of; placed confidence in] *the love that God hath to us. **God is love**; and he that dwelleth* [remains; abides] *in love dwelleth in God, and God in him"* (1 John 4:16).

Perhaps the most common phrase that believers use to express the essence of the Good News to an unbeliever is "God loves you!" This is a tremendous truth brought out in all its fullness in the New Testament. But it is sad, even shameful, that some believers talk of the God of love in the New Testament as though in contrast to a God of judgment in the Tanach. Don't they believe that He is the same God, the same loving, righteous Father from Genesis to Revelation?

It is important to avoid compartmentalizing God into the various characteristics of His nature. As A.W. Tozer expressed in his highly recommended book, *The Knowledge of the Holy*, "The words 'God is love' mean that love is an essential attribute of God. Love is something true of God but it is not God. It expresses the way God is in His unitary being, as do the words holiness, justice, faithfulness and truth. Because God is immutable He always acts like Himself, and because He is a unity He never suspends one of His attributes in order to exercise another."[3]

For this reason we should learn to see His mercy and love in action even in the midst of His judgments. One of the best examples of this doctrine is found in the story of Israel's exodus from Egypt. Instead of delivering Israel out of bondage without giving the Egyptians warning, the Lord sent ten plagues over a span of time not only to increase the faith of His people, but to give the Egyptians a chance to know that He, the LORD, is the Almighty God. *"And the Egyptians shall know that I am the LORD, when I stretch forth mine hand upon Egypt and bring out the children of Israel from among them"* (Exo 7:5).[4]

Not only does God judge in mercy, but He judges because He loves. We are redeemed because God is a God of judgment. Our sins separated us from Him (Isa 59:1-2). If God had not judged our sins on the Cross, then we would never have been able to approach or know Him. And Psalm 9:16a states exactly that, *"The LORD is known by the judgment which he executeth…"*

If our God is *"…the same yesterday, and today and forever"* (Heb 13:8), then He is a God of love in the *Tanach* as well as in the New Testament, and also a God of judgment in the New Testament as well as in the *Tanach*. Before we search the *Tanach* scriptures concerning His love, consider these New Testament verses concerning His judgment. He is the same God in all of Scripture.

The God of Judgment in the New Testament

"And fear not them which kill the body, but are not able to kill the soul [lit: breath; fig. life essence]*: but rather fear* [Gk *phobeo*, to be afraid of, be terrified of] *him which is able to destroy both soul and body in hell"* (Matt 10:28). Contrary to some explanations of this verse, Yeshua *is* telling His followers to fear God, in agreement with the many commandments in the *Tanach* that encourage the fear of the LORD.[5]

Acts 5:1-11 records God's judgment on Ananias and Sapphira because they lied to the Holy Spirit. The result was that *"…great fear* [dread, terror] *came upon all the church* [believers] *and upon as many as heard these things"* (v11).

"For we must all appear [lit: we must all be seen] *before the judgment seat of Messiah; that every one may receive the things*

done in his body...whether it be good or bad. Knowing therefore **the terror** *of the Lord, we persuade men..."* (2 Cor 5:10-11a). The Greek word translated "terror" is *"phobos"* from which we get "phobia." It literally means, fear; dread, or terror.[6]

The New Testament letter to the Hebrews contains two strong statements concerning God. *"For we know him that hath said, Vengeance* [revenge] *belongeth unto me, I will recompense* [pay back], *saith the Lord. And again, The Lord shall judge his people. It is* **a fearful thing** *to fall into* [be trapped by] *the hands of the living God"* (Heb 10:30-31). A few chapters later, the writer declares, *"For our God is a consuming* [destroying] *fire"* (Heb 12:29) in the context of encouraging godly fear.

In the final book of the New Testament, the gentle Lamb of God, our Messiah and Lord, Yeshua, gives two strong warnings – to believers! *"And* **I will kill her children with death***; and all the churches shall know that I am he which searcheth* [examines] *the reins* [inmost thoughts, feelings, and purposes] *and hearts* [mind, emotions and will]*: and I will give unto every one of you according to your works* [deeds]" (Rev 2:23); *"So then because thou art lukewarm* [fig. apathetic]*...I will* [intend to] *spue* [lit: vomit] *thee out of my mouth"* (Rev 3:16).

These New Testament verses reveal that God's justice and judgment are still valid even after the Cross. But is His love as clearly shown in the Tanach as is His justice in the New Testament?

The God of Love in the *Tanach*

Ahavah and *chesed* are two Hebrew words used in the *Tanach* to describe two different aspects of God's love. Both contribute to a solid understanding of Israel's and the Church's election and security in God's faithfulness.

The Election-Love of God - *Ahavah*

Ahavah, is the modern Hebrew term for "love." According to Norman Snaith in *The Distinctive Ideas of the Old Testament,*[7] *ahavah* in the *Tanach* stands for the "election-love" of God. He observes, "...when the [Hebraic root for *ahavah,* or *ahabah*] is used of loving persons, it is used of the attitude of a superior to an inferior" (p. 132). We will see later the same parameter for the biblical concept of grace, showing a superior favoring an inferior.

Snaith points out, *"ahabah* is the Election-love as against *chesed* [explained in the next section], which is the Covenant-love...the origin of the Covenant is due to Jehovah's *ahabah* (election-love)...She [Israel] is His elected people" (p. 133-134).

"The one thing of which all Old Testament writers are certain is that God's love for Israel was not because of anything that Israel had done or was" (p. 136). Already we see how close this idea conforms to New Testament "grace." Snaith says, "Either we must accept this idea of choice on the part of God with its necessary accompaniment of exclusiveness, or we have to hold to a doctrine of the Love of God other than that which is Biblical" (p. 139).

Finally, concerning God's command that His people love Him with all their heart, soul, mind and strength, Snaith states that the love of God which chose Israel is also the power which God gives them to obey Him. (p. 142).

Several different words are translated as "love" in the Bible. The word *ahavah* and its derivatives are translated "love" in many verses. Let us look at how these different words (**bolded**) are used.

In Deuteronomy 7:7-8a the Lord speaks to Israel through Moses as they are poised to enter the promised land. *"The LORD did not set his **love** [chashaq – longing or delight] upon you, nor choose you, because ye were more in number than any people; for ye were the fewest of all people: But because the LORD **loved** [ahavah] you..."*

Moses goes on to say that if Israel will listen to and do all that the Lord commands, then *"the LORD thy God shall keep unto thee the covenant and the mercy which he sware unto thy fathers: And he will **love** [ahavah] thee, and bless thee, and multiply thee..."* (vv 12b-13a). Remember, this promise is not New Testament; this is in the Law of Moses.

The following verse shows the difference between *chashaq*, a longing for and delight in someone, and *ahavah*. It also declares God's election of Israel. *"Only the LORD had a delight [chashaq] in thy fathers to **love** [ahavah] them, and he chose their seed after them, even you above all people, as it is this day"* (Deut 10:15).

In Deuteronomy 23:5 Moses refers to the Balaam incident found in Numbers 23-25 and states, *"Nevertheless the LORD thy God would not hearken unto Balaam; but the LORD thy God turned the curse into a blessing unto thee, because the LORD thy God **loved** [ahavah] thee."* In the same way, didn't the LORD through the Cross overturn the curse due to us? Didn't Yeshua take on Himself the judgment for breaking the Law and put in its place the blessing of our God who so abundantly loves us? Because of God's love, *"Messiah hath redeemed us from the curse of the law, being made a curse for us: for it is written, Cursed is every one that hangeth on a tree: That the blessing of Abraham might come on the Gentiles through Yeshua the Messiah"* (Gal 3:13-14a).

Isaiah 63:7-64:12 calls on God to remember His loving-kindness to Israel (v7) and to again turn to her because of His covenant relationship with her - a model for interceding for Israel. In this passage is found, *"In all their affliction he was afflicted, and the angel of his presence saved them: in his **love** [ahavah] and in his pity he redeemed them; and he bare [lifted] them, and carried them all the days of old"* (Isaiah 63:9).

Jeremiah 30:23-31:1 is a prophecy of Israel's final restoration. What is God's reason for restoring His people to His land and to Himself at the present time? Why does God say that He wants to draw Israel closer to Himself? Because of His love! Verse 31:3 states, *"The LORD hath appeared of old* [from afar] *unto me, saying, Yea* [Yes], *I have **loved*** [ahavah] *thee with an everlasting **love*** [ahavah]: *therefore with lovingkindness* [chesed – see below] *have I drawn thee."*

Ezekiel 16 is one of the classic Bible chapters on God's relationship with Israel. In the first part, verses 1-14, God recalls His love for Israel when He first chose her. Then He states Israel's harlotries against Him in verses 15-34. The reason God called Israel adulterous and a harlot is because He saw her as His wife! This is evident from verse 8, where God remembers His initial love for Israel. *"Now when I passed by thee, and looked upon thee, behold, thy time was the time of **love*** [Heb. *doe-deem'*, lit. loves, fig. marriage]; *and I spread my skirt over thee,*[8] *and covered thy nakedness: yea, I sware unto thee, and entered into a covenant with thee, saith the Lord GOD, and thou becamest mine."* And although, in Ezekiel 16:35-59, God announces her judgments, in verses 60-63 He prophesies that in the end He will establish an everlasting covenant with the house of Israel.

Hosea 14:4 is from the scripture portion read in synagogues on *Shabbat Shuvah,* the Sabbath of Repentance, which is the Sabbath falling between *Rosh haShanah,* the New Year, and *Yom Kippur,* the Day of Atonement. In Judaism the ten days between these two holy days are called "The Days of Awe," a time of heart-searching and of seeking reconciliation with God and man. This scripture from Hosea, so appropriate for such a sacred time, concerns the undying love of God for Israel. He only waits for her to acknowledge her sin and return to her Lord, her Husband.

Hosea urges in verses 1-2a, *"O Israel, return unto the LORD thy God; for thou hast fallen by thine iniquity. Take with you words, and turn* [return; repent] *to the LORD: say unto him, Take away all iniquity, and receive us graciously…"* The Lord responds with a promise that has kept the flame of hope alive in the Jewish people through many centuries of exile and darkness, *"I will heal their backsliding* [apostasy], *I will **love*** [ahavah] *them freely: for mine anger is turned away from him"* (14:4).

We do not have room to explore the many other verses in the *Tanach* which speak of God's *ahava.*[9] However, in ending this section we look into the Song of Songs which the famous second century Rabbi Akiva declared the "Holy of Holies" of the Holy Scriptures. Many see it as an allegory of the love between God and Israel and also between Yeshua and His Bride, whose character in the song says, *"He brought me to the banqueting house, and his banner* [flag, standard] *over me was love* [*ahavah*]" (Song 2:4). God's nature is unchanging and He has been a God of love from the beginning, from eternity.

> *"The LORD thy God in the midst of thee is mighty;*
> *he will save, he will rejoice over thee with joy;*
> *he will rest in his **love** [ahavah],*
> *he will joy over thee with singing" (Zeph 3:17).*

The Covenant-Love of God - *Chesed*

The Hebrew word *chesed* is central to explaining God's relationship with Israel, but it is a difficult concept to translate into English. The best explanation we have found is in Snaith's book.[10] He emphasizes, "...*ahabah* [see previous section] is God's Election-Love, whilst *chesed* is His Covenant-Love" (p.95). In the following sentence we have bolded Snaith's definition of *chesed*. "When the word came to be used predominantly of the covenant between Jehovah and Israel, it was realized by the prophets that such a covenant could be maintained only by that *persistent, determined, steadfast love of God, which transcends every other love by its nature and depth*" (p.99).

Although at times *chesed* is translated as "lovingkindness" or "mercy," Snaith points out that "these renderings are often far too weak to convey *the strength, the firmness, and the persistence of God's sure love... The most important of all the distinctive ideas of the Old Testament is God's steady and extraordinary persistence in continuing to love wayward Israel in spite of Israel's insistent waywardness*" (p.102). The same can be said for God's "extraordinary persistence in continuing to love" the Church, those of us who are now grafted into Israel's Olive Tree (see Rom 11:17).

Snaith declares that *chesed* underlies God's faithfulness to His Covenant with Israel. "...[Hosea] came to know that the *chesed* of God meant God's steadfast determination to be true to His share of the Covenant obligation whatever Israel did" (p.111). Snaith again, "But through all the troubles which beat against and broke the marriage covenant between Jehovah and Israel, there was one factor which never changed...God's sure love for Israel. Because of this sure, unswerving love, the Covenant can never be finally and completely broken" (p.113).

Snaith concludes, "Arising, then, out of this sure, unswerving love of God, we get the doctrine of the Remnant, and with it the belief that God will accomplish in Israel that repentance and turning to Him without which there can never be any hope of better days, or indeed any Remnant" (p.122). Romans 9-11 says the same.

Although sometimes confused, *chesed* is not the same as grace. Snaith points out that grace, *chen*, "tends to carry with it...the idea of unmerited favor..." He clarifies how both work together, "...the whole secret of God's mercy towards Israel was that they were the people of His choice [by love and grace]...[But] her hope of salvation was in God's persistent covenant-love (*chesed*)" (pp. 128-129).

In biblical times, as we have seen, a name was often an indication of character. In Exodus 33:18, when Moses asked the Lord, *"I beseech thee, shew me thy glory,"* God proclaimed His Name. In that passage, the KJV translates *chesed* with two different English words. *"And the LORD passed by before him, and proclaimed, The LORD, The LORD God, merciful and gracious, longsuffering, and abundant in **goodness** [chesed] and truth, Keeping **mercy** [chesed] for thousands, forgiving iniquity and transgression and sin, and that will by no means clear the guilty..."* (Exo 34:6-7a). We can see from this *Tanach* revelation of God's name that, although He does say that He must deal with sin, His character is one of covenant-love, mercy and grace.

After God redeems us by His grace, He leads us by His *chesed,* his faithful love, into what He has promised.[11] *"Thou in thy **mercy** [chesed] hast led forth the people which thou hast redeemed: thou hast guided them in thy strength unto thy holy habitation"* (Exo 15:13). Although this verse applies to the children of Israel in its original setting, according to the apostle Paul, the principles of the Lord's dealings with Israel also apply to His Church. *"Now all these things happened unto them* [Israel in the wilderness] *for ensamples* [patterns]*: and they are written for our admonition* [attention, warning]*, upon whom the ends* [also "goals" or "purposes"] *of the world* [ages, eternity] *are come* [have arrived]*"* (1 Cor 10:11).

Moses intercedes for Israel based on God's *chesed,* an essential aspect of who God is! *"Pardon* [forgive]*, I beseech thee, the iniquity of this people according unto the greatness of thy **mercy** [chesed], and as thou hast forgiven this people, from Egypt even until now"* (Num 14:19).

In Psalm 51:1, King David pleads for the Lord to forgive his murder and adultery. He bases his plea on a number of characteristics of God's nature, including *chesed. "Have mercy* [lit: grace; pity] *upon me, O God, according to thy **lovingkindness** [chesed]: according unto the multitude of thy tender mercies blot out my transgressions* [rebellion]*."* We see it in the context of repentance again in Psalm 86:5, *"For thou, Lord, art good, and ready to forgive; and plenteous in **mercy** [chesed] unto all them that call upon thee."*

David says that *chesed* enables God to deal with His people according to who He is and not according to what we deserve. *"He hath not dealt with us after our sins; nor rewarded us according to our iniquities. For as the heaven is high above the earth, so great* [strong; mighty] *is his **mercy** [chesed] toward them that fear* *him"* (Psa 103:10-11). Why does anyone, Jew or Gentile, ever have a chance to draw near to this holy God? Because of God's covenant love.

Psalm 136, the Great *Hallel*, has twenty-six verses, at the end of every one of which is, *"...for his **mercy** [chesed] endureth for ever."* David understood the concept of covenant love, trusting that God's relationship with Israel was based on His *chesed*.

Jeremiah pleads with apostate Israel to repent because God is a covenant-keeper and will have mercy on them. *"...Return, thou backsliding Israel, saith the LORD; and I will not cause mine anger to fall upon you: for I am **merciful** [from chesed], saith the LORD, and I will not keep anger for ever"* (Jer 3:12b). God's great *chesed* also endures forever for those who believe in Messiah Yeshua, then fall into unbelief, but finally repent.

Micah states that the reason God wants to forgive and be gracious is because He takes pleasure in acting on the basis of His *chesed*. *"Who is a God like unto thee, that pardoneth iniquity, and passeth by the transgression of the remnant of his heritage? he retaineth not his anger for ever, because he delighteth in **mercy** [chesed]"* (Mic 7:18).

Of all the *Tanach* verses that talk about God's *chesed*, one of the most moving is found in Lamentations. Jeremiah the prophet, author of this dirge, is watching the destruction of Jerusalem, the beloved city. He is witnessing horrible sights and sounds (see Lam 2:20; 4:10). He cries out his anguish to his God. Yet, in the midst of his heart-rending lament, Jeremiah utters one of the greatest expressions of faith in Scripture,

*"It is of the LORD's **mercies** [chesed] that we are not consumed,*
because his compassions fail not.
They are new every morning:
great is thy faithfulness" (Lam 3:22-23).

The God of Mercy

Although *chesed*, or covenant love, is often translated "mercy" or "mercies," there is another Hebrew word – *rachamim* – which is closer to the current English usage of the word "mercy." The word *rachamim* is always found in the *Tanach* in the plural, as in "mercies," and points to specific instances of God's compassion and patient love for His people. The root of this word is related to the Hebrew word for a mother's womb, *recham*. We do not serve an unfeeling God.

Yeshua said that if we have seen Him, we have seen the Father (John 14:6-11), and the gospels record many incidents when Yeshua evidenced his feelings: feeding and healing the multitudes in compassion (Matt 9:36; 14:14); crying over Lazarus' tomb (John 11:35)

and over Jerusalem (Luke 19:41); angry and grieved against the hard hearts of some of the people (Mark 3:5); angry at merchandise sellers in His Father's house (Matt 21:12-13); joyful over the disciples' works done in His name (Luke 10:17-22); disappointed with His disciples' unbelief (Matt 8:25-26; 14:29-31), etc.

Many of the Psalms read like excerpts from Yeshua's autobiography. In passages that express profound and powerful feelings,[12] we can rejoice in God's deep love for us – and share with Him a loathing for our sin.[13] He even commands us to join Him in hating evil. *"Ye that love the LORD, hate evil..."* (Psa 97:10a).[14]

In studying the word *rachamim*, we will look again at some of the same verses examined in the section on *chesed*, covenant-love. Remember, we cannot separate God's attributes or psychoanalyze Him. In fact, it is especially true of God that He is more than the sum of His characteristics.

A. W. Tozer writes, "Mercy is an attribute of God...which disposes God to be actively compassionate. Both the Old and New Testaments proclaim the mercy of God, but the Old has more than four times as much to say about it as the New."[15] As Tozer points out, probably the best definition for *rachamim* would be "actively compassionate." Just as love is a lifestyle, a choice, and not a feeling, so mercy, or mercies, are actions and not just feelings. Pity is a feeling, but mercy is an action "on" a recipient. *Rachamim* and its derivatives are **bolded** in the following texts.

As with *chesed*, covenant love, God declares that mercy, *rachamim*, is also His essential character, *"And the LORD passed by before him, and proclaimed, The LORD, The LORD God, **merciful** and gracious, longsuffering, and abundant in goodness [chesed] and truth...."* Mercy is the first attribute He lists after His Name (Exo 34:6).

In Deuteronomy 4 Moses prophesies that Israel will provoke the Lord to anger (v25), resulting in a God-driven global scattering (vv26-27). But He says that in the last days (v30), when Israel truly seeks God, they will find Him. Knowing all that Israel would do, how does Moses explain this conclusion? *"(For the LORD thy God is a **merciful** God;) he will not forsake thee, neither destroy thee, nor forget* [ignore] *the covenant of thy fathers which he sware unto them"* (Deut 4:31).

Nehemiah and Daniel, confessing Israel's constant rebellion against God, proclaim that Israel survives because of God's continual mercies to His people, *"Nevertheless for thy great **mercies'** sake thou didst not utterly consume them, nor forsake them; for thou art a gracious and **merciful** God"* (Neh 9:31), and, *"To the Lord our God belong **mercies** and forgivenesses, though we have rebelled against him;"* (Dan 9:9). King David puts this idea on an individual level. *"Have mercy* [lit: grace; pity – not *rachamim*] *upon me, O God,* *according to thy lovingkindness* [*chesed*]*: according unto the multitude of thy* **tender mercies** *blot out my transgressions"* (Psa 51:1).

Proverbs 28:13, concerning the result of confessing sin, says, *"He that covereth his sins* [lit: transgressions; rebellions] *shall not prosper: but whoso confesseth and forsaketh them shall have* **mercy***."* That is one of the root verses for John's declaration in 1 John 1:9, *"If we confess our sins, he is faithful and just to forgive us our sins, and to cleanse us from all unrighteousness."*

The prophets described God's merciful compassion as one of the "rewards" of repentance. *"Let the wicked forsake his way, and the unrighteous man his thoughts: and let him return* [repent] *unto the LORD, and he will have* **mercy** *upon him; and to our God, for he will abundantly pardon"* (Isa 55:7), and also, *"...rend your heart, and not your garments, and turn* [repent] *unto the LORD your God: for he is gracious and* **merciful***..."* (Joel 2:13a).

Look once more at that verse in Lamentations which contains both *chesed* and *rachamim. "It is of the LORD's mercies* [*chesed*, covenant-love] *that we are not consumed, because* **his compassions** [*rachamim*, mercies] *fail not. They are new every morning: great is thy faithfulness"* (Lam 3:22-23).

You probably know many of those verses and even quote some of them by heart. Such great revelations of God's character are found frequently in the Old Testament. The *Tanach* saints needed God's mercy as much as we do.

> *"Gracious is the LORD, and righteous;*
> *yea, our God is* **merciful** *"* (Psa 116:5).

The God of Grace

God never saved by means of the Law in the *Tanach*. Salvation by works does not exist anywhere in Scripture. God's way of salvation has always depended on grace through faith in His Word. "Grace" (Hebrew root word *chen*, sometimes translated "favor") can be defined as the pleasure, goodwill, and favor from a superior to an inferior; the stronger coming to the help of the weaker. God's grace means He delights in bestowing benefits on His undeserving children. The simplest theological definition of grace is God's unmerited favor on sinners.

His grace blooms everywhere in the *Tanach*. (The Hebrew word *chen* and its derivatives are **bolded** in the following verses.) Starting in Genesis, how were Noah and his family saved from the Flood? By God's grace. *"But Noah found* **grace** *in the eyes of the LORD"* (Gen 6:8), and Scripture only then talks about Noah being just and "perfect in his generations" (6:9).

Moses knew God's grace. In the previously discussed "show

me your glory" episode and its introduction (Exo 33:12-19; 34:5-9), the word *chen* ("grace," "gracious") is found nine times!

"And Moses said unto the LORD, See [consider], *thou sayest unto me, Bring up this people: and thou hast not let me know whom thou wilt send with me. Yet thou hast said, I know thee by name* [I know all about you], *and thou hast also found grace in my sight. Now therefore, I pray* [ask, plead with] *thee, if I have found grace in thy sight, shew me now* [lit: please let me know] *thy way, that I may know thee, that I may find grace in thy sight: and consider that this nation is thy people.*

"And he [God] *said, My presence shall go with thee, and I will give thee rest.*

"And he [Moses] *said unto him, If thy presence go not with me, carry us not up hence. For wherein shall it be known here that I and thy people have found grace in thy sight? is it not in that thou goest with us? so shall we be separated* [distinguished], *I and thy people, from all the people that are upon the face of the earth.*

"And the LORD said unto Moses, I will do this thing also that thou hast spoken: for thou hast found grace in my sight, and I know thee by name.

"And he [Moses] *said, I beseech thee, shew me thy glory.*

"And he [God] *said, I will make all my goodness pass before thee, and I will proclaim the name of the LORD* [which includes His characteristics] *before thee; and will be gracious to whom I will be gracious, and will shew mercy* [rachamim] *on whom I will shew mercy...*

"And the LORD descended in the cloud, and stood with him there,[16] *and proclaimed the name of the LORD. And the LORD passed by before him, and proclaimed, The LORD, The LORD God, merciful* [rachamim] *and gracious, longsuffering, and abundant in goodness* [chesed] *and truth, Keeping mercy* [chesed] *for thousands, forgiving* [bearing, carrying] *iniquity and transgression and sin, and that will by no means clear the guilty; visiting the iniquity of the fathers upon the children, and upon the children's children, unto the third and to the fourth generation.*

"And Moses made haste, and bowed his head toward the earth, and worshipped. And he said, If now I have found grace in thy sight, O Lord, let my Lord, I pray [ask, plead with] *thee, go among us; for it is a stiffnecked* [stubborn; obstinate] *people; and pardon our iniquity and our sin, and take us for thine inheritance."*

In pleading with God that He, and not just an angel,[17] would continue to accompany the children of Israel, Moses based his request on God's grace. Note the context; this dialogue occurs right after the sin of idolatry when Israel made and worshipped the golden calf (Exo 32-33). But here God reaffirms[18] grace, unmerited favor, as the basis of His relationship with Moses and the children of Israel.

God commanded Israel's priests to bless the children of Israel by placing His name on them, using the "Aaronic benediction." Part of this wonderful blessing asks God to deal with His children by grace. *"The LORD bless thee, and keep* [guard; protect] *thee: The LORD make his face shine upon thee, and be* **gracious** *unto thee: The LORD lift up his countenance upon thee, and give thee peace"* (Num 6:24-26). This peace, *shalom* in Hebrew, results from God's grace. It means much more than the cessation of strife. *Shalom* includes completeness, welfare, health, safety, contentment and prosperity.

Although oppressed by the king of Syria, Israel was not destroyed. *"And the LORD was* **gracious** *unto them, and had compassion* [rachamim] *on them, and had respect unto them, because of his covenant with Abraham, Isaac, and Jacob, and would not destroy them, neither cast he them from his presence as yet"* (2 Ki 13:23). There did come a time when Israel was "cast...from his presence," but even then God's promise not to destroy them still stood – as it does to this day (Jer 31:35-37; 51:5).

The plea for God's grace occurs at least twenty times in the Psalms, but it is often translated "mercy." *"Have* **mercy** *upon* [grace toward] *me, O LORD; for I am weak: O LORD, heal me; for my bones are vexed"* (Psa 6:2); *"I said, LORD,* **be merciful** [gracious] *unto me: heal my soul; for I have sinned against thee"* (Psa 41:4; also 4:1; 6:2; 9:13; 25:16; 51:1; 119:58, etc.).

Psalm 84:11 is a wonderful promise to those of us who are righteous in God's sight because of abiding in Messiah (2 Cor 5:21; Phil 3:9) and who are working out our salvation with fear and trembling (Phil 2:12b-13). Among the things God promises to us is more grace! *"For the LORD God is a sun and shield: the LORD will give* **grace** *and glory: no good thing will he withhold from them that walk uprightly."*

Psalm 102:13 is one of the verses that gives us hope. *"Thou shalt arise, and have mercy* [rachamim, active compassion] *upon Zion: for the time to* **favour** [from chen, grace] *her, yea, the set time,*[19] *is come."* Note that God deals with Israel because of His great compassion and grace – not because Israel is perfect or always obedient (cp. Jer 31:1-3). He deals with believers in the same way – for which we will be eternally thankful!

Proverbs 3:34 is a root verse that is used by James (4:6) and Peter (1 Pet 5:5), *"Surely he scorneth the scorners: but he giveth* **grace** *unto the lowly* [humble, meek, poor, broken hearted]."

We close this section on grace with two end time prophecies concerning Israel. In Isaiah 30:18-19, the prophet says that God is waiting for Israel's cry to Him, *"And therefore will the LORD wait, that he may be* **gracious** *unto you, and therefore will he be exalted,* *that he may have mercy [rachamim] upon you: for the LORD is a God of judgment [justice]: blessed are all they that wait for him. For the people shall dwell in Zion at Jerusalem: thou shalt weep no more: he will be very **gracious** unto thee at the voice of thy cry; when he shall hear it, he will answer thee."* This situation resembles one described in Ezekiel 36:37a - after the Lord promises to do many wonderful things for Israel, He waits for Israel to ask for them - *"Thus saith the Lord GOD; I will yet for this be inquired of by the house of Israel, to do it for them;"*

But when will Israel cry out to their God? Zechariah 12 gives a picture of all the nations coming against Jerusalem (vv2-11), and God still dealing with His people by grace! *"And I will pour upon the house of David, and upon the inhabitants of Jerusalem, the spirit of **grace** and of **supplications** [from the same root word as grace]: and they shall look upon [pay attention to; consider] me whom they have pierced, and they shall mourn for him, as one mourneth for his only son, and shall be in bitterness for him, as one that is in bitterness for his firstborn"* (Zech 12:10).

God had already stated this spiritual principle of crying out for His grace earlier in Zechariah when He said to Zerubbabel, whom some rabbis consider a foreshadow of the Messiah,

"This is the word of the LORD unto Zerubbabel, saying,
Not by might, nor by power, but by my spirit, saith the LORD of hosts.
Who art thou, O great mountain? before Zerubbabel thou shalt
become a plain:
and he shall bring forth the headstone thereof with shoutings, crying,
***Grace, grace** unto it"* (Zech 4:6b-7).

God our Father

For believers, being able to call God *"Abba, Father,"*[20] is one of the priceless benefits we obtain by our faith in Messiah. However, some have the impression that God's fatherhood was a new doctrine revealed by Yeshua. Like all New Testament doctrines, this one also has its roots in the *Tanach.* Here are some of the root verses in the *Tanach.*

God commanded Moses to approach Eygpt's king this way, *"And thou shalt say unto Pharaoh, Thus saith the LORD, **Israel is my son**, even my firstborn:"* (Exo 4:22). The Egyptians considered Pharaoh a god, and in a symbolic sense as a father. So God challenges Pharaoh, *"And I say unto thee, Let my son go, that he may serve me: and if thou refuse to let him go, behold, I will slay thy son, even thy firstborn"* (Exo 4:23).

Moses testified to God's father relationship with the children of Israel. In his final message to them, Moses declared, *"Ye are **the children of the LORD** your God..."* (Deut 14:1a). Later on in the same book, he asked Israel this pointed question, *"Do ye thus requite the LORD, O foolish people and unwise? is not he thy father that hath bought thee? hath he not made thee, and established thee?"* (Deut 32:6).

King David also had the revelation of God as a father to Israel. *"Wherefore David blessed the LORD before all the congregation: and David said, Blessed be thou, LORD God of Israel our father, for ever and ever"* (1 Chr 29:10).

Here are two interesting verses from the prophet Isaiah. In Isaiah 63:16, it appears that a believing remnant in Israel[21] is confessing that although they have not walked completely in the faith of their forefathers, Abraham and Israel, still, *"Doubtless thou art our father, though Abraham be ignorant of us, and Israel acknowledge us not: thou, O LORD, art our father, our redeemer; thy name* [reputation; character] *is from everlasting."* This remnant, having confessed their sins, pleads in Isaiah 64:8 for God to have mercy on Israel because of His father relationship to them. *"But now, O LORD, thou art our father; we are the clay, and thou our potter; and we all are the work of thy hand."*

The Lord justifies giving the people of Israel possession of the land of Israel, saying that when He saves her as a nation she will recognize Him as her Father and will serve and worship Him. *"But I said, How shall I put thee among the children, and give thee a pleasant* [precious] *land, a goodly* [prominent] *heritage of the hosts of nations? and I said, Thou shalt call me, My father; and shalt not turn away from me"* (Jer 3:19) and *"They shall come with weeping, and with supplications will I lead* [carry] *them: I will cause them to walk by the rivers of waters in a straight* [upright, righteous] *way, wherein they shall not stumble: for I am a father to Israel, and Ephraim is my firstborn"* (Jer 31:9). This last verse is a definite end time prophecy being fulfilled in a remnant of Israel today.

In the *Tanach* there are even instances of God being called a father of individuals. In declaring the Davidic covenant, God says about Solomon, *"I will be his father, and he shall be my son..."* (2 Sam 7:14a). There exists also a group of underprivileged individuals for whom God is declared to be a father. *"A father of the fatherless, and a judge of* [dispenser of justice for] *the widows, is God in his holy habitation"* (Psa 68:5).

We can see that before Yeshua came in the flesh, many *Tanach* verses had revealed God as our Father. Yeshua emphasized God's fatherhood more than anyone had before, but He could do so in total biblical correctness because of the deep *Tanach* roots that we have just reviewed.

The fatherhood of God also has a prominent role in rabbinic Judaism. A. Cohen observes that, "God is constantly addressed, or referred to, as 'Father Who is in heaven'...It was considered a mark of exceptional grace on His part that this intimate relationship exists and was revealed to man." He continues in his book *Everyman's Talmud*, "Especially when in the act of prayer, the individual was exhorted to think of himself as addressing his petitions to One Who stood to him in the relationship of Father."[22] In the traditional Hebrew prayer book, the *Siddur*, in the beautiful liturgical confession of sins read in every synagogue on *Yom Kippur*, the Day of Atonement, each line starts with *"Our Father, our King."*

"He shall cry unto me, Thou art my father,
my God, and the rock of my salvation" (Psa 89:26).

---

1   Walter Kaiser makes this observation. "Once in a while historical progress...allowed a full maturation of an aspect of the record, and at those points the text amazes us with the way in which meaning and teaching outstrip experience and the times." (Walter J. Kaiser Jr.,*Toward An Old Testament Theology*, Academie Books, Zondervan Pub. House, Grand Rapids, MI, 1978, pp. 8-9.)

2   *"And the Word* [Yeshua] *was made flesh, and dwelt among us, (and we beheld his glory, the glory as of the only begotten of the Father,) full of grace and truth"* (John 1:14); *"*[Yeshua]*... is the image of the invisible God...For it pleased the Father that in him should all fulness dwell;"* (Col 1:15a,19); *"*[God] *Hath in these last days spoken unto us by his Son...Who being the brightness of his glory, and the express image of his person, and upholding all things by the word of his power, when he had by himself purged our sins, sat down on the right hand of the Majesty on high;"* (Heb 1:2a,3).

3   A.W. Tozer, *The Knowledge of the Holy*, Harper & Row, Pub. Inc., New York, NY, 1961, p. 105.

4   See also Ex 7:16-17; 8:10,19,22; 9:14-16,20,29; 10:1-2; 11:7; 14:4,18,31.

5   Here are a few *Tanach* examples: *"O that there were such an heart* [mind, will, soul, inner man] *in them, that they would fear* [both revere and be afraid of] *me, and keep all my commandments always, that it might be well with them, and with their children for ever!"* (Deut 5:29).

   "Serve the LORD with fear, and rejoice with trembling" (Psa 2:11).

   "Surely his salvation is nigh them that fear him; that glory may dwell in our land" (Psa 85:9).

   "The fear of the LORD is the beginning of knowledge..." (Prov 1:7a).

   "But unto you that fear my name shall the Sun of righteousness arise with healing in his wings..." (Mal 4:2a).

   Other references on the fear of the Lord include: Josh 24:14; 1 Sam 12:14; Psa 19:9; Prov 1:7; Ecc 12:13; Isa 8:13.

6   *Strong's Concordance* #5401.

7   Norman H. Snaith, *The Distinctive Ideas of the Old Testament*, Schocken Books, NY, 1964, Chapter VI, "The Election-Love of God," pp. 131-142.

8 KJV "skirt," and the Hebrew "wing" both indicate betrothal. (Compare this to Ruth 3:9b, *"I am Ruth thine handmaid: spread therefore thy skirt over thine handmaid; for thou art a near kinsman* [my kinsman-redeemer].")

9 Here are a few more: 1 Ki 10:9; 2 Chr 2:11; Hos 3:1; 11:4.

10 Norman H. Snaith, *op. cit.*, pp. 94-130.

11 The New Testament describes God's faithfulness in many places. For example: Rom 16:25; 2 Cor 1:21; Phil 1:6; 2:13; Col 1:22; 1 Thes 5:24; 2 Thes 3:3-4; 2 Tim 4:18 and this incredible statement in Jude 24-25: *"Now unto him that is able* [has the power and authority] *to keep you from falling, and to present you faultless* [as an unblemished sacrifice] *before the presence of his glory with exceeding joy, To the only wise God our Saviour, be glory and majesty, dominion and power, both now and ever. Amen."*

12 For example, Psalm 22:1-22 [see Chapter 11, section "Psalm 22"]; 41:5-13; 69:4,7-9,19-26.

13 Prov 6:16; Isa 61:8; Jer 44:4; Amos 5:21; Zech 8:17. Yeshua hates things that pervert His Church. (Rev 2:6,15)

14 See also Psa 101:2-3; 119:104, 113, 128, 163; 139:21-22; Prov 8:13; Amos 5:14-15.

15 A.W. Tozer, *op. cit.*, pp. 96-97.

16 Who was this LORD who stood with Moses on the mount and revealed to him the essential nature of the God of Israel? According to John, it was the pre-incarnate Son of God: *"No man hath seen God at any time; the only begotten Son, which is in the bosom of the Father, he hath declared him"* (John 1:18).

17 See Ex 32:34-33:3.

18 We say reaffirmed because God chose Abraham, Isaac, and Jacob, and redeemed Israel from Egyptian bondage on the basis of His grace and love. Moses knows God's grace personally, and God reaffirms it here by saying yes to Moses' request.

19 The Hebrew word for "set time" is *moed.* It refers to a God-set appointment to meet with His people. Translated "feast" in Leviticus 23, which describes the "Feasts" of the LORD, it means more than just a holiday dinner.

20 Rom 8:15; Gal 4:6. *Abba* (Daddy) is heard in the streets and homes of Israel today.

21 As Paul indicates in Romans 9:27 and 11:5, there has always been a "remnant according to the election of grace."

22 A. Cohen, *Everyman's Talmud*, Schocken Books, New York, 1975 (reprint of 1949 ed. by EP Dutton), New York, pp. 20-21.

CHAPTER 3

Salvation in the *Tanach* - Passover

Passover Redemption

Participating in the feast of the Lord known as *Pesach,* or Passover, is a wonderful way to obtain a panoramic view of God's plan for salvation. By means of an unforgettable experience this "feast of [the] LORD" (see Lev 23)[1] portrays salvation by grace through faith in the blood of a lamb.

The story of Israel's redemption from slavery[2] and their subsequent freedom to receive God's Law at Mt. Sinai illustrates our redemption from the control of sin and Satan and of our freedom to live under God's rule. This is legitimate exegesis because, as we note in our comments on the covenant-love of God, Paul often used *Tanach* scriptures for examples of our walk with the Lord, explaining that *"all these things happened unto them* [Israel] *for ensamples* [warnings or prophetic types]: *and they are written for our admonition* [consideration], *upon whom the ends* [prophetic purpose or goal] *of the world* [lit: ages] *are come"* (1 Cor 10:11).

Besides teaching us spiritual truths, *Tanach* stories recount the penetration of world history by the God of the universe, the God of Israel. These episodes happened to a real flesh and blood people. Israel is never **just** a symbol.

Background

The book of Exodus opens with Israel in severe bondage to cruel taskmasters under a tyrant who is using them to build an empire and glorify himself. God hears their cries (Exo 2:23-25) and chooses an ambassador (apostle or "sent one"), an instrument to set His people free. God sends Moses as a prophet, in many ways a type of Yeshua,[3] to tell Pharaoh, whom the Egyptians claimed as a god, *"Thus saith the LORD God of Israel, Let my people go..."* (Exo 5:1b).[4]

Before Pharaoh ever hears this word, God tells Moses that Pharaoh will not listen. *"And I am sure* [I know] *that the king of Egypt will not let you go, no, not by a mighty hand"* (Exo 3:19). Pharaoh hardens his heart, then God hardens it further, allowing ample opportunity for God to display His power and draw many to Him. This process, stated in Exodus 9:16 by God and in Romans 9:17, shows God's sovereignty in the affairs of men. *"And in very deed for this cause have I raised thee* [Pharaoh] *up, for to shew in thee my power; and that my name* [character] *may be declared throughout all the earth"* (Exo 9:16).[5]

The display of God's sovereignty also attacks the concept of dualism, the idea of equally powerful good and evil forces fighting for the souls of men. Dualism undergirds many false religions but it cannot stand in light of the Scriptures which declare our God as Lord of heaven and earth. The following verses emphasize this:

"And I will sever [set apart, sanctify] *in that day the land of Goshen, in which my people dwell, that no swarms of flies shall be there; to the end* [in order that] *thou mayest know that **I am the LORD in the midst of the earth**"* (Exo 8:22).

*"And Moses said unto him, As soon as I am gone out of the city, I will spread abroad my hands unto the LORD; and the thunder shall cease, neither shall there be any more hail; that thou mayest know how that **the earth is the LORD's**"* (Exo 9:29).

"At that time Yeshua answered and said, I thank [lit: acknowledge; confess] *thee, O Father, **Lord of heaven and earth**..."* (Matt 11:25a).[6]

We are all familiar with the story of the ten plagues the Lord sent upon Egypt. The complete description is found in Exodus 7:14-12:30. These plagues pointedly attacked the many gods of Egypt. The last plague destroyed all the first-born animals and the first-born children (heirs) from every level of dynastic Egyptian society, including Pharaoh's son, the future god-king. *"For I will pass through the land of Egypt this night, and will smite all the firstborn in the land of Egypt, both man and beast; and against all the gods of Egypt I will execute judgment: I am the LORD"* (Exo 12:12).

God specified these judgments for the purpose of redemption, and not just Israel's, but also that of the Egyptians. The Lord states nine times that He sends these plagues so that *"...the Egyptians shall know that I am the LORD..."*[7] This is an excellent example of the thought in Psalm 9:16a, *"The LORD is known by the judgment which he executeth..."*

Our God still executes judgment and will continue to do so until the whole world knows that He is the God of Abraham,

Isaac and Jacob, the God of Israel. This has been and will continue to be accomplished through God's dealings with Israel. *"He hath remembered his mercy [chesed*[8]*] and his truth [lit: faithfulness] toward the house of Israel: all the ends of the earth have seen the salvation* [also deliverance, *yeshuah* – feminine form of Jesus' Hebrew name] *of our God"* (Psa 98:3).

On the Cross, the Father executed His judgment on our sin and laid it on Messiah Yeshua (see Isa 53:4-6) for the purpose of our redemption. God's righteous judgment removed the barrier separating us from Himself. Now we can enjoy a mutual love relationship with Him because of his judgment. *"Behold, the LORD's hand is not shortened, that it cannot save; neither his ear heavy* [insensitive]*, that it cannot hear: But your iniquities* [perversity; depravity] *have separated between* [divided] *you and your God, and your sins have hid* [concealed] *his face* [presence] *from you, that he will not hear"* (Isa 59:1-2).

As we saw above, God demonstrated His Lordship by protecting His people in Egypt from His wrath. After the first three plagues the "Israeli" neighborhood of Goshen was set apart *"...to the end thou mayest know that I am the LORD in the midst of the earth."* And at the last plague, *"But against any of the children of Israel shall not a dog move his tongue, against man or beast: that ye may know how that the LORD doth put a difference* [distinguishes] *between the Egyptians and Israel"* (Exo 11:7).[9]

Believers in Yeshua are also protected from God's wrath. We face the wrath of man (John 16:33), and the discipline of our Father (Heb 12:5-11), but in Yeshua, we will escape the wrath God will pour out on unbelievers. *"For God hath not appointed us to wrath* [His punishment or judgment]*, but to obtain salvation* [deliverance, rescue] *by our Lord Yeshua the Messiah"* (1 Thes 5:9).

Exodus 12 - The First Passover

The final book of the Bible proclaims Yeshua as *"the Lamb slain from the foundation of the world"* (Rev 13:8b). Why? Why is He called a lamb? Because the lamb *is* the Passover.

Exodus 12, the story of the Passover in Egypt, relates to our salvation through Yeshua and brings out facets of God's glorious redemption that the New Testament alone does not. The New Testament does not expand on many of these "root" issues because all of its writers assumed that believers would study and know Yeshua's Bible, the *Tanach*, as their scriptural foundation.[10] Here is a brief commentary on the Exodus account of the first Passover as it parallels our salvation. We encourage you to follow in your Bible.

12:1-2 By telling Moses and Aaron, *"This month shall be unto you the beginning of months: it shall be the first month of the year* *to you"* (v2), God indicates that redemption from bondage in Egypt will mark the start of a new life. We also start a new life when we trust in the sacrifice of Yeshua, our Passover Lamb (1 Cor 5:7), and become new creatures in the Messiah (2 Cor 5:17).

12:5 The *"lamb...without blemish"* is a type of the Messiah as a man without sin. *"For we have not an high priest which cannot be touched with the feeling of our infirmities* [weaknesses]*; but was in all points tempted* [tested; proved] *like as we are, yet without sin"* (Heb 4:15). The Hebrew word translated "without blemish," *tamiyim,* lines up perfectly with Yeshua's character, meaning complete, whole, entire, sound, innocent, having integrity and truth.[11] In the life of sheep, a *"male of the first year"* indicates a male in the prime of its life, as was Yeshua at 33 when He gave His life.

12:6 The lamb was examined for four days to see if there was any defect in it and only then was it killed. Yeshua walked and taught openly throughout the land of Israel for over three years so all could examine Him. He once asked, *"Which of you convicteth me of sin?"* (John 8:46). As Peter states, He is the spotless Lamb of God, *"Forasmuch as ye know that ye were not redeemed with corruptible* [perishable] *things, as silver and gold, from your vain* [profitless; empty] *conversation* [behavior, lifestyle] *received by tradition from your fathers; But with the precious blood of Messiah,* **as of a lamb without blemish and without spot:***"* (1 Pet 1:18-19).

12: 8-11 God commanded Israel to eat the flesh of the lamb, which is described in verse 11 as *"the LORD's Passover."* Comparing this with verses 21 and 27, we realize that in this chapter, God is often speaking of *the lamb* when He uses the term "the Passover." By the Holy Spirit, Paul said, *"Messiah our passover is sacrificed for us"* (1 Cor 5:7b). Therefore, calling Yeshua "our Passover" is parallel to calling Him 'the Lamb of God,*"* the title used of Yeshua more often than any other in the New Testament except for "the Messiah," "the Christ."[12] *"Messiah our Passover is sacrificed for us"* makes perfect sense against the background of Exodus 12.

What the Church calls Communion has roots in the annual Passover *Seder,* a meal God ordained to commemorate the Exodus from Egypt. Yeshua broke the bread, which is called "the bread of affliction" in the modern *Seder,* and told His disciples to eat it, saying, *"This is my body..."* (Luke 22:19). This bread was unleavened according to the commandment in Exodus 12:8. Leaven represents the spreading nature of sin (1 Cor 5:6-8). Yeshua, the sinless Lamb, used the Seder's unleavened bread to represent His body.[13]

Jewish *Seder* tradition names the cup of wine after supper "the cup of Messianic redemption." Yeshua said that this cup represented His blood which would seal the New Covenant promised in Jeremiah 31:31-34. *"Likewise also the cup after supper, saying, This cup is the new testament* [covenant] *in my blood, which is shed for you"* (Luke 22:20).

12:12 This verse identifies the one who destroys evil; the one who brings judgment on Egypt and its gods. The Lord God of Israel declares, *"For I will pass through the land of Egypt this night, and [I] will smite all the firstborn in the land of Egypt, both man and beast; and against all the gods of Egypt I will execute judgment: I am the LORD."* If we compare this with verses 13, 23, 27 and 29, we see that only in verse 23 is there a reference to *"...the destroyer..."* This is not Satan! Satan would not destroy his own kingdom, rooted so firmly in Egypt. God states four times that *He Himself* is the destroyer of Egypt's gods. We see this destroyer as none other than the pre-incarnate Son of God Who later destroyed the authority of the Devil over our lives at His first coming and will totally destroy Satan's kingdom at the end of time! *"For this purpose the Son of God was manifested, that he might destroy the works of the devil"* (I John 3:8b).

12:13 In verse 7, the children of Israel were commanded to smear the blood of the Passover lamb on the lintel and doorposts of their houses. They were then to go inside and eat the Passover meal. Once inside, they would no longer see the blood - it was a sign for God.

Yeshua presented His blood to His Father and the Father accepted it.[14] We trust in this blood sacrifice initially, and afterwards for forgiveness of each sin. God the Father is looking for the "sign" of the blood of His Son applied in our lives. When God sees the blood, His wrath will pass over us, while it falls on the world. *"And to wait for his Son from heaven, whom he raised from the dead, even* **Yeshua, which delivered** [rescued] **us from the wrath** [punishment] **to come**...*For God hath not appointed us to wrath, but to obtain salvation* [safety; deliverance] *by our Lord Yeshua the Messiah,"* (1 Thes 1:10; 5:9).

Another similarity to our salvation is that, unlike the later sacrificial system, the Passover was a "once for-all" deliverance from within enemy territory! *"Yea, though I walk through the valley of the shadow of death, I will fear no evil: for thou art with me; thy rod and thy staff they comfort me. Thou preparest a table before me in the presence of mine enemies: thou anointest my head with oil; my cup runneth over"* (Psa 23:4-5).

God commanded the children of Israel to eat this meal to forever remember His redemption. Jews and the gentiles who joined themselves to the house of Israel were to keep this feast (Exo 12:19,47-49) as a way to teach the next generation about God's goodness and power. *"And it shall come to pass, when your children shall say unto you, What mean ye by this service? That ye shall say, It is the sacrifice of the LORD's passover, who passed over the houses of the children of Israel in Egypt, when he smote the Egyptians, and delivered our houses. And the people bowed the head and worshipped"* (Exo 12:26-27). We declare redemption when we keep the Passover as well as when we celebrate Communion. *"For as often as ye eat this bread, and drink this cup, ye do shew* [publicly proclaim] *the Lord's death* [the Atonement] *till he come"* (1 Cor 11:26).

We encourage you to participate in a believers' Passover *Seder*. You will find it edifying and exciting, and will end up with a new appreciation of the continuity of God's great plan of salvation.

Conclusion

"Behold the Lamb of God which taketh away[15] *the sin of the world"* (John 1:29b). The Passover, while celebrating a historic event, also illustrates the dynamics of salvation *by grace through faith* in the blood of the Lamb. Grace applies because it was God who delivered the children of Israel when, through faith, they obeyed His instructions to apply the blood. They rested and ate under the protection of the blood until the Lord delivered them. We too apply the blood of God's Passover Lamb, rest in Him, partake of Him, and remain under His protection. We *"stand still, and see the salvation of the LORD..."* (Exo 14:13b).

"Oh, taste and see [consider] *that the LORD is good;*
blessed is the man that trusteth in him" (Psa 34:8).[16]

---

1   The seven yearly feasts in Leviticus 23 are divided into two seasons. The spring feasts: Passover (*Pesach* – v 5); Unleavened Bread (*Matzot* – vv 6-8); First Fruits [of the barley harvest] (*Bikkurim* – vv 9-14); Pentecost or Weeks (*Shavuot* – vv 15-21). Then the fall feasts: Day of the Blowing of the Shofar (*Yom Teruah*, known today as *Rosh haShanah*, i.e., the Jewish New Year – vv 24-25); The Day of Atonement (*Yom Kippur* – vv 26-32); finally Tabernacles or Booths (*Succot* – vv 33-43).

2   The children of Israel should have made a "clean break" from Egypt. They were no longer slaves and the gods of Egypt had been humiliated. Instead, in one of the great tragedies in the *Tanach*, many of the Israelites took Egyptian idols with them (See Ezek 20:7-8,16,18,24). Those who did, remained spiritual slaves. This is a picture of many believers in Messiah Yeshua who, although saved and set free from past sins, still hold on to their "idols" as well. The Israelites who professed love for the Lord, yet could not part with their idols, died in the wilderness.

3   Deut 18:15,18-19 *"The LORD thy God will raise up unto thee a Prophet from the midst of thee, of thy brethren, like unto me; unto him ye shall*

hearken...[the LORD said] I will raise them up a Prophet from among their brethren, like unto thee, and will put my words in his mouth; and he shall speak unto them all that I shall command him."

4   This is the first time in Scripture that God uses the name *"LORD God of Israel."*

5   See Dan 4:17,25,32, 34-35; 5:21.

6   See also Psa 2:1-9; 24:1; Isa 40:17-26; Hag 2:8; Acts 10:36.

7   See Ex 7:5,17; 8:10,19,22; 9:14,29; 14:4,18.

8   See Chapter 2.

9   See also Ex 9:4,26 and 10:23.

10 See 2 Tim 3:16-17 and Chapter 1.

11 Brown-Driver-Briggs Hebrew lexicon, *PC StudyBible*; Biblesoft Inc.

12 John 1:29,36; 1 Pet 1:19 plus 26 times in the book of Revelation!

13 Unleavened bread is called *matzah*. It is baked today as it was in Yeshua's day except then the shape was probably round. This special bread, representing Messiah's body, is pierced and has the appearance of being striped and bruised. It is broken before being eaten. *Matzah* is the most symbolic bread to use when taking Communion.

14 Acts 20:28; Eph 1:7; Heb 9:12,22.

15 "Takes away" is literally to lift up, carry away or bear on oneself. It is a Hebraism for atoning for, or redeeming from sin. Cp. Isaiah 53:4 – "he hath borne...carried;" 53:5 – "upon him;" 53:6 – "laid on him."

16 Alternative paraphrase: How happy is the valiant warrior that seeks refuge, flees for protection to, confides and hopes in Him.

Salvation in the *Tanach* - Grace and Faith

Salvation by Grace in the *Tanach*

We have seen that our God is a God of grace, that grace is just as much His nature as love or justice. The Passover story clarifies that God's salvation is *and always was* by grace through faith, and not through the "Law," as some have it. Unfortunately, for centuries many have been led to believe that in the Old Testament, salvation was accomplished only through works. That is a serious misconception of what the *Tanach* and the New Testament clearly teach.

Look at grace and the Law, or faith and works, in the *Tanach*. Think about the *"Law of Moses,"* also called the *"Law of the Lord"* even in the New Testament.[1] When was the "Law" (a better translation would be "Instruction" or "Teaching") first revealed to the children of Israel? It was given *after* they were freed from Egypt. By *faith* in God's Word to Moses they had already applied the blood of the Passover Lamb to their doorposts, and they had already been "baptized,"[2] in *faith* passing through the Red Sea at God's Word (Heb 11:29).

The children of Israel were redeemed and dedicated for His special purposes before they ever received His Law. At Sinai He said to His blood-bought,[3] water-baptized people, that He wanted His people to live by this Law, so as to be a kingdom of priests proclaiming His name to the nations.[4] The Law was given as a set of divine rules and instructions so the people of God would be holy (literally, "set-apart") and protected in the midst of the world and its traps.

Over time, and because of man's tendency to trust in works of the flesh, the Law became distortedly seen as the way of salvation (see Rom 9:31-32) - the thinking that one can do something to earn God's favor. But it has always been and ever will be that *"...the just shall live by his faith"* (Hab 2:4; Heb 10:38). The Law's nature never changed. According to Paul, the Law of God is still *"holy, and the commandment holy, and just, and good"* (Rom 7:12b).

Confusion has arisen due to translations saying that believers are no longer "under the Law." Bible expositors unfamiliar with Hebrew theology did not understand that "under the Law" is just a shortened way of saying "under the system for atonement found in the Mosaic Law." After all, what kind of believer would think it is now "legal" to break the Ten Commandments?

The Law of Moses no longer provides for an effective means of atonement for "Law-breakers" (sinners) because of the fulfillment in Messiah's blood atonement. However, the Law still contains God's standard of righteousness. Breaking the Law still requires blood atonement. The Jewish people no longer believe in blood atonement (animal blood is no longer accepted by God), and for that reason they are not saved outside of their Messiah Yeshua.[5] As for gentiles, so for Jews, for it has always been and ever will be that *"...the just shall live by his faith"* (Hab 2:4; Heb 10:38).

The doctrine of salvation by grace lies at the root of our proclamation of the Good News. Paul states, *"For by grace are ye saved through faith; and that not of yourselves: it is the gift* [or sacrificial offering] *of God: Not of works, lest any man should boast"* (Eph 2:8-9). And where do we find the root doctrine of grace? As we have seen, it appears in the Hebraic soil of the Old Testament as an attribute of God. But more than that, God actually saves us through His grace.

Here is another definition of grace which emphasizes its role in salvation. The Hebrew word most often translated "grace" or "favor" is *chen.* According to Colin Brown's *New International Dictionary of New Testament Theology,* this word "clarifies the meaning of 'grace' in history and actions. It denotes the stronger coming to the help of the weaker who stands in need of help by reason of his circumstances or natural weakness. [The stronger] acts by a voluntary decision, though he is moved by the dependence or the request of the weaker party."[6]

This is often expressed as "to find favor in someone's eyes," an idiom still in use in modern Hebrew. Brown makes the observation that *"chen* denotes relatively seldom the activity of God. It is used mostly in the sense of His undeserved gift in election."[7] Or as Paul puts it, *"In whom also we have obtained an inheritance, being predestinated according to the purpose of him who worketh all things after the counsel of his own will:"* (Eph 1:11b).

Tanach Verses

Here are some Tanach verses picturing God's grace, *chen* (in **bold**), variously translated as "grace" or "favor":

"But Noah found grace in the eyes of the LORD" (Gen 6:8). Although verse 9b says, *"Noah was a just* [righteous][8] *man and perfect* [had integrity] *in his generations, and Noah walked with God,"* yet the reason he acted righteously was because he had been chosen by God's grace. In that grace Noah responded as we all must, but ultimately, he and his household were saved by the grace of God.

After worshiping the golden calf in Exodus 32, Israel deserved death. Moses knew that it was not by any merit on the part of the children of Israel that he could approach the Lord and intercede for them. So he came on the basis of grace. God answered him on the same basis (33:17) and even stated that it is His divine nature to be "gracious" (34:6).[9] As we saw in this brief exchange between God and Moses, the word *chen*, or a word based on the same root, is used nine times.

Psalm 51 is David's prayer of confession, asking the Lord for forgiveness because of his sins of murder and adultery (2 Sam 11). *"Have mercy upon me, O God, according to thy lovingkindness* [*chesed*]*"* (Psa 51:1a). The word "mercy" in this verse comes from the Hebrew root meaning "grace." David realized that he was lost if God did not deal with him in accordance with His grace and mercy, based on God's *chesed,* His covenant love.[10] So David, the greatest king of Israel, like the great prophet Moses before him, came to his Lord on the basis of who God is and not with any merit of his own. Although David's life afterwards proved the spiritual principle that we reap what we sow (Gal 6:7-8), yet we must note that God did deal with His servant based on His grace – because according to His law, murder and adultery are worthy of the death penalty. (Lev 24:17; 20:10)

Proverbs 3:34 states, *"Surely he scorneth the scorners: but he giveth grace unto the lowly* [humble, meek, afflicted]*."* James and Peter quote the last part of this *Tanach* verse. James says, *"But he giveth more grace. Wherefore he saith, God resisteth the proud, but giveth grace unto the humble"* (Jam 4:6), and Peter says, *"...Yea, all of you be subject one to another, and be clothed with humility: for God resisteth the proud, and giveth grace to the humble"* (1 Pet 5:5b).

James 4:6 uses this principle of obtaining grace through humility to encourage believers to *"Submit yourselves therefore to God. Resist the devil..."* (Jam 4:7a). Peter brings out the same principle using slightly different terms as a proof text to encourage us to submit to God: *"Humble yourselves therefore under the mighty hand of God, that he may exalt you* [give grace/favor] *in due time:"* (1 Pet 5:6).

In Jeremiah's prophesied restoration of the nation of Israel (Chapters 30-33), God declares in 31:2, *"Thus saith the LORD, The people which were left* [lit: "survivors," or "remnant"] *of the sword found* **grace** *in the wilderness; even Israel, when I went to cause him to rest.*" God's rest is an example of His grace. The New Testament ties in God's rest with salvation. *"For he that is entered into his rest, he also hath ceased from his own works, as God did from his"* (Heb 4:10). Obviously, ceasing from trusting in our own works depends on trusting in God's grace through salvation.[11]

Zechariah 12:10 is a promise of Israel's national salvation (see Rom 11:26), the result of God's grace pouring out on them. *"And I will pour upon the house of David, and upon the inhabitants[12] of Jerusalem, the spirit of* **grace** *and of supplications: and they shall look upon* [intently regard] *me whom they have pierced, and they shall mourn for him, as one mourneth for his only son, and shall be in bitterness for him, as one that is in bitterness for his firstborn."* The Hebrew for "supplications" also comes from the same Hebrew root as "grace."

In just these six *Tanach* passages among the many showing God's grace, we have seen grace in connection with election, salvation, God's nature, the forgiveness of sin, and the national salvation of the house of Israel. These are the roots of that same grace proclaimed in the New Testament. And since our salvation is *"by grace through faith,"* let us look next at what the *Tanach* says about faith.

Salvation by Faith in the *Tanach*

As we have mentioned before, and contrary to what many believers think, salvation in the *Tanach* was never obtained just by obeying the Mosaic Law. God, who never changes (Mal 3:6), has always offered salvation to those who believe and trust in His Word. And His Word consistently points to salvation through faith in God's provision for atonement. This theme runs through the Old Testament as well as the New. As the following New Testament verses state, our God wants faith *with* works, not faith *in* works:

"Therefore whosoever heareth these sayings of mine, **and doeth them**, *I will liken him unto a wise man, which built his house upon a rock...And every one that heareth these sayings of mine,* **and doeth them not**, *shall be likened unto a foolish man, which built his house upon the sand:"* (Matt 7:24,26).

"If ye love me, **keep my commandments** *"* (John 14:15).[13]

"This is a faithful saying, and these things I will that thou affirm constantly, that they which have believed in God might **be careful to maintain good works** *..."* (Titus 3:8a).

Here is that often misunderstood section of James. *"What doth it profit, my brethren, though a man say he hath faith, and have not works? can faith save him?...Yea, a man may say, Thou hast faith, and I have works: shew me thy faith without thy works, and I will shew thee my faith by my works...But wilt thou know, O vain man, that faith without works is dead?...For as the body without the spirit is dead, so* **faith without works is dead** *also"* (James 2:14,18,20,26).

Works are the manifestation of the fruits of the Spirit. This fruit consists of the forming in us of godly characteristics (listed in Galatians 5:22-23) and includes faith and goodness. If we would keep in mind that our works are good only if they are validated by faith, our trusting and obeying God's Word to us, and empowered by His Spirit and not our own questionable motives, then all of the above verses make perfect sense.

The words "faith" and "belief" are commonly used in two different but valid ways. They are sometimes used to designate a creed or set of religious beliefs, for example: Christian belief, the Jewish faith, etc. However, in this section we use "faith" and "belief" in the usual biblical sense of trusting in, relying on, remaining steadfast in, and believing the Lord. Genesis 15:6 says about Father Abraham, *"And he believed in the LORD; and he counted it to him for righteousness"* or as the Amplified Version states, *"And* [Abram] *believed,* (trusted in, relied on, remained steadfast to the Lord)*; and He counted it to him as righteousness* [right standing with God].*"*

In Hebrew, three important words come from a single root. "Faith" (or "faithfulness"), "truth," and "amen" are linked linguistically and theologically. Their root word means "to build up or support; to foster as a parent; figuratively, to render [or be] firm or faithful, to trust or believe, to be permanent or quiet...to be true or certain" (*Strong's Concordance,* #539).

The Hebrew word for "faithful" denotes a trusting certainty, as well as faithfulness in the sense of dependability. This word is used of men:

"My servant Moses is not so, who is **faithful** *in all mine house"* (Num 12:7).

"And I will raise me up a **faithful** *priest* [Samuel],*that shall do according to that which is in mine heart..."* (1 Sam 2:35a).

"Thou art the LORD the God, who didst choose Abram, and broughtest him forth out of Ur of the Chaldees, and gavest him the name of Abraham; And foundest his heart **faithful** *before thee, and madest a covenant with him to give the land of the Canaanites..."* (Neh 9:7-8a).

This word is also used of God, the One to whom all true faith looks:

"Know therefore that the LORD thy God, he is God, the **faithful** *God, which keepeth covenant and mercy* [chesed] *with them that love him and keep his commandments to a thousand generations;"* (Deut 7:9).

"Kings shall see and arise, princes also shall worship, because of the LORD that is **faithful***, and the Holy One of Israel, and he shall choose thee"* (Isa 49:7b).

"It is of the LORD's mercies [chesed] that we are not consumed, because his compassions fail not. They are new every morning: great is thy faithfulness" (Lam 3:22-23). This word is also used of God's covenant, highlighting its reliability because God stands behind it. *"My mercy [chesed] will I keep for him for evermore, and my covenant shall stand fast with him"* (Psa 89:28).

Although the root word under discussion is not found in the following passage, this quote thoroughly embodies the concept of God's faithfulness to His covenant. *"Thus saith the LORD; If ye can break my covenant of the day, and my covenant of the night, and that there should not be day and night in their season; Then may also my covenant be broken* [frustrated; violated] *with David my servant, that he should not have a son to reign upon his throne; and with the Levites the priests, my ministers...Thus saith the LORD; If my covenant be not with day and night, and if I have not appointed the ordinances of heaven and earth; Then will I cast away* [or despise] *the seed of Jacob, and David my servant, so that I will not take any of his seed to be rulers over the seed of Abraham, Isaac, and Jacob: for I will cause their captivity to return, and have mercy on them"* (Jer 33:20-21,25-26).

The *Tanach* on Faith

Genesis 15:6 - *"And he* [Abraham] **believed** *in the LORD; and he counted it to him for righteousness."* More than once the New Testament uses this incident in the *Tanach* as a specific example of faith as trust. For example in James 2:23, *"And the scripture was fulfilled which saith, Abraham* **believed** [trusted] *God, and it was imputed* [accounted] *unto him for righteousness: and he was called the Friend of God."*[14] Paul also uses this verse to support his argument for salvation by faith in Romans 4, and also in Galatians 3:6 to encourage believers not to try to gain God's favor by works of the Law (Gal 5:4), but by continuing in faith (Gal 3:3).

Even the rabbis declare, "Our father Abraham, came into the possession of this world and the world hereafter [eternal life] only by the merit of his faith" (Mechilta 33a). In an interesting comment found in the *ArtScroll Tanach Series*, Hirsch explains in connection with this verse, "the concept of believing someone, in the sense that his promise is accepted, would be expressed as ["he believed him"]. The phrase in this verse, ["he believed *in* Him"], however, represents a much deeper concept than mere belief. It suggests total submission in the sense that one places his total confidence and seeks all his guidance and attitudes in God."[15]

The Tabernacle in the wilderness (Exo 25:1-40:38) symbolizes the pattern of our salvation, of how to relate to God His way. It ties together God's provision for the forgiveness of sins and our response of obedient service to Him in faith. Without the ordained priesthood and offerings, the tabernacle was just a pretty tent. Without God's order, timing and Law functioning in the tabernacle, all that man can offer is "profane fire" (Lev 10:1-5), "filthy rags" (Isa 64:6), and works and service through the flesh. Israel was saved through the Tabernacle not by bringing sacrifices, but only by acting in belief in what God said about blood, and atonement, and bringing sacrifices. There's a huge difference.

Leviticus 1:1-7:38 describes the sacrificial offerings. The sinner brought his sacrifice to the priest and confessed his sin over the head of the animal (Lev 4:29,33), then slew the offering. The priest applied the blood to the altar, making atonement for the sin. The sinner was then forgiven (Lev 4:31,35). What is the pattern? To gain acceptance by God, all the sinner needed to do was trust the Word of the Lord which told him that the blood of his sacrificial offering would atone for, literally "cover," his sin. The sinner did no work other than to trust and obey the Word! This atoning power of the shed blood models the forgiveness of sins. It is a foreshadow of our salvation accomplished on the Cross through our sacrificial offering, Yeshua. All we "do" for salvation is believe God's Word and trust Him to fulfill it; and the fruit of that faith comes when we obey God's commands.

We read in 2 Chronicles 20:20b, *"Hear me, O Judah, and ye inhabitants of Jerusalem;* **Believe** *in the LORD your God, so shall ye be established;* **believe** *his prophets, so shall ye prosper."* The Hebrew in that verse has the same wording as in Genesis 15:6, to believe *in* the Lord. This charge, given by King Jehoshaphat to the nation of Judah when they were about to be attacked by a greatly superior army, demonstrates the Hebrew concept behind the word "faith," translated here as "believe." We are "established," "built up," when we trust in God's Word (see Matt 7:24-27). In fact the Hebrew for *"so shall ye be established,"* has the same Hebrew root as "believe"!

The negative side of the above verse is found in Isaiah 7:9b, *"If ye will not* **believe**, *surely ye shall not be established."* Again, the word translated "believe," means to trust, to be certain, and has the same root as the word translated *"ye shall...be established."*

Habakkuk 2:4 is one of the most important of the "faith" verses found in the *Tanach, "Behold, his soul which is lifted up is not upright in him: but the just shall live by his* **faith** [or faithfulness]." That second part is quoted several times in the New Testament as a proof text for our life of faith:

"For I am not ashamed of the gospel of Messiah: for it is the power of God unto salvation to every one that **believeth**; *to the Jew first, and also to the Greek. For therein is the righteousness of*

God revealed [disclosed] *from faith to faith: as it is written, The just shall live by faith "* (Rom 1:16-17).

"But that no man is justified [rendered righteous] *by the law in the sight of God, it is evident* [obvious]*: for, The just shall live by faith"* (Gal 3:11).

"For yet a little while, and he that shall come will come, and will not tarry. Now the just shall live by faith" (Heb 10:37-38a).

When the New Testament authors wanted to give solid examples of men and women of God who lived by faith, they pointed to the heroes of the *Tanach*. The most quoted chapter in this regard is Hebrews 11 which presents a "great cloud of witnesses" (Heb 12:1) who overcame, stood in their faith, trusting in God through all kinds of trials, including death.

Scripture emphatically states that these saints of God pleased Him (Heb 11:6), not through their works *per se*, although we see their faith by their works, but through trusting the One who did the works through them. Here is the key - not faith in our faith or in our ability to believe, but faith/trust in the living God of the Scriptures, who is faithful. *"Looking unto Yeshua the author* [leading example] *and finisher* [perfector] *of our faith; who for the joy that was set before him endured the cross, despising the shame* [disgrace]*, and is set down at the right hand of the throne of God"* (Heb 12:2).

Paul mentions God's faithfulness as the pillar of Abraham's faith, *"He staggered* [withdrew] *not at the promise of God through unbelief; but was strong in faith, giving glory to God; And being fully persuaded that,* **what he had promised, he was able also to perform**. *And therefore it was imputed* [accounted] *to him for righteousness"* (Rom 4:20-22).

Paul further tells us in 2 Timothy 2:13 that we can trust in God because of who He is. It is God's character to be faithful - *"If we believe not, yet he abideth* [remains] **faithful**: *he cannot* [is not able to] *deny himself."*

Finally, in Revelation 3:14 Yeshua calls Himself *"...the **Amen**, the **faithful** and **true** witness...,"* combining all three of the major concepts rooted in the Hebrew word for "faith." Yeshua, and He alone, must be the focal point of our faith.

*"Thus saith the LORD, the Redeemer of Israel, and his Holy One, to him whom man despiseth, to him whom the nation abhorreth, to a servant of rulers, Kings shall see and arise, princes also shall worship, because of the LORD that is **faithful**, and the Holy One of Israel, and he shall choose thee"* (Isaiah 49:7).

1   *"And when the days of her purification according to* **the law of Moses** *were accomplished, they brought him to Jerusalem, to present him to the Lord; (As it is written in* **the law of the Lord**, *Every male that openeth the womb shall be called holy to the Lord;) And to offer a sacrifice according to that which is said in* **the law of the Lord**, *A pair of turtledoves, or two young pigeons"* (Luke 2:22-24).

2   *"Moreover, brethren, I would not that ye should be ignorant, how that all our fathers were under the cloud, and all passed through the sea; And were all* **baptized** *unto Moses in the cloud and in the sea;"* (1 Cor 10:1-2).

3   See Ex 15:16; cp. with Acts 20:28.

4   Here is that paraphrase as it appears in the KJV: *"And Moses went up unto God, and the LORD called unto him out of the mountain, saying, Thus shalt thou say to the house of Jacob, and tell the children of Israel; Ye have seen what I did unto the Egyptians, and how I bare you on eagles' wings, and brought you unto myself. Now therefore, if ye will obey my voice indeed, and keep my covenant, then ye shall be a peculiar treasure unto me above all people: for all the earth is mine: And ye shall be unto me a kingdom of priests, and an holy nation. These are the words which thou shalt speak unto the children of Israel"* (Exo 19:3-6).

5   For this reason, any attempts to help the Jewish people rebuild their Temple and reinstitute animal sacrifices are misguided and hindering their salvation.

6   *The New International Dictionary of the New Testament*, ed. Colin Brown, Vol. 2, p.116.

7   Ibid., p. 116.

8   As Isaiah 64:6a states: *"But we are all as an unclean thing, and all our righteousnesses are as filthy rags."*

9   See Chap. 2, section "God of Grace" for a more complete look at this section of scripture.

10 See Chap. 2, section "The Covenant-Love of God - *Chesed"*

11 *"Even so then at this present time also there is a remnant according to the election of grace. And if by grace, then is it no more of works: otherwise grace is no more grace. But if it be of works, then is it no more grace: otherwise work is no more work"* (Rom 11:5-6; also Eph 2:8-9).

12 This word in modern Hebrew is translated "settlers." Considering the current uproar over the "Israeli settlers," it is good to know that these people will also be recipients of God's grace.

13 See also John 14:21-24; 1 John 2:3-5; 5:2-3.

14 See also Rom 4:3-6,9,20-25 and Gal 3:6-14. Also see Hebrews 11:8 for another New Testament use of Abraham as someone whose faith should provoke us to jealousy.

15 *ArtScroll Tanach Series, Bereshis (Genesis)*, Mesorah Publications, Brooklyn, Vol. 1., p. 512.

CHAPTER 5

Doctrines in the *Tanach* - Sin, Blood, Atonement

Having studied some basic concepts of salvation illustrated in the feast of Passover, we turn our attention to *Yom Kippur*, the Day of Atonement, another *Tanach* holy day in which several teachings of our faith take root. We will look at teachings in four areas: sin, blood atonement, forgiveness, and the mediation of the High Priest.

Sin

As mentioned before, Rabbi Shaul (Apostle Paul), who had been carefully educated in *"the holy scriptures"* (called the *Tanach* or "Old Testament" - 2 Tim 3:15), referred to or quoted the *Tanach* about sixty times in his one letter to the Romans. Only by doing so could he have proven that the major New Testament doctrines are of God. Paul knew that for a doctrine to be true it must confirm what God had previously said in the *Tanach*. The Lord stated this through His prophet Isaiah, *"To the law and to the testimony: if they speak not according to this word, it is because there is no light in them"* (Isa 8:20).

So do we find in the *Tanach* any sweeping statements about sin like Paul's declaration in Romans 3:23, *"For all have sinned and come short of the glory of God?"*

As early as Genesis 6:5, before the Flood, the Bible observes, *"And GOD saw that the wickedness of man was great in the earth, and that every imagination* [purpose, idea] *of the thoughts of his heart was only evil continually"* ("continually" in the Hebrew is *kol yom*, literally, all or every day). After the Flood God declares that He will *"...not again curse the ground any more for man's sake; for the imagination* [purpose] *of man's heart is evil from his*

47

youth..." (Gen 8:21b). In these verses God focuses on the state of the "heart," which in both Hebrew and Greek stands for the inner man, the mind, emotions and will. In both verses, the condition of man's heart is described as "evil" all through his life. Or as God declares through the prophet Jeremiah, *"The heart is deceitful* [sly; insidious; lit: slippery] *above all things, and desperately wicked* [incurably sick]*: who can know it?"* (Jer 17:9).

In the *Yom Kippur* instructions found in Leviticus 16, which we will study in a later section, the High Priest made atonement for everyone in the camp of Israel, including himself. No one was free from the need of atonement for his sins.[1]

King Solomon, whom the scriptures declare was the wisest man who ever lived (1 Kin 3:12; 4:29-34), knew about our tendency to sin. When dedicating the Temple in Jerusalem, he prayed to God, *"If they sin against thee, (for there is no man that sinneth not,)..."* (1 Kin 8:46a). In Proverbs 20:9, Solomon has this insight, *"Who can say, I have made my heart clean, I am pure from my sin?"* Later in life, he came to a further realization, *"For there is not a just man upon earth, that doeth good, and sinneth not"* (Ecc 7:20). Even the righteous person who wants to please God does not avoid all sin.

The prophet Isaiah says in 64:6a, *"But we are as an unclean* [impure; defiled] *thing, and all our righteousnesses are like filthy rags..."* These last two verses reprove those who try to earn their salvation. Not only is there *"no man,"* not even a *"just man"* who never sins, but the literal Hebrew declares that even our righteous acts are, in His sight, like clothing that has been soiled and stained.

The Psalmist exclaims in 130:3, *"If thou, LORD, shouldest mark iniquities, O Lord, who shall stand?"* In Psalm 143:2, King David pleads with the Lord, *"And enter not into judgment with thy servant: for in thy sight shall no man living be justified."* If God judged us according to His legal right as our Creator, insisting that we walk before Him without fault, as He says in both the *Tanach* and the New Testament,[2] no one would be found blameless. Isaiah confirms this in 53:6a, *"All we like sheep have gone astray; we have turned every one to his own way..."*

In the New Testament Paul says that we have inherited our "old man," our propensity to sin, from our father Adam, the natural head of the human race.[3] Can we find the roots of that truth in the *Tanach?*

Psalm 51:5 (*"Behold, I was shapen in iniquity; and in sin did my mother conceive me."*) and Psalm 58:3 (*"The wicked are estranged from the womb: they go astray as soon as they be born, speaking lies."*) indicate that babies are born with the first Adam's nature. If you have ever seen a precious little baby suddenly change into a screamer because it could not have its way, you have seen a perfect demonstration of a rebellious spirit whose vocabulary is largely limited to "I," "Me" and "Mine."

In Genesis 5:1-3 we have an insightful commentary by Moses on the result of Adam's sin. *"This is the book of the generations of Adam. In the day that **God created man, in the likeness of God** made he him; Male and female created he them; and blessed them, and called their name Adam, in the day when they were created. And Adam lived an hundred and thirty years, and **begat a son in his own likeness, after his image**; and called his name Seth:"*

Since *"God is a Spirit..."* (John 4:24), it was Adam's spirit that was created in God's likeness. That likeness died when Adam and Eve sinned (Eph 2:1,5) and all their offspring were then born with *their* spiritual likeness - the tendency to sin, which we all have inherited. Only by being "born from above" are our spirits reborn or resurrected in God's likeness (John 3:6-7). Our lives then begin to be conformed into the likeness of the life of the Son of God, Yeshua (Rom 8:29).

The *Tanach* scriptures given above undergird the New Testament doctrine that all people are sinners. Here are specific terms that the *Tanach* uses to describe manifest sin: unbelief, lack of trust, hardness of heart, disobedience, stiff-neck, rebellion.

Atonement and Blood

The Hebrew root word *kopher,* means literally "to cover," but figuratively "to pay" or "to ransom." We have a good example of it in Exodus 21:30, *"If there be laid on him a sum of money, then he shall **give for the ransom** of his life whatsoever is laid upon him,"* or as it states in the NKJV, *"...he shall **pay** [kopher] to redeem his life..."* The Hebrew noun for atonement, *kaphar,* is derived from this root word.

Kaphar, atonement, literally means a protective covering, but figuratively it takes on the meaning of forgiveness, including the "covering" and "payment" for sins. The *Theological Wordbook of the Old Testament* states the following about *kaphar:* "From the meaning of *kopher,* 'to ransom', the meaning of *kaphar* can be understood...'to atone by offering a substitute'."[4]

Hebrews 9:22, contains the clearest position statement on blood atonement in the New Testament, *"And almost all things are by the law purged* [cleansed] *with blood; and without shedding of blood is no remission* [forgiveness; pardon]*"* (based on Lev 17:11 - see following). That verse occurs in the context of the writer's argument that Yeshua's blood sacrifice was necessary to establish a new covenant between God and man. The phrase "make a covenant" literally says in Hebrew "cut a covenant," referring to a blood sacrifice to seal the covenant.[5]

When we realize that sealing a covenant requires blood to be shed we obtain a better understanding of Yeshua's words spoken over the cup of wine during His last supper (the Passover meal), *"And he took the cup, and gave thanks, and gave it to them, saying, Drink ye all of it; For this is my blood of the new testament* [covenant], *which is shed for many for the remission* [forgiveness; pardon] *of sins"* (Matt 26:27-28).[6]

Throughout the Scriptures God makes it clear that blood is not some arbitrary magical substance that provides atonement. Blood is required because it contains the life of the creature. The Lord states, *"The soul that sinneth, it shall die"* (Ezek 18:20a). "Soul" (Hebrew - *nephesh*) *"...*denotes the 'life' of an individual."[7] Look at Leviticus 17:11-12. *"For the life* [*nephesh*] *of the flesh is in the blood: and I have given it to you upon the altar to make an atonement* [covering] *for* [or over] *your souls* [nephesh]: *for it is the blood that maketh an atonement for the soul* [*nephesh*]. *Therefore I said unto the children of Israel, No soul* [*nephesh*] *of you shall eat blood, neither shall any stranger that sojourneth among you eat blood."*

Forty years later, as Israel prepared to enter the promised land, Moses reminded them of that commandment (Deut 12:23). This divine instruction was not new; it had been given to all mankind from the time that God made a covenant with Noah after the Flood. Included in His instructions to Noah and his sons is, *"But flesh with the life* [nephesh] *thereof, which is the blood thereof, shall ye not eat"* (Gen 9:4).[8]

God uses the physical red liquid as a symbol for the life of the flesh. The NKJV translates the Hebrew word "blood" as "life." Leviticus 19:16b in the NKJV reads *"...against the **life** of your neighbor";* but in the King James Version and the original Hebrew it is *"...against the **blood** of your neighbor."* A sacrifice whose blood was sprinkled on the altar of God became a substitute for the sinner's soul, that is, the sinner's life, which would have been forfeit through sin. It fulfilled the divine Law of a life [*nephesh*] for a life [*nephesh*] (Exo 21:23; Deut 19:21).

Our salvation depends on that fact. Yeshua gave His life for us by offering His blood as our substitute/sacrifice; His life for our lives. Matthew 20:28 says, *"Even as the Son of man came not to be ministered unto* [to be served], *but to minister* [to serve], *and to give his life a ransom for many."*[9]

As mankind's substitute, Yeshua had to die in a certain way. He could not be suffocated or poisoned. His blood had to be shed like that of a sacrificed animal.[10] This legally satisfied God's justice while releasing His mercy in forgiveness. *"For all have sinned, and come short of the glory of God; Being justified* [rendered righteous] *freely* [undeservedly] *by his grace through the redemption that is in Messiah Yeshua: Whom God hath set forth to be a propitiation* [satisfaction of divine justice] ***through faith in his blood...*** *"* (Rom 3:23-25a).

The following was prophesied in Isaiah 53:10, *"Yet it pleased the LORD* [the LORD willed] *to bruise* [crush] *Him; he hath put him to grief: when thou shalt make his soul* [nephesh] *an offering for sin..."* It was Yeshua's soul, His life, His blood, that was offered for our sin. As Judas finally realized, *"I have sinned in that I have betrayed the innocent blood"* (Matt 27:4a). God is proclaiming that the sinless life of Yeshua was exchanged for our sinful lives by His blood poured out on the Cross.

Isaiah 53 analyzes the exchange our Lord accomplished by dying in our place. It states that Yeshua took our griefs and carried our sorrows (53:4); He was wounded for our transgressions, bruised for our iniquities and the chastisement for our peace was upon Him (53:5); He had the iniquity of us all laid on Him (53:6); Yeshua was stricken for the transgression of the people (53:8); His soul was an offering for sin (53:10); and He bore the sin of many (53:12).

All of that was made possible because as Yeshua said, *"Think not that I am come to destroy the law, or the prophets: I am not come to destroy, but to fulfil"* (Matt 5:17). In this case, with reference to His death on the Cross, he fulfilled, brought to its ultimate goal, the doctrine of substitutionary blood sacrifice as spelled out in the *Tanach*.

How did the people who offered sacrifices to God obtain forgiveness before Yeshua's atonement? *"But without faith it is impossible to please Him..."* (Heb 11:6a). Remember that in the *Tanach* "faith" is often found embodied in the word "trust." The author of Hebrews goes on to give examples of this biblical faith by looking to that *"great...cloud* [vast multitude] *of witnesses"* (Heb. 12:1), heroes and heroines of the *Tanach*.[11]

So it was, that before Yeshua's death, as a witness of the truth of God's Word, any member of Israel instructed in God's Word, realizing that he needed atonement for his sin, brought a substitutionary sacrifice to the priests. He believed/trusted what God said was true, that blood must be shed in order for sins to be forgiven. The sinner acted on that Word and was reconciled to God. Even Yeshua commanded this before His death, telling the leper to offer what Moses commanded as a testimony/witness to the priests of his healing (Matt 8:2). However, *if* the rite was performed not in belief but only as dead tradition, God, who has always looked on the condition of the heart, would not forgive.[12]

Works do not, and never did, lead to salvation. However, coupled with faith, they evidence and witness to a relationship with the living God, as Paul emphasizes to Titus, *"Looking for that blessed hope, and the glorious appearing of the great God and our Saviour Yeshua the Messiah; Who gave himself for us, that he might redeem us from all iniquity* [lawlessness], *and purify unto himself a peculiar people,* **zealous of good works** ...*This is a faithful saying, and these things I will that thou affirm constantly* [confidently; strongly], *that* **they which have believed** *in God might be careful to* **maintain** [give attention to; practice] **good works**. *These things are good and profitable unto men...And let ours also learn to* **maintain good works** *for necessary uses, that they be not unfruitful"* (Tit 2:13-14; 3:8,14). Works without faith are just as dead as faith without works (Jam 2:20), but together faith and works make an unbeatable combination.

> *"And they overcame him by the blood of the Lamb*
> *and by the word of their testimony* [witness],
> *and they loved not their lives unto the death"*
> (Rev 12:11).

---

1   See Lev 16:6, 11, 17, 24, 33-34.

2   Lev 11:44-45; 1 Pet 1:16.

3   Rom 5:14-21; 1 Cor 15:21-22.

4   Harris, Archer, Waltke, *Theological Wordbook of the Old Testament*, Vol. I, p. 453.

5   *Ibid.*, p. 128.

6   Obviously the wine was not literal blood. Yeshua was speaking symbolically. His Jewish listeners would have understood this. Drinking blood is absolutely forbidden under both Old and New Covenants. See Lev 17:10 and Acts 15:29.

7   Harris, Archer, Waltke, *op. cit.*, Vol. 2, p. 589.

8   Even in the New Testament, the Jerusalem council included this injunction as one of the four things gentile believers needed to do so that Jew and gentile in the Body of Messiah could have fellowship together. See Acts 15:29 where three of the four "necessary things" had to do with food laws! How do *we* deal with these New Testament commandments?

9   See also John 6:47-54; 1 John 3:16.

10 Incredible as this sounds to some ears, the Bible specifically claims that when Yeshua died on the tree, it was **God's blood** that was shed: *"Take heed therefore unto yourselves, and to all the flock, over the which the Holy Ghost hath made you overseers, to feed the church of God, which* **he hath purchased with** [through] **his own blood** *"* (Acts 20:28).

A similar thought is brought out in Israel's victory song on the other side of the Red Sea: *"Thou in thy mercy* [chesed – covenant love] *hast led forth **the people which thou hast redeemed**: thou hast guided them in thy strength unto thy holy habitation. The people shall hear, and be afraid: sorrow shall take hold on the inhabitants of Palestina...Fear and dread shall fall upon them; by the greatness of thine arm they shall be as still as a stone; till thy people pass over, O LORD, **till the people pass over, which thou hast purchased***" (Ex 15:13-14,16).

11 Our word "martyr" comes from the Greek word meaning "witness." But, though all these died in the faith, not all witnesses are killed because of their faith.

12 See for example, Genesis 4:4, cp. Heb 11:4; 1 Sam 15:22; Psa 34:22; 51:16-19; Prov 21:27; Isa 1:10-20; Jer 7:21-23; Hos 6:6; Amos 5:21-24; Mic 6:6-8; Mal 3:3; Mark 12:33-34.

CHAPTER 6

Day of Atonement - Yom Kippur

Atonement in Yom Kippur

Yom Kippur, the sixth of the seven annual convocations instituted by God (Lev 23:26-32), occurs on the tenth day of the seventh month of the Hebrew calendar (*Tishrei*), and has been observed as a complete fast in Judaism at least since the time of the Second Temple.[1] On that day, according to Scripture, atonement was made for all of Israel's iniquities, transgressions, and sins (See comments on Lev 16:21 below). God says that He has provided a way to make atonement. *"For the life of the flesh is in the blood: and I have given it to you upon the altar to make an atonement for your souls: for it is the blood that maketh an atonement for the soul"* (Lev 17:11).

This has always been the most solemn day of the year for the Jewish people. On this day religious Jews spend the day in synagogues fasting, praying prayers of repentance, and believing that God will hear and answer their prayers. The whole nation of Israel shuts down to observe this biblical holy day. The city of Jerusalem is closed, and except for an occasional ambulance, there is no traffic.[2]

Concerning this day we agree with Matthew Henry's statement in his *Commentary*, "The Day of Atonement...has as much gospel in it as perhaps any of the...ceremonial law."[3]

Leviticus 16

Leviticus 16 gives a detailed description of the duties of the high priest on Yom Kippur. Without an understanding of that chapter it is impossible to fully comprehend the New Testament book of Hebrews which declares Yeshua as the High Priest of all believers. *"Wherefore, holy brethren, partakers of the heavenly calling, consider the Apostle and High Priest of our profession* [confession], *Messiah Yeshua;"* (Heb 3:1).

"Now of the things which we have spoken this is the sum [summary]*: We have such an high priest, who is set on the right hand* [metaphorically, the place of honor and/or authority] *of the throne of the Majesty* [God] *in the heavens; A minister* [public servant; priest] *of the sanctuary, and of the true tabernacle, which the Lord pitched, and not man"* (Heb 8:1-2).[4]

After each of the verses quoted below, we give a brief description of the God-ordained rituals for this most holy of days and their fulfillment by Yeshua, our High Priest.

Lev 16:2 *"And the LORD said unto Moses, Speak unto Aaron thy brother, that he come not at all times into the holy place within the veil before the* **mercy seat***, which is upon the ark; that he die not: for I will appear in the cloud upon the mercy seat."*

These instructions applied originally to the Tabernacle in the wilderness and later to the Temple in Jerusalem. The Lord warned that Aaron, the first high priest, should not come through the veil into the Holy of Holies except yearly on that one day. Aaron needed to approach God in God's way, bringing something to cover his sin, making an atonement. The word translated "mercy seat" in this verse comes from a Hebrew word, *kaporah*, literally meaning a protective cover,[5] and is derived from the same word from which Hebrew also derives the word for "atonement."

Lev 16:3 *"Thus shall Aaron come into the holy place: with a young bullock for a sin offering, and a ram for a burnt offering."*

Aaron needed protection, a covering. The penalty for his own sin first needed to be purged by the blood of a sin offering and a burnt offering before he could enter into the presence of Israel's holy God. In the next chapter of Leviticus God says He has provided a way to make atonement, *"For the life of the flesh is in the blood: and I have given it to you upon the altar to make an atonement for your souls: for it is the blood that maketh an atonement for the soul"* (Lev 17:11).

Yeshua presented Himself as the offering for sin by His own blood (Heb 9:12-14,22). He was also the perfect burnt offering, offering His whole life completely to His Father's will (Heb 10:5-10). *"But Messiah being come an high priest of good things to come, by a greater and more perfect* [complete] *tabernacle, not made with hands, that is to say, not of this building* [creation]*; Neither by the blood of goats and calves, but* **by his own blood he entered in once into the holy place***, having obtained eternal redemption for us"* (Heb 9:11-12). He is there in the true Tabernacle (Heb 8:2; 9:24), interceding for us now (Rom 8:27,34).

Believers have continual access to God's presence, but not because we are priests. Regular priests were never allowed to enter that special place. We have access because of the blood of our Messiah *and* because we are part of the body of the High Priest (Eph 5:30-32). Therefore, we belong within the veil. *"Having therefore, brethren, boldness* [assurance] *to enter into the holiest by the blood of Yeshua, By a new and living way, which he hath consecrated* [initiated] *for us, through the veil, that is to say, his flesh;"* (Heb 10:19-21).

Lev 16:4 *"He shall put on the holy linen coat, and he shall have the linen breeches upon his flesh, and shall be girded with a linen girdle, and with the linen mitre shall he be attired: these are holy garments; therefore shall he wash his flesh in water, and so put them on."*

The high priest needed to wear ordained holy garments made out of unadorned linen when entering God's presence. Holy means separated from the world *and* consecrated to God. Linen is symbolic of righteous deeds. *"And to her* [the wife of the Lamb] *was granted that she should be arrayed in fine linen, clean* [pure] *and white* [shining]: *for the fine linen is the righteousness* [righteous deeds of faith] *of saints"* (Rev 19:8; see also Eph 2:10). The high priest wore these symbolic yet simple garments in the Holy of Holies when he represented the people before a holy God. When he appeared as God's representative to the people (v23), he changed into his elegantly adorned high priest's garments symbolizing God's glory and majesty (see Exo 39:1-31).

Lev 16:5 *"And he shall take of the congregation of the children of Israel two kids of the goats for a sin offering, and one ram for a burnt offering."*

These offerings made atonement for the sins of the people of Israel (see v15). Other than here and in Leviticus 14:2-7, there is no other instance of two animals presented together as one offering. We will see what this represents in verse 22.

Lev 16:6 *"And Aaron shall offer* [lit: come near with] *his bullock of the sin offering, which is for himself, and make an atonement for himself, and for his house."*

Aaron, or any human high priest, needed to deal with his own sin before he could stand in the gap for the sins of the people. Yeshua did not need to do that since He was without sin. *"For such an high priest became* [was suitable for] *us, who is holy, harmless* [free from guilt], *undefiled, separate from sinners, and made higher* [more exalted] *than the heavens; Who needeth not daily, as those high priests, to offer up sacrifice, first for his own sins, and then for the people's: for this he did once, when he offered up himself"* (Heb 7:26-27). Because He had no sin, nothing separated Him from His Father (see Isa 59:2).

Lev 16:7-8 *"And he shall take the two goats, and present them before the LORD at the door of the tabernacle of the congregation.*

And Aaron shall cast lots upon the two goats; one lot for the LORD, and the other lot for the scapegoat."
After presenting the bull's blood for his own sins, Aaron was able to mediate for Israel. He took both goats to the door of the Tabernacle before the Lord and cast lots. One goat became the Lord's and was killed as a sin offering. The other goat, called *"azazel"* in Hebrew or "scapegoat" in some English versions, was released in the wilderness. (See vv20-21 farther on for a detailed discussion on the scapegoat.)

Lev 16:9 *"And Aaron shall bring the goat upon which the LORD's lot fell, and offer him for a sin offering."*
The Lord's goat was slain to be a propitiation, a satisfaction of divine justice. *"The soul that sinneth, it shall die"* (Ezek 18:4b,20a). *"For the wages of sin is death..."* (Rom 6:23a). Justification is what Yeshua's death on the cross accomplished for all who believe. *"Being justified freely by his grace through the redemption that is in Messiah Yeshua: Whom God hath set forth to be a propitiation through faith in his blood..."* (Rom 3:24-25a).

Lev 16:10 *"But the goat, on which the lot fell to be the scapegoat, shall be presented alive before the LORD, to make an atonement with him, and to let him go for a scapegoat into the wilderness."*
This is an amazing ritual. The live goat released in the wilderness was also part of the atonement. But atonement for sin can only be accomplished through the shedding of blood (Lev 17:11). We will reconcile that contradiction in a later section (vv20-22).

Lev 16:11 *"And Aaron shall bring the bullock of the sin offering, which is for himself, and shall make an atonement for himself, and for his house, and shall kill the bullock of the sin offering which is for himself."*
This repeats verse 6 with the added detail that Aaron is the one who killed the sin offering. Yeshua laid down His life. *"No man taketh it from me, but I lay it down of myself"* (John 10:18a, see also 1 John 3:16).

Lev 16:12-13 *"And he shall take a censer full of burning coals of fire from off the altar before the LORD, and his hands full of sweet incense beaten small, and bring it within the vail: And he shall put the incense upon the fire before the LORD, that the cloud of the incense may cover* [clothe or conceal] *the mercy seat that is upon the testimony, that he die not:"*
Aaron brought incense into the Holy of Holies to cover the mercy seat so that he would not die (v2). Incense is a type of the prayers of the saints (Rev 5:8; 8:3-4), a sweet smelling offering to God. We may not see our prayers as always pleasing God but in Proverbs 15:8, Solomon writes, *"The sacrifice of the wicked is an abomination to the LORD: **but the prayer of the upright is his delight**..."* Since He sees us as righteous by our position in Messiah Yeshua,[6] our prayers are His delight!

Lev 16:14 *"And he shall take of the blood of the bullock, and sprinkle it with his finger upon the mercy seat eastward; and before the mercy seat shall he sprinkle of the blood with his finger seven times."*

In the Holy of Holies, the high priest sprinkled the blood once on the mercy seat and seven times on the ground. "This act constituted the rite of expiation [atonement]..."[7] The blood-sprinkled mercy seat is a foreshadow of Messiah Yeshua's atonement. In fact, in the Greek New Testament, the same word used for "mercy seat" in Hebrews 9:5 is also used for "propitiation" in Romans 3:25. Commenting on this, C.I. Scofield states that the "mercy seat was sprinkled with the atoning blood on the Day of Atonement (Lev 16:14)[8], representing that the righteous sentence of the Law had been executed, changing the judgment seat into a mercy seat (Heb 9:11-15; cp. "throne of grace," Heb 4:14-16; place of communion, Exo 25:21-22)."[9] On the basis of Yeshua's finished work, we can boldly enter the Holy of Holies to meet with our God.

Lev 16:15 *"Then shall he kill the goat of the sin offering, that is for the people, and bring his blood within the vail, and do with that blood as he did with the blood of the bullock, and sprinkle it upon the mercy seat, and before the mercy seat:"*

That verse foreshadows the point at which Yeshua as the High Priest begins His ministry for us. All the sacrifices to that point in Leviticus 16 were for the sins of the high priest. Yeshua, being sinless, had no need to offer these sacrifices for Himself (see Heb 7:26-27, under Lev 16:6 above). An incredible thing about God's Messiah is that He is our High Priest *and* our sacrifice. *"For even the Son of man came not to be ministered unto, but to minister [serve], and to give his life a ransom [redemption price, atonement] for many"* (Mark 10:45); *"Behold the Lamb of God, which taketh away [carries upon oneself] the sin of the world"* (John 1:29b). By crying out, *"It is finished"* (John 19:30b), Yeshua indicated that the payment for our salvation was accomplished by His voluntary death, His blood freely offered for us.

Another important point that Leviticus 16:15 brings to mind is the biblical concept of a mediator. How cleverly the Enemy has deceived multitudes into thinking they can be on good terms with God without needing a mediator. Israel needed one. *"And [Aaron] stood between the dead and the living; and the plague was stayed [stopped]"* (Num 16:48; see 41-48 for the context of that incident). Even righteous Job (Job 1:1,8) recognized his need for a mediator. *"For he is not a man, as I am, that I should answer him, and we should come together in judgment. Neither is there any daysman [mediator] betwixt us, that might lay his hand upon us both"* (Job 9:32-33). You cannot find any verse in the Scriptures saying that God did away with the necessity of a mediator to stand between us and Him.

God had given the priesthood to Israel. He desired them to become a nation of mediators between Him and the rest of the world, but they had to keep His covenant and obey His voice. *"Now therefore, if ye will obey my voice indeed, and keep my covenant, then ye shall be a peculiar* [specially chosen] *treasure unto me above all people: for all the earth is mine: And ye shall be unto me a **kingdom of priests**, and an holy [separated] nation..."* (Exo 19:5-6a).

But only Messiah Yeshua, as the representative of the children of Israel,[10] was able to live in perfect obedience to God's Word. He was the long awaited mediator. *"For there is one God, and one mediator* [intercessor; reconciler] *between God and men, the man Messiah Yeshua;"* (1 Tim 2:5); *"And if any man sin, we have an advocate* [intercessor; helper] *with the Father, Messiah Yeshua the righteous:"* (1 John 2:1b).

Lev 16:16 *"And he shall make an atonement for the holy place, because of the uncleanness* [impurity] *of the children of Israel, and because of their transgressions* [rebellions] *in all their sins: and so shall he do for the tabernacle of the congregation, that remaineth among them in the midst of their uncleanness."*

This verse explains what God desired when He gave the plans for the Tabernacle and what He desires from us as His Temple.[11]   He wants to dwell among us (Exo 25:8), but our sin prevents it. Both the Tabernacle in the wilderness and then the Temple in Jerusalem provided a way for sins to be covered, or "atoned for," by the blood of a sacrifice. And ever since the Cross, the blood of God's own Son covers our sins, allowing God to dwell in our midst, even inside of us - by His Spirit. *"Yeshua answered and said unto him, If a man love me, he will keep my words: and my Father will love him, and we will come unto him, and make our abode* [home] *with him"* (John 14:23).

Lev 16:17 *"And there shall be no man in the tabernacle of the congregation when he goeth in to make an atonement in the holy place, until he come out, and have made an atonement for himself, and for his household, and for all the congregation of Israel."*

No one could help the high priest; he had to face God alone. So too, Yeshua was the only one who could accomplish His Father's will and become a ransom for us. *"Neither is there salvation in any other: for there is none other name under heaven given among men, whereby we must be saved"* (Acts 4:12).

Yeshua knew He must do it alone to fulfill Zechariah 13:7 - *"Awake, O sword, against my shepherd, and against the man* [valiant warrior] *that is my fellow* [associate; comrade], *saith the*

LORD *of hosts: smite* [even "slay"] *the shepherd, and the sheep shall be scattered: and I will turn mine hand upon the little ones."* [12]

Lev 16:18-19 *"And he shall go out unto the altar that is before the LORD, and make an atonement for it; and shall take of the blood of the bullock, and of the blood of the goat, and put it upon the horns of the altar round about. And he shall sprinkle of the blood upon it with his finger seven times, and cleanse it, and hallow it* [sanctify; set apart] *from the uncleanness* [spiritual impurity] *of the children of Israel."*

The blood was ordained by God to make atonement; to cleanse and sanctify men and things.

Lev 16:20-21 *"And when he hath made an end of* [accomplished; finished] *reconciling* [lit: making atonement for] *the holy place, and the tabernacle of the congregation, and the altar, he shall bring the live goat: And Aaron shall lay both his hands upon the head of the live goat, and confess over him all the iniquities of the children of Israel, and all their transgressions in all their sins, putting them upon the head of the goat, and shall send him away by the hand of a fit man into the wilderness:"*

Here the high priest's concentration turned to the live goat, the other part of the composite sin offering. He laid hands on the head of the "scapegoat" and confessed, or literally "cast" or "threw," the sins of Israel onto it, transferring them onto the goat. This is more than symbolism. The Israelite received forgiveness (see v30) and sanctification *by faith* because the ritual was done in obedience to God's direct word as found in this chapter of Leviticus.

Therefore for sin, God's forgiveness came through faithful, obedient animal sacrifice. However, under this sacrificial system no indwelling Spirit routinely brought to the moral conciousness the purifying fire, the agony of conviction of sin. That had to wait for the better sacrifice of the blood of God's Son. Hebrews 9:13-14 puts these two truths together like this, *"For if the blood of bulls and of goats, and the ashes of an heifer sprinkling the unclean, sanctifieth to the purifying of the flesh: How much more shall the blood of Messiah, who through the eternal Spirit offered himself without spot to God, purge* [cleanse] *your conscience from dead works to serve* [obey and worship] *the living God?"*

What does the Hebrew word for the scapegoat signify? "'Azazel' [is] a rare Hebrew noun meaning, 'dismissal' or, 'entire removal'...It is the ancient technical term for the entire removal of sin and guilt of the community..."[13] What sins did God forgive on Yom Kippur? Here are the Hebrew meanings for "iniquities," "transgressions" and "sins." See how truly forgiving God was through the Law:

"iniquities" - crookedness; disobedience; denotes a willful departure from the Law of God.

"transgressions" - the Hebrew is strong, literally meaning rebellion.

"sins" - missing the mark; unintentional deviation from the right path.

Although in the *Tanach* God provided forgiveness for sins through a believing obedience, Yeshua dealt with the root of sins - our "old man." By taking our death penalty on Himself, He made it possible for us to consider our "old man" dead and buried (Rom 6:4), making new creations of us who trustingly depend on Him. When we abide in Him, walking in His Spirit and repenting as needed, we appropriate His newness of life.[14]

Lev 16:22 *"And the goat shall bear upon him all their iniquities unto a land not inhabited: and he shall let go the goat in the wilderness."*

The live goat was released in the wilderness to carry away all the sins of Israel. The ideas of "to bear or carry" and "to forgive" are often covered by the same Hebrew verb [**bolded**], as we read in Isaiah 53. *"Surely he hath **borne** our griefs, and carried our sorrows...he hath poured out his soul unto death: and he was numbered with the transgressors; and he **bare** the sin of many, and made intercession for the transgressors"* (Isa 53:4a,12b). The same verb is bolded in Psalm 32, *"Blessed is he whose transgression is **forgiven**, whose sin is covered...I said, I will confess my transgressions unto the LORD; and thou **forgavest** the iniquity of my sin. Selah"* (Psa 32:1,5b).

The scapegoat part of the offering carried away each sin, never to be seen again. Micah, in a declaration full of prophetic hope, states the conclusion of the matter when he says, *"He will turn again, he will have compassion upon us; he will subdue* [conquer] *our iniquities; and thou wilt cast all their sins into the depths of the sea"* (Mic 7:19).

Why did God use two animals to represent one sin offering? All that Yeshua accomplished in purchasing our salvation could not be demonstrated by either one alone. The Lord's goat represents Yeshua's death on the Cross, and the scapegoat, His resurrection. His death atoned for our sins (Rom 3:25) and His resurrection declared us justified (Rom 4:25). His resurrection was God's formal announcement that our sins had been carried away to be remembered no more. Two goats; one offering. The first one dead; the other alive. Our Redeemer is portrayed in these two, dead and then alive. We too, if living sacrifices to our God, are to be dead to self but alive to Him (Rom 6:2-8, 11-12).

Lev 16:23-24 *"And Aaron shall come into the tabernacle of the congregation, and shall put off the linen garments, which he put on when he went into the holy place, and shall leave them there: And he shall wash his flesh with water in the holy place, and put on his garments, and come forth, and offer his burnt* *offering, and the burnt offering of the people, and make an atonement for himself, and for the people."*

By our count, that is the 27th of 32 statements in Leviticus saying that a priest makes atonement for the people. We may be assured that sinners need a mediator to atone for their sins (see v15). We are not able to do it by ourselves.

The type we see is this. The high priest made atonement by presenting the sacrificial blood on the mercy seat in the Most Holy place. That he remained alive and came back out to the people indicated that God accepted the sacrifice. Those who by faith believed what God said about this ritual, were then forgiven their sins.

The anti-type is this - Yeshua's death on the cross made atonement for us. Three days later He rose from the dead, demonstrating His Father's approval of His sacrifice as acceptable payment for sin. Those who believe this Good News are forgiven.

Lev 16:27 *"And the bullock for the sin offering, and the goat for the sin offering, whose blood was brought in to make atonement in the holy place, shall one carry forth without the camp; and they shall burn in the fire their skins, and their flesh, and their dung."*

The remains of the sin offering, whose blood was brought within the veil, were burned outside the camp. The writer to the Hebrews sees that verse as a foreshadow of Messiah Yeshua's sacrifice and encourages us to join Him outside the camp of this world's religions and values. Our eyes should be fixed on the city whose builder and maintainer is God (Heb 11:10). Here is what he says in Hebrews 13:11-14, *"For the bodies of those beasts, whose blood is brought into the sanctuary by the high priest for sin, are burned without [outside] the camp. Wherefore Yeshua also, that he might sanctify the people with his own blood, suffered without the gate. Let us go forth therefore unto him without the camp, bearing his reproach. For here have we no continuing [permanent] city, but we seek one to come."*

Lev 16:29 *"And this shall be a statute for ever unto you: that in the seventh month, on the tenth day of the month, ye shall afflict [humble] your souls, and do no work at all, whether it be one of your own country, or a stranger that sojourneth among you:"*

Afflicting or humbling ourselves before God has been interpreted by Jewish and Christian commentators as fasting. This interpretation can be derived from several verses in the Bible: *"Then I proclaimed a **fast** there, at the river of Ahava, that we might **afflict** [humble] **ourselves** before our God"* (Ezra 8:21a); *"**I humbled my soul with fasting**;"* (Psa 35:13b); *"When I wept, and **chastened my soul with fasting**, that was to my reproach"* (Psa 69:10); *"Therefore also now, saith the LORD, turn ye even to me with all your heart, and with **fasting**, and with*

63

weeping, and with mourning:" (Joel 2:12). This day has been a complete fast throughout the history of the Jewish people.

Notice to whom the Lord directs this command. The Lord states that this day's observance be *"...a statute for ever..."* for the children of Israel *and* for the *"...stranger that sojourneth among you:"* The "strangers," who are non-Jews who had chosen to live with the children of Israel and follow the God of Israel, are a foreshadow of the non-Jewish part of the Body of Messiah.[15]

Lev 16:30 *"For on that day shall the priest make an atonement for you, to cleanse [purify] you, that ye may be clean from all your sins before the LORD."*

Here is the reason why this day is called the holiest day of the year in Judaism. Not only did the atonement accomplished on Yom Kippur enable the sinner to be forgiven all his/her sins, but, since the words "the priest" are not in the Hebrew, some rabbis say that the day itself provides atonement to the person who humbles himself and confesses his sins before God. As believers, we know that Messiah and not fasting, repentance, or a special day provides atonement, but we still see the importance of the day as a divinely appointed time to commune with God and to pray for Israel and the Church.

Verse 30 also offers further proof that forgiveness of sins was available to those who lived in obedience to the Law of God concerning atonement (see 16:21-22 above). Of course, Yeshua's atoning death has made continuing these blood sacrifices unnecessary and ineffectual for the cleansing of sins. *"For Messiah is not entered into the holy places made with hands, which are the figures of the true; but into heaven itself, now to appear in the presence of God for us: Nor yet that he should offer himself often, as the high priest entereth into the holy place every year with blood of others; For then must he often have suffered since the foundation of the world: but now once in the end of the world* [completion of the ages] *hath he appeared to put away* [abolish; annul] *sin by the sacrifice of himself"* (Heb 9:24-26).

Lev 16:31 *"It shall be a sabbath of rest unto you, and ye shall afflict* [humble] *your souls, by a statute for ever."*

This was to be a day of complete rest which is called in Hebrew *"shabbat shabbaton."* The high priest did all the work required to remove the sins; the sinner rested in that work and was required only to recognize his need of forgiveness. The Day of Atonement perfectly illustrates God's grace at work.

Lev 16:32 *"And the priest, whom he shall anoint, and whom he shall consecrate to minister in the priest's office in his father's stead, shall make the atonement, and shall put on the linen clothes, even the holy garments:"*

The priest who made the atonement for Israel was anointed (the same Hebrew root from which we get the word *"Mashiach,"* Messiah, Anointed One - translated "Christ" in English from the Greek)[16] and consecrated to minister in his father's stead. This foreshadows Yeshua, who is consecrated to the High Priest's office as a representative of His Father and of us, His brethren. *"For there is one God, and one mediator between God and men, the man Messiah Yeshua;"* (1 Tim 2:5); *"Wherefore, holy brethren, partakers* [sharers] *of the heavenly calling, consider the Apostle and High Priest of our profession* [declaration or confession], *Messiah Yeshua;"* (Heb 3:1).

Summary

As we have seen from the *Tanach*, God declares that without His grace we are all hopelessly lost in our sins. But Leviticus 16 has shown us the Day of Atonement when the high priest entered into the Holy of Holies, going behind the veil, making atonement for sins with the blood of the God-ordained sin offering. We heard him confess the people's sins as he laid them on the head of the scapegoat. We watched that goat driven into the wilderness never to be seen again. Israel's iniquities, transgressions and sins were forgiven and removed. God provided for His people this way of purification so that He could dwell among them. This divine illustration of forgiveness in the *Tanach* points unmistakably to the death and resurrection of Messiah Yeshua.

"Having therefore, brethren, boldness [confidence]
to enter into the holiest by the blood of Yeshua,
By a new and living way,
which he hath consecrated [renewed or inaugurated] *for us,*
through the veil, that is to say, his flesh;
And having an high priest over the house of God;
Let us draw near with a true heart in full assurance of faith,
having our hearts sprinkled [purified] *from an evil* [bad] *conscience,*
and our bodies washed with pure water"
(Heb 10:19-22).

---

1   Zech 7:5; Acts 27:9.

2   What other nation shuts down for a full day just because God's Word says so? Despite this nation's large measure of unbelief at this time, she is still a witness to the eternal truth of God's Word.

3   Matthew Henry, *Matthew Henry's Commentary*, Vol. 1, p. 504.

4   See also Heb 2:17; 4:14-15; 5:10; 6:20; 7:26-28; 9:11; 10:21.

5   Scripturally it was used in describing pitch's ability to protect from water. It also described the protection afforded by a village.

Idiomatically it was used to denote protection money - used for both good (a ransom) or bad (a bribe).

6 See 1 Cor 1:30 and 2 Cor 5:21 and compare with these *Tanach* verses: Psa 119:40; Isa 45:24-25; 46:12-13; 54:17; Jer 23:5-6.

7 Dr. J. H. Hertz, ed., *The Pentateuch and Haftorahs*, p. 482.

8 Concerning sprinkling, see comments on Isaiah 52:15a, in Chap. 10, section "Isaiah 52:13-53:12."

9 *The New Scofield Reference Bible*, Oxford University Press, p. 1214; note #4, Rom 3:25.

10 In Isaiah 49:3, the servant of the Lord is called "Israel" and in the context of that chapter specifically means the Messiah.

11 See 1 Cor 3:16-17; 6:19-20; 2 Cor 6:16; Eph 2:19-22; 1 Pet 2:5.

12 See Matt 26:31,56; John 16:32.

13 Dr. J. H. Hertz, ed., *op. cit.*, p. 481.

14 For example, see Romans chapter 5-6 and 2 Cor 5:17.

15 In Part Three we see how this statement proves accurate.

16 In Matthew 24:23-25 and Mark 13:21-23, Yeshua warns about "false christs" arising in the last days. Literally, this terms translates into false "anointed-ones."

CHAPTER 7

The New Birth

Since some believers endorse the mistaken idea that God required only outward works of ritual and sacrifice in the *Tanach*, they may also think that after the inauguration of the New Covenant, He is concerned only with "inward works," the spiritual condition of our hearts. However, neither of these views agrees with the Word of God. In both the *Tanach* and the New Testament, God's emphasis is the faith of the heart manifested through works of obedience.

A New Heart

The concept of being born again, or born from above, is so central to our belief, that Yeshua said if a person is not born again he cannot enter the kingdom of God (John 3:3). Yeshua stated, *"Marvel not that I said unto thee, Ye must be born again"* (John 3:7). He was talking to Nicodemus, a ruler of the Jews, who many scholars believe was the leading teacher in Israel at that time. Nicodemus was surprised at His statement, but Yeshua indicated that it should not have taken him by surprise, asking, *"Art thou a master of Israel, and knowest* [understand] *not these things?"* (John 3:10b). He was implying that this crucial belief is found in the *Tanach*, Nicodemus' Bible.

"Born again" - what does it mean? "Regeneration, or new birth, is an inner re-creating of fallen human nature [spirit] by the gracious sovereign act of the Holy Spirit..."[1]

In the *Tanach* and the New Testament "heart" refers to the soul, and at times the spirit, that must be renewed or regenerated. Look at what "heart" means in the original Hebrew and Greek.

Hebrew – lev: "..the heart, the center, or the middle of something...it is common to interpret the term [in the *Tanach*] as the totality of man's inner or immaterial nature...In the Bible, the whole spectrum of human emotions is attributed to the heart...Wisdom and understanding reside in the heart (1 Kin 3:12; Prov 16:23). It is almost a synonym for "mind" (2 Chr 9:23) or perceptive nature (1 Kin 3:12). However, it can be deceived (Isa 44:20). The heart is the seat of the will [self] (Num. 16:28 [in Hebrew, the "mind" of the KJV, and the "will" in the NKJV is *lev*, heart.]; Jud 9:3; 2 Chr 12:14). To refuse to make the right choice is to harden the heart (Exo 10:1; Josh 11:20). The heart is the seat of moral evil (Jer 17:9)."[2]

Greek – *kardia*: "The Scriptures attributed to the heart thoughts, reasonings, understanding, will, judgment, designs, affections, love, hatred, fear, joy, sorrow, and anger...Therefore, the heart is used for the mind in general (Matt 12:34; John 13:2; Rom 2:15;10:9-10); the understanding (Luke 3:15; Acts 28:26-27; Rom 1:21; 2 Cor 4:6); the will (Acts 11:23;13:22); the memory (Luke 1:66; 2:51); the intention, affection or desire (Matt 6:21;18:35; Mark 7:6; Luke 1:17; Acts 8:21); the conscience (1 John 3:20-21)."[3]

According to the above definitions and biblical usage the term "heart" refers to the inner man, the mind, emotions and will together, or any of those parts separately or in combination.

The Heart of the Issue in the New Testament

God wants our hearts to be humble and upright before Him. One of the chief benefits of the "born again" experience is that God begins to purify our hearts by faith. *"And God, which knoweth the **hearts**, bare them [the gentiles] witness, giving them the Holy Ghost, even as he did unto us; And put no difference between us and them, purifying [cleansing] their **hearts** by faith"* (Acts 15:8-9); *"To the end he may stablish your **hearts** unblameable in holiness before God, even our Father, at the coming of our Lord Yeshua the Messiah with all his saints"* (1 Thes 3:13).

Here are some other New Testament scriptures that label as "heart" the sphere God changes through regeneration, the theological term for being "born again" (born from above, given a new spirit, saved, redeemed, etc.). Speaking to His disciples, Yeshua declares, *"Blessed are the pure in **heart**: for they shall see God"* (Matt 5:8). But speaking to some of the religious leaders of His day, He says, *"Ye hypocrites, well did [Isaiah] prophesy of you, saying, This people draweth nigh [near] unto me with their mouth, and honoureth me with their lips; but their **heart** is far from me"* (Matt 15:7-8).

The writer of Hebrews gives us this warning, *"Take heed, brethren, lest there be in any of you an evil **heart** of unbelief, in departing from the living God"* (Heb 3:12).

In Paul's Spirit-led prayer for believers, he uses a parallelism to identify our inner man with our heart, asking that the Spirit of Messiah would abide there – in His spiritual temple. *"That he would grant you, according to the riches of his glory, to be strengthened with might by his Spirit in the **inner man**; That Messiah may dwell in your **hearts** by faith..."* (Eph 3:16-17a).

In Romans 10, Paul shows the difference between the righteousness of works versus the righteousness of faith. He demonstrates that both are mentioned in the Law but that, even there, God points to faith as essential to approach and be reconciled to Him.[4] *"But what saith it?*[5] *The word is nigh thee, even in thy mouth, and in thy **heart**: that is, the word of **faith**, which we preach; That if thou shalt confess* [declare; acknowledge] *with thy mouth the Lord Yeshua, and shalt believe in thine **heart** that God hath raised him from the dead, thou shalt be saved. For with the **heart** man believeth* [trusts] *unto righteousness; and with the mouth confession is made unto salvation"* (Rom 10:8-10, see Acts 8:37).

From just these few New Testament examples, we see God dealing with the heart in and after the new birth. But the term "heart" as used throughout the Bible has other associations as well.

Tanach Roots of Regeneration

Using the biblical definition of "heart," we now discover the roots of being "born again" in the *Tanach*. The most graphic metaphor used is "heart circumcision." "In [*Tanach*] prophecies, regeneration is depicted as the work of God renovating, circumcising, and softening Israelite hearts, writing His laws upon them, and thereby causing their owners to know, love, and obey Him as never before (Deut 30:6; Jer 31:31-34; 32:39-40; Ezek 11:19-20; 36:25-27). It is a sovereign work of purification from sin's defilement (Ezek 36:25; cf. Psa 51:10)."[6]

Many *Tanach* passages concerning the heart are referenced in the above quote taken from a theological dictionary. We will look at several of these. Here are two which promise Israel's final salvation after she is restored to God's land. We see these promises coming to pass today. *"And I will give them **one heart**, and one way, that they may fear*[7] *me for ever, for the good of them, and of their children after them: And I will make* [lit: cut] *an everlasting covenant with them, that I will not turn away from them, to do them good; but I will put my fear **in their hearts**, that they shall not depart* [turn away] *from me"* (Jer 32:39-40).

The second passage, from Ezekiel, is arguably the best description of what it means to be "born again" in all of Scripture. *"Then will I sprinkle clean water upon you, and ye shall be clean* [pure; undefiled]*: from all your filthiness, and from all your idols, will I cleanse* [purify] *you. A **new heart** also will I give you, and a **new spirit** will I put* *within you: and I will take away the stony heart out of your flesh, and I will give you an heart of flesh. And I will put my spirit within you, and cause you to walk in my statutes, and ye shall keep my judgments, and do them"* (Ezek 36:25-27).

In other "heart" verses, the *Tanach* states the precise demands that God makes on those who desire to approach Him. One example would be Psalm 24:3-4, *"Who shall ascend into the hill of the LORD? or who shall stand in his holy place? He that hath clean* [innocent] *hands, and a pure* [purified] *heart; who hath not lifted up his soul unto vanity* [falsehood], *nor sworn deceitfully."* The same criteria is found in Matthew 5:8, *"Blessed are the pure in heart: for they shall see God."*

David in Psalm 51:10 implores his King to, *"Create in me a clean* [purified, cleansed] *heart, O God; and renew a right spirit within me."* The Hebrew word "create" in that verse is the same word used in Genesis 1:1 for God's creation of the universe out of nothing. David, like Paul, understood that in his flesh dwelt no good thing (Rom 7:18). For David to be able to conquer his sin, it was necessary for God to make of him a new creature (2 Cor 5:17).

As we saw in the last chapter, the *Tanach* declares that all have sinned; all people have chronic and terminal "heart disease." God pinpoints this problem through the prophet Jeremiah. *"The sin of Judah is written with a pen of iron, and with the point of a diamond: it is graven upon the table of their heart...The heart is deceitful above all things, and desperately wicked* [incurably sick]: *who can know it?"* (Jer 17:1a,9).

To make us aware that we need heart "surgery" ("heart circumcision" in the *Tanach*), God challenges us to do it ourselves. Through Moses, the Lord says, *"Circumcise therefore the foreskin of your heart, and be no more stiffnecked* [stubborn, rebellious]*"* (Deut 10: 16). The results of any attempts to follow this most important command show us we cannot do it without Him.

Moses continues to list all that God requires from us if we choose to live by our own righteousness. Yet as Moses frequently reminds us in Deuteronomy, which is a divine summary of God's Law, the heart is the core issue.[8] Finally in Chapter 30:6, Moses prophesies about the new birth, *"And the LORD thy God will circumcise thine heart, and the heart of thy seed, to love the LORD thy God with all thine heart, and with all thy soul,* [so] *that thou mayest live."* God performs the heart surgery. As Paul states, we are saved by grace (Eph 2:8).

Results of the New Birth

In these times, with a what-can-God-do-for-me attitude permeating the Church, it is important we understand why God saves us. He saves us so we can love and obey Him with our whole lives. Yeshua says that loving Him (not Him loving us) entails obeying His commands, His words, in other words, the Word of God. *"If ye love me, keep my commandments...He that hath my commandments, and keepeth them, he it is that loveth me...If a man love me, he will keep my words ...He that loveth me not keepeth not my sayings..."* (John 14:15,21a,23b,24a; John restates this in 1 John 2:3-6).

In the *Tanach* God promised to the houses of Israel and Judah that the new birth into the new covenant would make possible that obedience! Through Jeremiah God prophesies about the New Covenant, *"Behold, the days come, saith the LORD, that I will make* [lit: cut] *a **new covenant** with the house of **Israel**, and with the house of **Judah**: Not according to the covenant that I made with their fathers in the day that I took them by the hand to bring them out of the land of Egypt; which my covenant they brake* [violated], *although I was an husband unto them, saith the LORD: But this shall be the covenant that I will make with the house of Israel; After those days, saith the LORD, **I will put my law in their inward parts, and write it in their hearts**; and will be their God, and they shall be my people. And they shall teach no more every man his neighbour, and every man his brother, saying, Know the LORD: for they shall all know me, from the least of them unto the greatest of them, saith the LORD: for* [because] *I will forgive their iniquity, and I will remember their sin no more"* (Jer 31:31-34).

That entire passage becomes the longest *Tanach* quote in the New Testament. It is quoted or referred to twice in the book of Hebrews (8:8-12; 10:16-17). The writer uses these verses to prove that Yeshua's High Priestly ministry and sacrifice instituted that "new covenant" of which Jeremiah spoke.

The writer of Hebrews goes on to say in 8:13 that the "old" was now obsolete. The question is, "old what?" That "old" referred to the system of the Levitical priesthood and animal sacrifices for sin. It did not, indeed, could not, refer to "the Law" because God's Law, or literally, Teaching, is holy, just and good (Rom 7:12). The word "Law" (in the Hebrew *"Torah"*) means God's instruction, His teachings, His way, His guidance, and not just a list of commands and restrictions.

The Lord never said either in Jeremiah or Hebrews that the New Covenant would replace His Law, but that by the New Covenant He would sovereignly place His Law in our minds and write it on our hearts. Paul says, *"That the righteousness of the law might be fulfilled in us, who walk not after the flesh, but after the Spirit"* (Rom 8:4). Paul implies that only those who are born from above and led by the Spirit can fulfill God's Law, His *Torah*. The new birth provides new wineskins for the new wine, the indwelling Holy Spirit.

Ezekiel also talks about the new birth. In 11:19, the prophet proclaims that God will give Israel one heart and put a new spirit in them. Why? *"That they may walk in my statutes, and keep mine ordinances, and do them: and they shall be my people, and I will be their God"* (Ezek 11:20).

Do we remember that our Lord Yeshua and the writers of the New Testament said that as well? Yes, we *are* saved by grace through faith. It *is* a gift of God that does not depend on anything we do so that we have no reason to boast (Eph 2:8-9). But how do we live after salvation? Can we claim to be believers and do what we want, or are we commanded in the New Testament to do the good works God has ordained for us?

In the beginning of the Sermon on the Mount, Yeshua says to His disciples (Matt 5:1-2), *"Let your light so shine before men, that they may see your good works, and glorify your Father which is in heaven"* (Matt 5:16). And He sums up that teaching by stating, *"Therefore whosoever heareth these sayings of mine, and doeth them, I will liken him unto a wise man, which built his house upon a rock:"* (Matt 7:24).

A few people may protest that these sayings of Yeshua were spoken before He died and do not apply to believers after the Cross. Or they may say that all these statements were made to Jewish believers and do not apply to gentiles in Messiah. However, consider the following verses written to the universal community of believers *after* Yeshua's resurrection:

"Looking for that blessed hope, and [even] *the glorious appearing of the great God and our Saviour Yeshua the Messiah; Who gave himself for us, that he might redeem us from all iniquity* [lawlessness], *and purify unto himself a peculiar people, zealous of good works "* (Titus 2:13-14).

"This is a faithful saying, and these things I will that thou affirm constantly, that they which have believed [placed their confidence] *in God might be careful to maintain good works. These things are good and profitable unto men...And let ours also learn to maintain good works for necessary uses, that they be not unfruitful"* (Titus 3:8,14).

"What doth it profit, my brethren, though a man say he hath faith, and have not works? can faith save him?...Even so faith, if it hath not works, is dead, being alone. Yea, a man may say, Thou hast faith, and I have works: shew me [give proof of] *thy faith without* [apart from] *thy works, and I will shew thee my faith by my works "* (James 2:14,17-18).

"Here is the patience [steadfastness] *of the saints: here are*

*they that **keep the commandments of God, and the faith of Yeshua** "* (Rev 14:12).

From Genesis through Revelation God's constant appeal is to the heart of man, which He alone can read (Jer 17:9-10). When we see our need of Him, beginning with trusting His atonement for our sins, then our Father gives us new hearts and new spirits. In time we will do what God created us for - worship (serve) Him in faith through obedient works that bring Him glory.

"Let your light so shine before men,
*that they may see your **good works**,*
and glorify your Father which is in heaven" (Matt 5:16).

"Hear, O Israel: The LORD our God is one LORD:
*And thou shalt **love the LORD thy God with all thine heart**,*
and with all thy soul, and with all thy might.
And these words, which I command thee this day,
*shall be **in thine heart**:"* (Deut 6:4-6).

---

1   Walter A. Elwell, ed., *Evangelical Dictionary of Theology*, p. 924.

2   Spiros Zodhiates, Th.D., ed., *Lexical Aids to the Old Testament, The Hebrew - Greek Key Study Bible*, p. 1603.

3   Ibid., p. 1701.

4   See Chapter 9, section "Saved by Faith" for a more detailed explanation of these verses from Romans 10.

5   This "it" refers back to "the righteousness which is of faith" in verse 6, which is taken from the *Tanach* in Deut. 30:14.

6   Walter A. Elwell, *op. cit.*, p. 925.

7   This Hebrew word occurring over 300 times in scripture is here correctly translated "to fear" and includes to be afraid, fearful or to make afraid.

8   See Deut 4:9,29: 5:29; 8:2,5; 9:4-5; 10:12; 17:17; 28:47; 30:14.

PART TWO

Teachers

Old Testament Scripture roots filled the hearts and minds of Yeshua and the New Testament writers. Only by nourishing those roots in them could the Spirit of God use these men to "fulfill" - metaphorically, to explain and exemplify the true meaning of - the Law of God.

CHAPTER 8

The Prophet Like Moses

Deuteronomy 18:15-19

Deuteronomy contains many prophecies of the coming Messiah. But the prophetic promise found in Chapter 18:15-19 stands out like a beam of sunlight on a shaded landscape.

*"The LORD thy God will raise up unto thee a Prophet from the midst of thee, **of thy brethren**, **like unto me**; unto him ye shall hearken* [hear with the intent to obey]; *According to all that thou desiredst of the LORD thy God in Horeb in the day of the assembly, saying, Let me not hear again the voice of the LORD my God, neither let me see this great fire any more, that I die not. And the LORD said unto me, They have well spoken that which they have spoken.* **I will raise them up a Prophet from among their brethren, like unto thee, and will put my words in his mouth; and he shall speak unto them all that I shall command him. And it shall come to pass, that whosoever will not hearken unto my words which he shall speak in my name, I will require it of him."**

The Prophet in The New Testament

The New Testament actually refers to these verses on several occasions, but if we are not aware of the perspective of the speakers, we lose the full implication of what they are saying. For example, why do people in the following New Testament verses all refer to the "prophet"? Because the Jewish people of Yeshua's time were looking for the one promised in Deuteronomy 18.

"And they asked him [John the Baptist], *What then? Art thou Elias* [Elijah]? *And he saith, I am not. Art thou **that prophet**? And he answered, No...And they asked him, and said unto him, Why baptizest*

thou then, if thou be not that Messiah, nor Elias [Elijah], *neither **that prophet**?"* (John 1:21, 25).

*"Then those men, when they had seen the miracle that Jesus did, said, This is of a truth **that prophet** that should come into the world"* (John 6:14).

*"Many of the people therefore, when they heard this saying, said, Of a truth this is **the Prophet**. Others said, This is the Messiah..."* (John 7:40-41a).

After Yeshua's resurrection, the disciples used the Deuteronomy passage as an apologetic to declare that Yeshua is *that* Prophet, and then stated that He is the Messiah, the Anointed One. Note how Peter tied these together. *"But those things, which God before had shewed* [promised] *by the mouth of all his prophets, that Messiah should suffer, he hath so fulfilled...For Moses truly said unto the fathers, A **prophet** shall the Lord your God raise up[1] unto you of your brethren, like unto me; him shall ye hear in all things whatsoever he shall say unto you. And it shall come to pass, that every soul, which will not hear that **prophet**, shall be destroyed from among the people. Yea, and all the prophets from Samuel and those that follow after, as many as have spoken, have likewise foretold of these days"* (Acts 3:18, 22-24).

Stephen's message to the Sanhedrin also uses this prophecy to demonstrate that Israel had a history of not believing Moses. *"This is that Moses, which said unto the children of Israel, A **prophet** shall the Lord your God raise up[2] unto you of your brethren, like unto me; him shall ye hear"* (Acts 7:37). In fact, Yeshua pointed out this issue as a stumbling block to Israel believing in Him. *"For had ye believed Moses, ye would have believed me: for he wrote of me* [He could be referring to Deuteronomy 18]. *But if ye believe not his writings, how shall ye believe my words?"* (John 5:46-47). Isn't not believing Moses one of the major problems in the Church? The word *believe* in this passage means to have faith, confidence, or trust in. How many really believe that what Moses wrote is still foundational for us today?

The Prophet To Be Like Moses

The Deuteronomy prophecy promises the coming of a prophet like Moses. Even the rabbis point out that the coming Messiah would be like Moses. "The Rabbinic literature often presents parallels between similar types of fact...*One of the most frequently used parallels is the likening of the Messiah to the 'first savior', Moses.*"[3] (emphasis in the original) So we should expect that the lives of Moses and Yeshua should contain some parallels, and they do - extensive ones. Let's look at some of these.

Lineage

Moses and Yeshua are both children of Israel, what we would today call Jews, descendants of Abraham through Isaac and Jacob (Israel).

*"The book of the generation of Yeshua the Messiah, the son of David, the **son of Abraham** "* (Matt 1:1).

*"Who are **Israelites**; to whom pertaineth the adoption, and the glory, and the covenants, and the giving of the law, and the service of God, and the promises; Whose are the fathers, and **of whom as concerning the flesh Messiah came**, who is over all, God blessed for ever. Amen"* (Rom 9:4-5).

Childhood

The parallels here are so astounding that we can truly call them supernatural! Both Moses and Yeshua were born when the people of Israel were under gentile rule, Moses in Egypt (Exo 1:8-10) and Yeshua in Roman occupied Israel (Luke 2:1,3-5).

Both were, out of necessity, placed by their mothers in unusual beds, Moses in a waterproof basket (Exo 2:3), and Yeshua in a feeding trough (Luke 2:7). Each was saved from a death decree placed on many of the Hebrew boys by the ruling gentile king; Moses was saved from the decree of Pharaoh (Exo 1:22), and Yeshua from the decree of Herod (Matt 2:13b,16).

They were not only rescued in their infancy, but also preserved miraculously in the same foreign country. Moses was rescued and raised by Pharaoh's daughter (Exo 2:5-6), although God even arranged to have Moses' own mother nurse him (Exo 2:9). Yeshua, like Moses, was preserved in Egypt because Joseph believed the Word of the Lord brought by an angel. *"When he arose, he took the young child and his mother by night, and departed into Egypt: And was there until the death of Herod: that it might be fulfilled which was spoken of the Lord by the prophet, saying, Out of Egypt have I called my son"* (Matt 2:14-15). The women who raised them were both daughters of a kingly line, Pharaoh's daughter (Exo 2:5-10), and Miriam, who was a direct descendant of King David (Luke 1:26-33; 3:23-32).[4]

Finally, they were raised in the home of men who were not their real fathers. Moses was raised in Pharaoh's house, as the *Tanach* and New Testament point out (Exo 2:9-10; Acts 7:21-22). In Yeshua's case, Matthew states that Joseph obeyed the Lord and took Miriam to be his wife when an angel told him about Yeshua's miraculous conception (Matt 1:18-25).

Other Life Similarities

Here are some other interesting parallels that we find between the lives of Israel's Lawgiver and Israel's Messiah: they had to flee the land of their birth because of a king's wrath, Moses from Pharaoh (Exo 2:15), and Yeshua from Herod (Matt 2:13). Each returned to that land and was used by the God of Israel to perform many miracles there (Exo 4:21; Matt 2:19-21).

They shared the experience of being criticized and challenged by family members and fellow Israelis. *"And when Pharaoh drew nigh, the children of Israel lifted up their eyes...and they were sore afraid: and the children of Israel cried out unto the LORD. And they said unto Moses, Because there were no graves in Egypt, hast thou taken us away to die in the wilderness? wherefore hast thou dealt thus with us, to carry us forth out of Egypt?"* (Exo 14:10-11). And again Moses is criticized. *"And Miriam and Aaron* [Moses' sister and brother] *spake against Moses because of the Ethiopian woman whom he had married: for he had married an Ethiopian woman"* (Num 12:1).

In Yeshua's case, *"His brethren therefore said unto him, Depart hence, and go into Judaea, that thy disciples also may see the works that thou doest...If thou do these things, shew thyself to the world. For neither did his brethren believe in him"* (John 7:3-5). And again, *"But though he had done so many miracles before them, yet they believed not on him: That the saying of [Isaiah] the prophet might be fulfilled...Lord, who hath believed our report? and to whom hath the arm of the Lord been revealed?"* (John 12:37-38).

They endured murmuring from God's people. *"And the people murmured against Moses, saying, What shall we drink?"* (Exo 15:24, see 16:2). *"The Jews then murmured at him* [Yeshua], *because he said, I am the bread which came down from heaven"* (John 6:41).

Moses and Yeshua had seventy chosen helpers at some point in their ministries. *"And the LORD said unto Moses, Gather unto me seventy men of the elders of Israel, whom thou knowest to be the elders of the people, and officers over them; and bring them unto the tabernacle of the .congregation, that they may stand there with thee"* (Num 11:16). *"After these things the Lord* [Yeshua] *appointed other seventy also, and sent them two and two before his face into every city and place, whither he himself would come"* (Luke 10:1).

They each sent out twelve men on special missions. *"And the LORD spake unto Moses, saying, Send thou men, that they may search the land of Canaan, which I give unto the children of Israel:*

of every tribe [12] *of their fathers shall ye send a man, every one a ruler among them"* (Num 13:1-2). *"And when he* [Yeshua] *had called unto him his twelve disciples, he gave them power against unclean spirits, to cast them out, and to heal all manner of sickness and all manner of disease...These* **twelve** *Yeshua sent forth..."* (Matt 10:1,5a).

They experienced forty day fasts. *"And he* [Moses] *was there with the LORD* **forty** *days and forty nights; he did neither eat bread, nor drink water. And he wrote upon the tables the words of the covenant, the ten commandments"* (Exo 34:28). *"Then was Yeshua led up of the Spirit into the wilderness to be tempted of the devil. And when he had fasted forty days and forty nights, he was afterward an hungred"* (Matt 4:1-2).

Moses and Yeshua are spoken of as men of deep humility despite their greatness and position. *"(Now the man Moses was* **very meek**, *above all the men which were upon the face of the earth)"* (Num 12:3). *"Come unto me, all ye that labour and are heavy laden, and I will give you rest. Take my yoke upon you, and learn of me; for I* [Yeshua] *am* **meek and lowly** *in heart: and ye shall find rest unto your souls. For my yoke is easy, and my burden is light"* (Matt 11:28-30).

They fed multitudes through miraculous means. *"And when the children of Israel saw it, they said one to another, It is manna: for they wist not what it was. And Moses said unto them, This is the bread which the LORD hath given you to eat...And the children of* **Israel did eat manna** *forty years..."* (Exo 16:15,35a). *"And he* [Yeshua] *commanded the multitude to sit down on the grass, and took the* **five loaves, and the two fishes**, *and looking up to heaven, he blessed, and brake, and gave the loaves to his disciples, and the disciples to the multitude. And* **they did all eat**, *and were filled...And they that had eaten were about five thousand men, beside women and children"* (Matt 14:19-21).

Both of these servants of God had a supernatural experience of having their faces shine with God's glory. *"...when Moses came down from mount Sinai with the two tables of testimony in Moses' hand...Moses wist not that the skin of* **his face shone** *while he talked with him. And when Aaron and all the children of Israel saw Moses, behold, the skin of his face shone; and they were afraid to come nigh him"* (Exo 34:29-30). *"And after six days Yeshua taketh Peter, James, and John his brother, and bringeth them up into an high mountain apart, And was transfigured before them: and* **his face did shine** *as the sun, and his raiment was white as the light"* (Matt 17:1-2).

We are not half finished but already we see a likeness of Yeshua to Moses that goes far beyond coincidence. As a friend of ours has said, it is a "God-incidence"!

Their Relationship with God
In Numbers 12 God describes His relationship with Moses as one that no lesser prophet would ever have, an extraordinary relationship which is best described as *"face to face."* *"...Hear now my words: If there be a prophet among you, I the LORD will make myself known unto him in a vision, and will speak unto him in a dream. My servant Moses is not so, who is faithful in all mine house. With him will I speak **mouth to mouth**, even apparently, and not in dark speeches; and the similitude of the LORD shall he behold: wherefore then were ye not afraid to speak against my servant Moses?"* (Num 12:6-8). Deuteronomy confirms this special relationship, *"And there arose not a prophet since in Israel like unto Moses, whom the LORD knew face to face"* (Deut 34:10).

Messiah Yeshua also had a singular relationship with His Father that could also be described as talking *"face to face"* (see examples below). This idiomatic term can be interpreted as having direct access to God and His revelation. In fact, we see examples of God speaking audibly to both of them.

*"And the LORD said unto Moses, Lo, I come unto thee in a thick cloud, that the people may hear when I speak with thee, and believe thee for ever. And Moses told the words of the people unto the LORD...And when the voice of the trumpet sounded long, and waxed louder and louder, Moses spake, and **God answered him by a voice**"* (Exo 19:9,19; see also 34:5-6).

*"And Yeshua answered them, saying, The hour is come, that the Son of man should be glorified...Now is my soul troubled; and what shall I say? Father, save me from this hour: but for this cause came I unto this hour. Father, glorify thy name. Then came there **a voice** from heaven, saying, I have both glorified it, and will glorify it again"* (John 12:23,27-28).

Because of their direct access to the Father, both spoke as oracles of God. *"And Moses came and told the people all the words of the LORD, and all the judgments: and all the people answered with one voice, and said, All the words which the LORD hath said will we do"* (Exo 24:3, cp. 20:18-19). *"I [Yeshua] have many things to say and to judge of you: but he that sent me is true; and I speak to the world those things which I have heard of him"* (John 8:26). *"For I* [Yeshua] *have not spoken of myself; but the Father which sent me, he gave me a commandment, what I should say, and what I should speak. And I know that his commandment is life everlasting: whatsoever I speak therefore, even as the Father said unto me, so I speak"* (John 12:49-50).

Their special relationship with God was based on God's sovereign choice in sending them to the children of Israel and was maintained by faithfulness to Him. *"My servant Moses is not so, who is faithful in all mine house"* (Num 12:7). *"Wherefore... consider the Apostle and High Priest of our profession, Messiah Yeshua; Who was faithful to him that appointed him, as also Moses was faithful in all his house"* (Heb 3:1-6).

Of course, their being sent by God is another divine parallel. *"I will send thee unto Pharaoh, that thou mayest bring forth my people the children of Israel out of Egypt...And Moses said unto God, Behold, when I come unto the children of Israel, and shall say unto them, The God of your fathers hath sent me unto you; and they shall say to me, What is his name? what shall I say unto them? And God said unto Moses, I AM THAT I AM...Thus shalt thou say unto the children of Israel, I AM hath sent me unto you... The LORD God of your fathers, the God of Abraham, the God of Isaac, and the God of Jacob, hath sent me unto you: this is my name for ever, and this is my memorial unto all generations"* (selections from Exo 3:10-15).

John the Baptist testified of Yeshua, *"For he whom God hath sent speaketh the words of God: for God giveth not the Spirit by measure unto him"* (John 3:34). And Yeshua described Himself as "sent." *"Say ye of him, whom the Father hath sanctified, and sent into the world, Thou blasphemest; because I said, I am the Son of God?"* (John 10:36).

Mediator

Moses was called on to be a mediator between God and Israel; he passed on God's words and commands to them. *"(I* [Moses] *stood between the LORD and you at that time, to shew you the word of the LORD: for ye were afraid by reason of the fire, and went not up into the mount;)"* (Deut 5:5). *"But as for thee, stand thou here by me* [God], *and I will speak unto thee all the commandments, and the statutes, and the judgments, which thou shalt teach them, that they may do them in the land which I give them to possess it"* (Deut 5:31).

Messiah Yeshua also acted as such a mediator – as a vessel to bring God's words, thoughts, and actions to man, to express the Father's name or nature. *"Then answered Yeshua and said unto them, Verily, verily, I say unto you, The Son can do nothing of himself, but what he seeth the Father do: for what things soever he doeth, these also doeth the Son likewise. For the Father loveth the Son, and sheweth him all things that himself doeth: and he will shew him greater works than these, that ye may marvel"* (John 5:19-20). *"I have many things to say and to judge of you: but he that sent me is true; and I speak to the world those things which I have heard of him"* (John 8:26).

They were used by God as mediators of a covenant which was sealed with blood. *"And he [Moses] took the book of the covenant, and read in the audience of the people: and they said, All that the LORD hath said will we do, and be obedient. And Moses took the **blood**, and sprinkled it on the people, and said, Behold the **blood of the covenant**, which the LORD hath made with you concerning all these words"* (Exo 24:7-8). *"And as they were eating, Jesus took bread, and blessed [God], and brake it, and gave it to the disciples, and said, Take, eat; this is my body. And he took the cup, and gave thanks, and gave it to them, saying, Drink ye all of it; For this is my **blood of the new testament**, which is shed for many for the remission of sins"* (Matt 26:26-28).

Intercessor

Moses interceded by standing in the gap between God's righteous anger and sinful man, in this case Israel, to turn that anger aside. *"Therefore he said that he would destroy them, had not Moses his chosen stood before him in the breach, to turn away his wrath, lest he should destroy them"* (Psa 106:23, see Exo 32:11-14). *"And Moses returned unto the LORD, and said, Oh, this people have sinned a great sin, and have made them gods of gold. Yet now, if thou wilt forgive their sin—; and if not, blot me, I pray thee, out of thy book which thou hast written"* (Exo 32:31-32, see also Deut 9:13-20; 10:10).

Yeshua is the Anointed One (Messiah) whose sacrifice turns aside God's wrath from sinful, but repentant, man. *"For even the Son of man came not to be ministered unto, but to minister, and to give his life a ransom for many"* (Mark 10:45). *"For there is one God, and one mediator between God and men, the man Messiah Yeshua; Who gave himself a ransom for all, to be testified in due time"* (1 Tim 2:5-6). *"Therefore will I divide him a portion with the great, and he shall divide the spoil with the strong; because he hath poured out his soul unto death: and he was numbered with the transgressors; and he bare the sin of many, and made intercession for the transgressors"* (Isa 53:12).

Moses interceded in prayer for Israel. Here are some examples: *"And when the people complained, it displeased the LORD: and the LORD heard it; and his anger was kindled; and the fire of the LORD burnt among them, and consumed them that were in the uttermost parts of the camp. And the people cried unto Moses; and when **Moses prayed** unto the LORD, the fire was quenched"* (Num 11:1-2). *"And the LORD spake unto Moses and unto Aaron, saying, Separate yourselves from among this congregation, that I may consume them in a moment. And they **fell upon their faces, and said**, O God, the God of the spirits of all flesh, shall one man sin, and wilt thou be wroth with all the congregation?"* (Num 16:20-22).

Yeshua also used prayer to intercede for God's people. *"I pray for them: **I pray** not for the world, but for them which thou hast given me; for they are thine"* (John 17:9). *"And when they were come to the place, which is called Calvary, there they crucified him, and the malefactors, one on the right hand, and the other on the left. Then **said Yeshua, Father, forgive** them; for they know not what they do"* (Luke 23:33-34a).

Of course, He is still interceding for us today. *"Who is he that condemneth? It is Messiah that died, yea rather, that is risen again, who is even at the right hand of God, who also maketh intercession for us"* (Rom 8:34). *"Wherefore he is able also to save them to the uttermost that come unto God by him, seeing he ever liveth to make intercession for them"* (Heb 7:25).

Deliverer

God chose Moses to deliver Israel from slavery in Egypt. *"Now therefore, behold, the cry of the children of Israel is come unto me: and I have also seen the oppression wherewith the Egyptians oppress them. Come now therefore, and I will send thee unto Pharaoh, that thou mayest **bring forth my people** the children of Israel out of Egypt"* (Exo 3:9-10). *"For he supposed his brethren would have understood how that God by his hand would **deliver** them: but they understood not"* (Acts 7:25).

So too, God chose Yeshua to deliver us from slavery to sin and from other afflictions. At the start of His public ministry, Yeshua claimed that what God had prophesied in Isaiah was fulfilled in Himself, *"The Spirit of the Lord is upon me, because he hath anointed me to preach the gospel to the poor; he hath sent me to heal* [make whole] *the brokenhearted, to preach **deliverance*** [freedom, pardon] *to the captives, and recovering of sight to the* *blind, to **set at liberty*** [same as "deliver"] *them that are bruised* [lit: crushed, shattered], *To preach the acceptable year of the Lord"* (Luke 4:18-19).

Paul explains deliverance from slavery to sin in a comprehensive way in Romans 6. This verse seems to sum up his thoughts. *"But God be thanked, that ye were the **servants of sin**, but ye have obeyed from the heart that form of doctrine which was delivered you. Being then **made free from sin**, ye became the servants of righteousness."* (Rom 6:17-18; see in context 6:16-23).

To accomplish this salvation, both contended with evil. Moses resisted the magicians of Pharaoh (Exo 7:11,22), and when finally free from Egypt, he became the spiritual focal point of Israel's fight with Amalek (Exo 17:8-13). Then in Exodus 32:26-28 he called those on the Lord's side to himself. The Levites responded and obeyed, killing three thousand idolaters in the camp of Israel.

Yeshua was confronted by Satan but resisted his temptations in the wilderness (Matt 4:1-11). He also freed people from demons on many occasions (for example Matt 8:28-32; 17:14-18).

Another important parallel is that deliverance by Moses from Egypt and by Yeshua from sin were accomplished through the shedding of blood - which in both instances provided protection against God's righteous judgment. The Passover Lamb is the anti-type of Yeshua, the Lamb of God.[5]

The Lord told Moses, *"And they shall take of the **blood** [of the lamb], and strike it on the two side posts and on the upper door post of the houses, wherein they shall eat it...[The lamb] is the LORD's passover. For I will pass through the land of Egypt this night, and will smite all the firstborn in the land of Egypt, both man and beast; and against all the gods of Egypt I will execute judgment: I am the LORD. And the **blood** shall be to you for a token upon the houses where ye are: and when I see the **blood**, I will pass over you, and the plague shall not be upon you to destroy you, when I smite the land of Egypt"* (Exo 12:7,11b-13).

The writer to the Hebrews teaches about Yeshua's blood atonement, *"But Messiah being come an high priest of good things to come...by his own **blood** he entered in once into the holy place, having obtained eternal redemption for us. For if the blood of bulls and of goats, and the ashes of an heifer sprinkling the unclean, sanctifieth to the purifying of the flesh:[6] How much more shall the **blood** of Messiah, who through the eternal Spirit offered himself without spot to God, purge your conscience from dead works to serve the living God? And for this cause he is the mediator of the new testament [covenant], that by means of death, for the* *redemption of the transgressions that were under the first testament, they which are called might receive the promise of eternal inheritance"* (Heb 9:11-15).

Moses and Yeshua each established covenant meals to help us remember and give thanks to God for His great deliverance/ salvation. God commanded Israel to keep a meal on Passover as a memorial for them and their children (Exo 12:3-11, 25-27, 42-49; Lev 23:5). Of course, when Yeshua instituted Communion, it was during the Passover meal (Luke 22:14-20; 1 Cor 11:26). And the New Testament goes on to identify Yeshua as the Passover Lamb, *"For even Messiah our passover is sacrificed for us:"* (1 Cor 5:7b).[7]

Authority

Both Yeshua and Moses were empowered to declare God's word with authority. Deuteronomy 18:18 states that the promised prophet would speak in God's name with God's authority! *"I will raise them up a Prophet from among their brethren, like unto thee, and will put my words in his mouth; and he shall speak unto them all that I shall command him."*

Moses displayed this power in his ministry, it being promised him by God when He first called him to go to Egypt. *"Now therefore go, and I will be with thy mouth, and teach thee what thou shalt say"* (Exo 4:12). At Mt Sinai, the children of Israel recognized that Moses spoke the words of the Lord to them. They had pleaded to hear them from him rather than directly from God, *"And they said unto Moses, Speak thou with us, and we will hear: but let not God speak with us, lest we die"* (Exo 20:19).

Yeshua also revealed the authority of God when He spoke and/or performed miracles. *"And they went into Capernaum; and straightway on the sabbath day he entered into the synagogue, and taught. And they were astonished at his doctrine: for he taught them as one that had **authority**, and not as the scribes...And they were all amazed, insomuch that they questioned among themselves, saying, What thing is this? what new doctrine is this? for with **authority** commandeth he even the unclean spirits, and they do obey him"* (Mark 1:21-22,27; see also Matt 7:28-29; Luke 4:20-21). *"Verily, verily, I say unto you, He that heareth my word, and believeth on him that sent me, hath everlasting life, and shall not come into condemnation; but is passed from death unto life...The hour is coming, and now is, when the dead shall hear the voice of the Son of God: and they that hear shall live. For as the Father hath life in himself; so hath he given to the Son to have* *life in himself; And hath given him **authority** to execute judgment also, because he is the Son of man"* (John 5:24-27).

Judge

Moses became the supreme judge in Israel. At His return, Yeshua will be the Judge of the whole world. Although Jethro gave Moses the idea to have faithful men help him, Moses was still the final authority when it came to difficult cases, as Jethro said, *"Moreover thou shalt provide out of all the people able men, such as fear God, men of truth, hating covetousness; and place such over them, to be rulers of thousands, and rulers of hundreds, rulers of fifties, and rulers of tens: And let them judge the people at all seasons: and it shall be, that **every great matter they shall bring unto thee**, but every small matter they shall judge: so shall it be easier for thyself, and they shall bear the burden with thee"* (Exo 18:21-22, see context: vv 13-23).

Yeshua stated that He did not come the first time as a judge. *"Ye judge after the flesh; **I judge no man**. And yet if I judge, my judgment is true: for I am not alone, but I and the Father that sent me"* (John 8:15-16). *"And if any man hear my words, and believe not, **I judge him not**: for I came not to judge the world, but to save the world"* (John 12:47).

Of course He will be *the* judge when He returns, and not just of Israel, but of all the earth. *"Let the field be joyful, and all that is therein: then shall all the trees of the wood rejoice; Before the LORD: for he cometh, for he cometh to **judge** the earth: he shall **judge** the world with righteousness, and the people with his truth"* (Psa 96:12-13). *"For we must all appear before the **judgment seat of Christ**; that every one may receive the things done in his body, according to that he hath done, whether it be good or bad"* (2 Cor 5:10). *"I charge thee therefore before God, and the Lord Jesus Christ, who shall **judge** the quick and the dead at his appearing and his kingdom;"* (2 Tim 4:1; see also Matt 25:31-46; Acts 10:40-42; Rev 19:11).

Shepherd

Moses and Yeshua are called shepherds of God's people. *"Thou leddest thy people like a flock by the hand of Moses and Aaron"* (Psa 77:20). *"Then he remembered the days of old, Moses, and his people, saying, Where is he that brought them up out of the sea with the **shepherd** of his flock?"* (Isa 63:11a).

*"I [Yeshua] am the good **shepherd**: the good **shepherd** giveth his life for the sheep...I am the good **shepherd**, and know my sheep, and am known of mine. As the Father knoweth*

*me, even so know I the Father: and I lay down my life for the sheep. And other sheep I have, which are not of this fold: them also I must bring, and they shall hear my voice; and there shall be one fold, and one **shepherd*** " (John 10:11,14-16, see also Heb 13:20; 1 Pet 2:5; 5:4).

Miracles

Both men demonstrated the Kingdom of God in word and power as they performed many mighty public miracles. Yet each was constrained to do only what they were told by God the Father.

In Moses' life all ten plagues on Egypt were commanded by God. *"And I will stretch out my hand, and smite Egypt with all my wonders which I will do in the midst thereof: and after that he will let you go"* (Exo 3:20, see also 4:28). *"Thus saith the LORD, In this thou shalt know that I am the LORD: behold, I will smite with the rod that is in mine hand upon the waters which are in the river, and they shall be turned to blood"* (Exo 7:17, see also 8:2,16,21, etc.).

Also in the wilderness, God specifically showed Moses what miracles He would do through him. *"And the people murmured against Moses, saying, What shall we drink? And he cried unto the LORD; and the LORD shewed him a tree, which when he had cast into the waters, the waters were made sweet: there he made for them a statute and an ordinance, and there he proved them,"* (Exo 15:24-25). *"And the LORD said unto Moses, Go on before the people, and take with thee of the elders of Israel; and thy rod, wherewith thou smotest the river, take in thine hand, and go. Behold, I will stand before thee there upon the rock in Horeb; and thou shalt smite the rock, and there shall come water out of it, that the people may drink. And Moses did so in the sight of the elders of Israel"* (Exo 17:5-6).

Yeshua said He did only what He saw His Father doing, so He also obeyed, performing only miracles God ordained Him to perform. *"Then answered Jesus and said unto them, Verily, verily, I say unto you, The Son can do nothing of himself, but what he seeth the Father do: for what things soever he doeth, these also doeth the Son likewise. For the Father loveth the Son, and sheweth him all things that himself doeth: and he will shew him greater works than these, that ye may marvel"* (John 5:19-20).

Their Deaths

The deaths of both were previously revealed in Scripture by God. *"So Moses the servant of the LORD died there in the land of Moab, according to the word of the LORD"* (Deut 34:5, cp. 32:48-52). *"For I delivered unto you first of all that which I also received, how that Messiah died for our sins according to the scriptures; And that he was buried, and that he rose again the third day according to the scriptures:"* (1 Cor 15:3-4).

Amazingly, each reappeared after death. Moses actually did "enter" the promised land when he appeared with Elijah talking to Yeshua on the mountain of transfiguration. *"And, behold, there appeared unto them Moses and* [Elijah] *talking with him"* (Matt 17:3).

Of course, Yeshua's resurrection from the dead climaxes the gospel story (Luke 24:13ff; Acts 1:3, etc.).

Relationship with Israel

Since God sent both Moses and Yeshua to Israel we would expect them to have a special relationship with the Jewish people. Again the parallels are quite extraordinary.

Each was initially rejected by Israel. *"And it came to pass...when Moses was grown, that he went out unto his brethren, and looked on their burdens: and he spied an Egyptian smiting an Hebrew, one of his brethren. And he looked this way and that way, and when he saw that there was no man, he slew the Egyptian, and hid him in the sand.*

"And when he went out the second day, behold, two men of the Hebrews strove together: and he said to him that did the wrong, Wherefore smitest thou thy fellow? And he said, **Who made thee a prince and a judge over us?** *intendest thou to kill me, as thou killedst the Egyptian? And Moses feared, and said, Surely this thing is known"* (Exo 2:11-14).

In Acts 7:23-28, Stephen reviews this part of Moses' story adding in verse 35, *"This Moses whom they refused, saying, Who made thee a ruler and a judge? the same did God send to be* **a ruler and a deliverer** *by the hand of the angel which appeared to him in the bush."*

The majority of Israel also rejected Yeshua at His first appearing although perhaps one-third believed Him to be the promised Messiah.

After Israel rejects them, they each obtain a gentile bride. Moses married Zipporah, daughter of Jethro, the priest of Midian (Exo 2:16-21), and also an Ethiopian woman (Num 12:1). And Paul writes to the *gentiles* in Corinth, *"For I am jealous over you with godly jealousy: for I have espoused you to one husband, that I may present you as a chaste virgin to the Messiah"* (2 Cor 11:2). And in the letter to the Ephesians, which most biblical scholars view as a general letter to the Church, he says, *"For we are members of his body, of his flesh, and of his bones. For this cause shall a man leave his father and mother, and shall be joined unto his wife, and they two shall be one flesh. This is a great mystery: but I speak concerning Messiah and the church"* (Eph 5:30-32).

Although it is true that the initial Church was made up exclusively of Messianic Jews and that there has always been a Jewish remnant in the Church throughout history,[8] it is also true that the overwhelming majority of the Church in membership and culture for the past two millennia has been non-Jewish.

When Moses returned to Israel, he was accepted. *"And Moses and Aaron went and gathered together all the elders of the children of Israel: And Aaron spake all the words which the LORD had spoken unto Moses, and did the signs in the sight of the people.* **And the people believed***: and when they heard that the LORD had visited the children of Israel, and that he had looked upon their affliction,* **then they bowed their heads and worshipped** *"* (Exo 4:29-31).

Yeshua also will be accepted when He returns to Israel. Paul says so, *"For I would not, brethren, that ye should be ignorant of this mystery, lest ye should be wise in your own conceits; that blindness in part is happened to Israel, until the fulness of the Gentiles be come in. And so* **all Israel shall be saved***: as it is written, There shall come out of Sion the Deliverer, and shall turn away ungodliness from Jacob:"* (Rom 11:25-26).[9]

Conclusion

This extensive look at the parallels between the lives of Moses and Yeshua, the prophet promised to be like Moses, proves that when the Lord God states something in His word, He means it. *"So shall my word be that goeth forth out of my mouth: it shall not return unto me void, but it shall accomplish that which I please, and it shall prosper in the thing whereto I sent it"* (Isa 55:11). God's faithfulness should be a source of great comfort and encouragement for us as we look at all the wonderful promises He has made to Israel, and to the Church. He will fulfill His Word. No wonder Messiah Yeshua said to Israel, *"Search the scriptures; for in them ye think ye have eternal life: and they are they which testify of me"* (John 5:39).

Finally, rabbis knew that the greatness of the Messiah would overshadow the greatness of Moses! "In fact the Messiah is such a prophet as it is stated in the *Midrash*[10] on the verse, 'Behold my servant shall prosper'...Moses by the miracles which he wrought drew but a single nation to the worship of god, but the Messiah will draw all nations to the worship of God."[11]

"Philip found Nathanael and said to him,
'We have found Him of whom Moses in the law,
and also the prophets, wrote -
Yeshua of Nazareth, the son of Joseph" (John 1:45).

---

1   This Greek word is also used for being raised from the dead. For example: Mark 8:31; 9:9-10; 12:23-25; Luke 9:8,19; 16:31; 24:46; John 6:54; 11:23-24; 20:9; Acts 2:24,32; 13:33-34; Eph 5:14; 1 Thes 4:14,16.

2   See Endnote 1.

3   Risto Santala, *The Messiah in the Old Testament in the Light of Rabbinical Writings*, Keren Ahvah Meshihit, Jerusalem, 1992.

4   Most commentators say that the genealogical record in Luke traces Miriam's family line, while the one in Matthew traces Joseph's side of the family.

5   The New Testament uses the title "Lamb" to describe Yeshua more often than any other title except "Messiah" and the most frequent use is in the Book of Revelation.

6   The New Testament says that the *Tanach* blood sacrifices sanctified the offerers from sins of the flesh. Those sacrifices could not deal with our inherited sin nature, but Messiah's sacrifice made each of us *"a new creature"* in the Messiah (2 Cor 5:17).

7   See Chap. 3 on Passover.

8   Note in Rom 11:17, *"among them,"* and in 11:25 *"blindness in part."*

9   Standing before the Sanhedrin, Stephen emphasizes the Second Coming when he compares Yeshua's life with the patriarch Joseph's and says, *"And **at the second time** Joseph was made known to his brethren..."* (Acts 7:13a).

10 A *midrash* is a Jewish commentary on the Scriptures.

11   F. Kenton Beshore, *The Messiah of the Targums, Talmuds and Rabbinical Writers*, 1971, Chart 17 quoting R. Levi ben Gershom.

CHAPTER 9

The Gospel
According to the *Tanach*

Where Are the Roots of the Gospel Found?

The Gospel, literally "good news,"[1] was not totally unexpected when the angel announced to the Jewish virgin Miriam that she would give birth to the promised Messiah. Many in Israel were waiting for His appearing, for example Simeon and Anna. (See Luke 2:25-38). In fact we see that the inspired writers of the New Testament are constantly pointing back to the *Tanach* as their proof text for what they proclaim about Messiah Yeshua, His life and ministry, His miracles, and most importantly His death on the cross, His burial, and His resurrection.

We want to look at a number of New Testament texts that will demonstrate that the Gospel, the "good news" we have believed, was based on the Word of God found in the *Tanach*.

The New Testament Looks Backward For Proof

From the opening line of the New Testament, our attention is focused on what went before, "*The book of the generation of Yeshua the Messiah, the son of **David**, the son of **Abraham**"* (Matt 1:1). Why was it so important that Yeshua was the son, or descendant, of both Abraham and David? Because God covenanted with them that one of their offspring would be the promised Messiah.

To Abraham, God said, *"Get thee out of thy country, and from thy kindred, and from thy father's house, unto a land that I will shew thee: And I will make of thee a great nation, and I will bless thee, and make thy name* [reputation, fame] *great; and thou shalt be a blessing: And I will bless them that bless thee, and curse him that curseth[2] thee: **and in thee shall all families of the earth be blessed** "* (Gen 12:1b-3). We have already seen in Chapter 1 that according to Paul, that phrase prophesied the Gospel to the gentiles, *"And the scripture, foreseeing that God would justify* [make righteous] *the heathen* [*ethnos*³] *through faith, preached before the gospel unto Abraham, saying, In thee shall all nations* [*ethnos*] *be blessed"* (Gal 3:8). Even from Matthew 1:1, the New Testament looks backward to God's promises to Abraham and forward to the message going out to the whole world.

God also promised that David's greater Son would be the Messiah who would reign on David's throne forever. *"And when thy days be fulfilled, and thou shalt sleep with thy fathers, I will set up thy seed after thee, which shall proceed out of thy bowels, and I will establish his kingdom. He shall build an house for my name* [honor, glory], ***and I will stablish the throne of his kingdom for ever***. *I will be his father, and he shall be my son...And thine house and thy kingdom shall be established* [confirmed] *for ever before thee: thy throne shall be established for ever"* (2 Sam 7:12-14a,16).

Solomon, although a type, was not the final fulfillment of these promises because a natural son could not possibly fulfill them. Yeshua, called the "Son of David" in many New Testament verses, is the Promised One.⁴

Incidentally, both Abraham and David were also promised the inheritance of the Land of Israel, making Matthew 1:1 one of several New Testament texts which affirm that the coming of Israel's Messiah did not do away with God's promises to the Jewish people concerning that inheritance. See Genesis 12:1 above for the promise to Abraham. To David, God states in 2 Samuel 7:10a, *"Moreover I will appoint a place for my people Israel, and will plant* [establish] *them, that they may dwell* [abide, settle] *in a place of their own, and move* [move with fear, be agitated] *no more;"*

Matthew continually points back to the *Tanach* by using the following or similar phrases repeatedly, *"Now all this was done* [brought into being], ***that it might be fulfilled which was spoken of the Lord by the prophet***..." (Matt 1:22).⁵

John,⁶ like Matthew, is also careful to link his Gospel account with the fulfillment of *Tanach* prophecies. He often uses that same phrase. For example: *"But though he had done so many miracles before them, yet they believed not on* [did not put confidence in] *him: **That the saying of** [Isaiah] **the prophet might be fulfilled**, which he spake, Lord, who hath believed our report? and to whom hath the arm of the Lord been revealed? Therefore they could not* [were not able to, did not have the power to] *believe, because that* ***[Isaiah] said again***, *He hath blinded their eyes, and hardened their heart* [understanding]*; that they should not see with their eyes, nor understand* [comprehend] *with their heart, and be converted*

[handwritten margin note: Land promised to Abraham + David]

[turned around 180 degrees], *and I should heal them"* (John 12:37-40).[7] This does not refer to all the Jewish people. If it did, the Gospel would never have spread to the gentiles. It did not even refer to all the Levitical priests, many of whom believed![8] In the original context of the quote from Isaiah (Isa 6), the previous chapter (Isa 5) speaks about self-indulgent and corrupt nominal believers in Israel and Judah who were already under God's judgment.

Yeshua Points to the *Tanach*

Imagine for a moment you are walking on the road to Emmaus with the resurrected Messiah, but your eyes have been blinded to His identity. Writing the script for this fantasy, wouldn't you have Him say something like, "Hey - wake up! It's me. I am risen from the dead. Look at Me, touch Me – and believe!" But what did Yeshua really say to His disciples on that road? *"'...O fools, and slow of heart* [mind, inner man] *to believe* [be persuaded, place confidence in] *all that the prophets have spoken: Ought not Messiah to have suffered these things, and to enter into his glory?"*

What did He do next? *"And beginning at Moses and all the prophets, he expounded unto them in all the scriptures the things concerning himself"* (Luke 24:25b-27). Yeshua's proof of his Messiahship is based on what the Word of God, the *Tanach*, states and *not* just physical evidence – no matter how miraculous.[9] God's people in Yeshua's day, just like many of His people today, were seeking signs and a miraculous deliverance. Yeshua strongly warned against signs becoming their main focus.[10] Instead, He turned His disciples' attention back to the Word.

Many Jews were crucified in the first century AD and several Jews were even resurrected in the gospel accounts – Lazarus, a widow's son, and a synagogue ruler's little girl. So Yeshua's crucifixion or resurrection alone do not prove He is Messiah. His birth, crucifixion, burial, and resurrection prove He is Israel's promised Anointed One, and the world's Savior, *only* because they exactly fulfill what the *Tanach* prophesied concerning the Jewish Messiah!

How did Yeshua challenge those who doubted He was the Messiah? *"Search the scriptures* [the *Tanach*]; *for in them ye think ye have eternal life: and they are they which testify* [bear witness] *of me...Do not think that I will accuse you to the Father: there is one that accuseth you, even Moses, in whom ye trust. For had ye believed Moses, ye would have believed me: for he wrote of me. But if ye believe not his writings, how shall ye believe my words?"* (John 5:39,45-47). That particular saying of the Messiah is a stumbling block to many in the Church when it should be a foundation. If we do not have confidence that what Moses wrote is still the Word of our God, then how can we really trust in Yeshua as Messiah, Savior, and Lord? Yeshua *always* used the *Tanach* as proof of His Messiahship.

God wants us to believe in what Moses wrote – forever! *"And the LORD said unto Moses, Lo, I come unto thee in a thick cloud,* [in order] *that the people may hear when I speak with thee, **and believe thee for ever**. And Moses told the words of the people unto the LORD"* (Exo 19:9).

A Rabbi Satisfied with Yeshua's Messiahship

Why was Rabbi Saul, the apostle Paul, so convinced that Yeshua was the true Messiah? Because he found that the Gospel was the fulfillment of what the *Tanach* says. He declared before both Roman and Jewish authorities, *"But this I confess unto thee, that after the way which **they** call heresy, so worship* [and serve] *I the God of my fathers, **believing** [trusting in] **all things which are written in the law and in the prophets**:"* (Acts 24:14).

In Romans 1:1-2 Paul not only calls the *Tanach* "the holy scriptures," but he states that the Gospel was promised in the Tanach, *"Paul, a servant* [slave] *of Yeshua the Messiah, called to be an apostle, separated unto the gospel of God, **(Which he had promised afore by his prophets in the holy scriptures**)...."* [11]

Saved by Faith

In Romans 10:5-8, the apostle quotes Moses, arguing in favor of God's righteousness imparted through trusting God, as opposed to the idea that man can achieve righteousness by keeping all of God's Law. Although what follows may sound like Moses was contradicting himself, he was not. Moses only points out that if a person wants to be righteous in God's sight by his own works, he must perfectly keep all of God's Law. But Moses knows this is impossible. He then says that there is another way of being righteous with God, a way that achieves its goal, and that is by faith.

Paul uses these points from Moses in his argument, *"For Moses describeth the righteousness which is of the law, That the man which doeth those things shall live by them (Lev 18:5)."* He then contrasts that impossible approach to righteousness **by again quoting from Moses,** *"But the righteousness which is of faith speaketh on this wise, Say not in thine heart, Who shall ascend into heaven* [Deut 30:12]*? (that is, to bring Messiah down from above:) Or, Who shall descend into the deep? (that is, to bring up Messiah again from the dead.) **But what saith it? The word** is nigh thee, even in thy mouth, and in thy heart* [Deut 30:14] [12]*: that is, **the word of faith**, which we preach."*

So to establish what God means by *"the righteousness which is of faith,"* Paul has quoted Moses - he quotes the Law! In the Law (lit: Teaching), both types of righteousness are proclaimed. Righteousness by faith never negates the righteousness of the Law, but rather upholds it as a standard (Rom 3:31).

Paul continues presenting his Gospel evidence from the *Tanach* (here in **bold**) throughout Romans 10:9-21, *"That if thou shalt confess with thy mouth the Lord Yeshua, and shalt believe* [trust] *in thine heart that God hath raised him from the dead, thou shalt be saved. For with the heart man believeth unto righteousness; and with the mouth confession is made unto salvation. For the scripture* [the *Tanach*] *saith,* **Whosoever believeth on** [trusts in] **him shall not be ashamed** [Isa 28:16; 49:23]. *For there is no difference between the Jew and the Greek: for the same Lord over all is rich unto all that call upon him.* **For whosoever shall call upon the name of the Lord shall be saved** [Joel 2:32]. *How then shall they call on him in whom they have not believed? and how shall they believe* [trust] *in him of whom they have not heard? and how shall they hear without a preacher? And how shall they preach, except they be sent? as it is written,* **How beautiful are the feet of them that preach the gospel of peace, and bring glad tidings of good things** [Isa 52:7; Nah 1:15]. *But they have not all obeyed the gospel. For* [Isaiah] *saith,* **Lord, who hath believed our report?** [Isa 53:1] *So then faith cometh by hearing, and hearing by the word of God.*[13] *But I say, Have they not heard? Yes verily,* **their sound went into all the earth, and their words unto the ends of the world** [Psa 19:4]. *But I say, Did not Israel know? First Moses saith,* **I will provoke you to jealousy by them that are no people** [ethnos], **and by a foolish nation** [ethnos] **I will anger you** [Deut 32:21]. *But* [Isaiah] *is very bold, and saith,* **I was found of them that sought me not; I was made manifest unto them that asked not after me** [Isa 65:1]. *But to Israel he saith,* **All day long I have stretched forth my hands unto a disobedient** [rebellious] **and gainsaying** [unwilling, contrary] **people** [Isa 65:2]."

At this point in Paul's argument in Romans, you might think that God is finished with Israel. After all, the *Tanach* verses that Paul quotes are critical of God's chosen people. But the Spirit of God knew that many people might reach this conclusion and so continued in the very next verse[14] with this statement, *"I say then, Hath God cast away* [rejected] *his people? God forbid"* (Rom 11:1a). And to prove this, Paul quotes from or alludes to the *Tanach* in many other verses.[15]

In Paul's classic chapter on the resurrection of the dead, again and again he uses the *Tanach* as God's sanctified foundation for his belief. *"For I delivered* [committed, transmitted] *to you first of all what I also received, how that Messiah died for our sins* **according to the scriptures** [the *Tanach*]; *that he was buried, and he rose again the third day* **according to the scriptures** [the *Tanach*]" (1 Cor 15:3-4).

It should be quite obvious by now that if Paul cannot find the "roots" of some doctrine in the *Tanach*, he will not ask you to believe it in the New Covenant. Even with an issue like speaking in tongues, Paul finds a *Tanach* proof text, "*In the law it is written*, *With men of other tongues and other lips will I speak unto this people; and yet for all that will they not hear me, saith the Lord. Wherefore tongues are for a sign, not to them that believe, but to them that believe not: but prophesying serveth not for them that believe not, but for them which believe*" (1 Cor 14:21-22).

Other New Testament Proofs

The letter to the Hebrews states also that the Gospel was preached to the children of Israel in the wilderness *after* the Law was given. "*Let us therefore fear, lest, a promise being left us of entering into his rest, any of you should seem to come short of it.* **For unto us was the gospel preached, as well as** [lit: exactly as] **unto them**: *but the word preached did not profit them,* **not being mixed with faith** *in them that heard it. For we which have believed* [trusted, have confidence] *do enter into rest,* **as he said, As I have sworn in my wrath, if they shall enter into my rest** [Psa 95:11]: *although the works were finished from the foundation of the world*" (Heb 4:1-3).

This is similar to another *Tanach* verse in which God said to Israel through the prophet Jeremiah, "*Thus saith the LORD, Stand ye in the ways, and see, and ask for the old* [lit: everlasting, eternal] *paths, where is* **the good way**, *and walk therein, and ye shall find* [attain] **rest for your souls**. *But they said, We will not walk therein*" (Jer 6:16).

Finally, Peter declares that the Word of the Lord as found in the *Tanach* was the same Word that the apostles used to preach the Gospel, the good news of Yeshua the Messiah. And why not? It was the only Word of God they had. "*Being born again, not of corruptible seed, but of incorruptible, by* [through] *the* **word of God, which liveth and abideth for ever**. *For all flesh is as grass, and all the glory* [beauty, influence, dignity] *of man as the flower of grass. The grass withereth, and the flower thereof falleth away:* **But the word of the Lord endureth for ever** [Isa 40:6,8]. **And this is the word which by the gospel is preached unto you**" (1 Pet 1:23-25).

In Conclusion

Try this most informative, eye-opening, and profitable word study. Trace all the places where the New Testament uses the word "scripture" and in your mind substitute *"Tanach."* You are not doing a disservice to the text – in fact just the opposite. You will be reading the text with the mindset of the writers whom God used to write it.

Here is the question. Do you think your own personal theological view of the Old Testament is as "high and holy" as that of the New Testament authors and Messiah Yeshua? If not, why not?

We cannot afford to believe in just the New Testament. *"Yeshua answered and said unto them, Ye do err* [go astray, are deceived and in error], *not knowing* [understanding] *the scriptures* [the *Tanach*], *nor the power of God"* (Matt 22:29). We cannot afford such error. Why call ourselves "New Testament believers?" We should more accurately call ourselves "Bible believers." We must realize that the *Tanach* is vital to our faith.

"For I am not ashamed of the gospel of Messiah:
for it is the power of God unto salvation
to every one that believeth;
to the Jew first, and also to the Greek.
For therein is the righteousness of God revealed
from faith to faith:
as it is written *[in Hab 2:4], The just shall live by faith"*
(Rom 1:16-17).

---

1 Proverbs 25:25.

2 The two words translated "curse" in this verse are not the same in Hebrew. Paraphrased, it reads: "I will bitterly curse, or put under a curse, them that treat you with contempt, make you despicable and dishonor you."

3 The Greek *ethnos* and the Hebrew *goyim* can be translated as heathens, or nations, according to the context.

4 See Chapter 14, section "God's Son."

5 See also Matt 2:15, 23; 8:17; 12:17; 13:35; 21:4.

6 Many scholars list John's as the least Jewish of the gospels, but according to *Tanach* rabbinic thinking, it would be one of the more "kosher" accounts, as seen by John's frequent *Tanach* references.

7 See also John 15:25; 17:12; 18:9; 19:24, 28, 36-37.

8 Acts 6:7.

9 See also Luke 24:44.

10 Matt 24:24; Mark 13:22; John 4:48; 2 Thess 2:9.

11 Whenever the New Testament mentions "scriptures," in the historical context it is referring only to the *Tanach*. How many believers in Messiah Yeshua today understand that their Holy Scriptures must include the Old Testament?

12 Through Paul, the Spirit of God gives this inspired commentary, or *midrash,* on what the *Tanach* says.

13 In some manuscripts, *"the word of Christ."*

14 In the original Greek and Hebrew scriptures there were no chapter or verse divisions. The current numbering system, although very helpful, can at times cut through the thought flow. Often it is helpful, before tackling the beginning of a new chapter, to read the last couple of verses in the previous chapter to check for a vital connection.

15 Rom 11:2-4, 7-12, 15-16, 20-21, 24-29, 33-36.

CHAPTER 10

The Cross in the *Tanach* - Part 1

Believers can run into many problems if they don't fully understand what Scripture says about the Cross. However, to comprehend what happened on the Cross, we need to know more than just what the New Testament reveals. We can safely assume that the New Testament authors depended on their readers studying and knowing the *Tanach*. Although the cross as a means of execution was first used only a couple of centuries before Yeshua, yet there are prophecies in the *Tanach* from much earlier which give deep insight about what was to occur on that "tree."

The New Testament says that the prophets had many things revealed to them about the Messiah except the exact time of His coming. *"Of which salvation the prophets have inquired and searched diligently* [in the *Tanach*], *who prophesied of the* **grace** *that should come unto you: Searching what, or what manner of* **time** *the Spirit of Messiah which was in them did signify* [make clear; give understanding], *when it testified beforehand the* **sufferings of Messiah**, *and the glory that should follow"* (1 Pet 1:10-11).

One of the most complete revelations of *"Yeshua the Messiah and Him crucified"* (1 Cor 2:2) is found in Isaiah 52:13-53:12. The following verse-by-verse discussion of this and other passages will demonstrate the necessity of looking into the *Tanach* in order to fully understand the New Testament.

Isaiah 52:13-53:12[1]

52:13 *"Behold,* **My Servant** *shall deal prudently* [prosper, deal wisely, succeed in that for which He is sent], *He* **shall be exalted** [raised up on high, lit. and/or fig.] *and extolled, and be very high."*

In Yeshua's time there were Aramaic translations of the *Tanach* with commentaries, called the *targums*. They give insight into the thinking of the Jewish people of that day. *Targum Jonathan* translates the verse: "Behold, My Servant Messiah ...shall be exalted..."[2] Yeshua must have had this verse in mind when He said, *"And I, if I be lifted up from the earth, will draw all men unto me"* (John 12:32).

Here is an interesting quote: "Our Rabbis expound this [verse]...of the King Messiah, saying, 'He shall be higher than Abraham, exalted above Moses, and loftier than the ministering angels.'"[3] It is difficult to see how this interpretation could apply to any mere human. It sounds similar to what the New Testament writer to the Hebrews says about Messiah Yeshua in the first three chapters of his letter (Heb 1,2,3).

In both the Hebrew and Greek, the word "servant" can also be translated "worshipper." Servants obey, and Yeshua was obedient - even to his death on the Cross. Obedience is the essence of worship. Simply put, to serve and worship God we must obey Him.

52:14 *"Just as many were astonished* [appalled, horrified] *at you, so **His visage*** [appearance] ***was marred** more than any man, and His form **more than the sons of men**;"*

Yeshua received a beating and scourging before His crucifixion. By the time Messiah was crucified He was a bleeding, shocking sight. If we remember that Messiah was standing in our place, taking the punishment for sin that we rightly deserve from a holy God, we can understand why our sin repulses God. Just as it marred Yeshua's body, it destroys what is holy, the likeness of God in man.

52:15a *"So shall He **sprinkle** many nations [goyim - gentiles]."*

The Hebrew word translated "sprinkle" is used for ceremonial cleansing through the sprinkling of blood. Peter refers to this section of Isaiah several times in his first letter. For example: *"Elect according to the foreknowledge of God the Father, through sanctification of the Spirit, unto obedience and **sprinkling of the blood** of Jesus Christ: Grace unto you, and peace, be multiplied"* (1Pet 1:2).

52:15b *"**Kings** shall shut their mouths at Him; for what had not been told them they **shall see**, and what they had not heard they shall consider* [discern, understand]."*

Compare this with Isaiah 49:7: *"Thus saith the LORD, the Redeemer of Israel, and his Holy One, to him **whom man** [nephesh – lit. a soul] **despiseth**, to him **whom the nation** [in context – Israel] **abhorreth**, to a servant of rulers, **Kings shall see** and arise, **princes also shall worship**, because of the LORD that is faithful, and the Holy One of Israel, and he shall choose thee."*

These two verses prophesy that the Servant of the LORD, the Messiah, will be revealed to, and worshipped by, gentiles and their leaders. In fact, Isaiah 49:7 (above) states that the reason Israel will despise, but the gentiles accept, this Sent One, is because God is faithful to His promises to Israel! This perhaps startling thought is confirmed by Paul in Romans 11.[4]

53:1a *"Who has believed our report?"*

John 12:37-38 gives the reason more Jewish people did not believe in Yeshua despite His miracles. *"But though he had done so many miracles before them, yet **they believed not** on him: **That the saying of** [Isaiah] **the prophet might be fulfilled**, which he spake, Lord, who hath believed our report? and to whom hath the arm of the Lord been revealed?"*

God was confirming His Word by executing it. He blinded Israel's eyes as John says in the verses following: *"Therefore they **could** not believe, because that* [Isaiah] *said again, He hath blinded their eyes* [metaphorically, the mind, the faculty of knowing], *and hardened their heart* [soul, mind, will, understanding]*; that they should not see* [know, perceive] *with their eyes, nor understand with their heart, and be converted* [lit. turn back; fig. change one's mind]*, and I should heal* [to free from errors and sins; save] *them"* (John 12:39-40). Remember, in context this referred to the unbelievers among the Jews and many of the religious authorities, not to *all* Israel.

In Romans 10 Paul shows that although the Gospel was preached as was prophesied, not all believed, also as was prophesied. By combining Isaiah 52:7 with 53:1 in the following verse, he demonstrates the scriptural principle of God watching over His Word to perform it (see Jer 1:12). *"And how shall they preach, except they be sent? as it is written, How beautiful are the feet of them that preach the gospel of peace, and bring glad tidings of good things! But they have not all obeyed the gospel. For* [Isaiah] *saith, Lord, who hath believed our report?"* (Rom 10:15-16).

Paul confirms the divine blinding of most of Israel for the sake of the salvation of gentiles: *"For I would not, brethren, that ye should be ignorant of this mystery,[5] lest ye should be wise in your own conceits; that blindness* [hardness] ***in part*** *is happened to Israel, until the fulness of the Gentiles be come in"* (Rom 11:25).

53:1b *"And to whom has **the arm of the LORD** been revealed?"*

Isaiah 52:10 proclaims that *"The **LORD has made bare His holy arm** in the eyes of all the nations; and all the ends of the earth shall see **the salvation**[6] **of our God**."* In context (Isa 52:7-10), this occurs when Israel receives her salvation. That scripture is part of the *Tanach* foundation for Paul's theology that the salvation of Israel as a nation will bring even greater blessings to the world. *"Now if the fall of them be the riches of the world,* *and the diminishing of them the riches of the Gentiles; how much more their fulness?...For if the casting away of them be the reconciling of the world, what shall the receiving of them be, but life from the dead?"* (Rom 11:12,15).

Faith for salvation comes only by revelation; it is a gift from God (Eph 2:8). Yeshua gave His Father all the glory for "opening Peter's eyes," making sure that "flesh and blood" did not get any credit for Peter's ability to "see" that He was *"the Messiah, the Son of the living God"* (Matt 16:16-17).

53:2 *"For He shall grow up before Him* [in God's presence] *as a tender plant, and as a **root out of dry ground**. He has **no form or comeliness*** [appearance or excellence]*; and when we see Him, there is **no beauty** that we should desire* [take pleasure, delight in] *Him."*

This verse describes Yeshua's humanity and Israel's spiritual condition at the time of the first coming of Messiah. Yes, there was a righteous remnant, but most of the community could be described as "dry ground."

Isaiah 11:10 declares that one of the names of the Messiah is "Root of Jesse": *"And in that day there shall be a **root of Jesse**, which shall stand for an ensign* [*nes* – banner, sign, standard lifted up, a rallying point; can be translated as "miracle"] *of the people; to it shall the Gentiles seek: and his rest shall be glorious."*

53:3 *'He is despised and rejected by men, a man of sorrows* [or pain] *and acquainted with* [knows intimately] *grief* [also sickness, both physical and mental]. *And we hid, as it were, our faces from Him; **He was despised**, and we did not esteem Him."*

Some rabbis and *Targum Jonathan* saw this verse as referring to the Messiah whom Israel would despise.[7] Read Matthew 27:30-31 with this verse in mind.

53:4a *"Surely* [or but] *He has **borne our griefs and carried our sorrows*** [borne = lifted; carried = carried away]:*"

This was and still is fulfilled in Yeshua's healing ministry. *"When the even was come, they brought unto him many that were possessed with devils: and he cast out the spirits with his word, and healed all that were sick: That it might be fulfilled* [accomplished] *which was spoken by* [Isaiah] *the prophet, saying, **Himself took our infirmities, and bare our sicknesses**"* (Matt 8:16-17).

53:4b *"...yet we esteemed* [thought, judged] *him stricken, **smitten by God**, and afflicted.*

Psalm 69:26 also predicts this attitude: *"For they persecute him whom **thou hast smitten**; and they talk to the grief of those whom thou hast wounded."* This last phrase literally translates as *"...they recount near the anguish of the fatally-pierced."* In other words this means: in the presence of the agony of the Crucified, they recite His faults.

53:5 *"But **He** was wounded* [profaned, defiled, pierced] *for **our** transgressions* [rebellion], ***He** was bruised* [crushed, broken] *for **our** iniquities* [faults, perversity, depravity]; *the chastisement for **our** peace* [completeness, well-being, prosperity] *was upon **Him**, and by **His** stripes* [lashings] ***we** are healed."*
Four times "He" and "we" are contrasted, emphasizing that His suffering was *for us*, a substitutionary atonement. The first two times explain the reason He suffered - for our sins; the last two times present us with the results of His suffering - our peace and healing. Rabbi Simeon ben Yochai states: "...since the Messiah bears our iniquities, which produce the effect of His being bruised, it follows that whosoever will not admit that the Messiah thus suffers for our iniquities, must endure and suffer for them himself."[8]
Another rabbinic comment: "And when Israel is sinful, the Messiah seeks for mercy upon them, as it is written, 'By His stripes we were healed, and He carried the sins of many; and made intercession for the transgressors'." [9]
53:6 *"All we like sheep have gone astray* [erred, wandered, been seduced, been deceived, staggered as if drunk]; *we have turned, every one, to his own way; and the LORD has laid on* [made fall upon; same root word is used for "intercession"] *Him the iniquity of us all."*
"...we have turned, every one, to his own way..." is a short but encompassing definition of sin.
53:7 *"He was oppressed, and He was afflicted, yet **He opened not His mouth**; He was led as a lamb to the slaughter, and **as a sheep** before its shearers is **silent**, so **He opened not His mouth**."*
This verse predicts the Servant's lamb-like quiet submission, which we see clearly in Mark 15:3-5: *"And the chief priests accused him of many things: but **he answered nothing**. And Pilate asked him again, saying, **Answerest thou nothing?** behold how many things they witness against thee. But Yeshua yet **answered nothing**; so that Pilate marvelled."*
Messiah Yeshua's death as the slain Lamb is extolled in heaven and crowns the Lamb's glory: *"And I beheld, and, lo, in the midst of the throne and of the four beasts, and in the midst of the elders, stood a **Lamb as it had been slain**, having seven horns and seven eyes, which are the seven Spirits of God sent forth into all the earth. And he came and took the book out of the right hand of him that sat upon the throne.*
*"And when he had taken the book, the four beasts and four and twenty elders fell down before **the Lamb**, having every one of them harps, and golden vials full of odours, which are the prayers of saints. And they sung a new song, saying, **Thou art worthy** to*

*take the book, and to open the seals thereof: **for thou wast slain**, and hast redeemed us to God by thy blood out of every kindred, and tongue, and people, and nation; And hast made us unto our God kings and priests: and we shall reign on the earth.*

*"And I beheld, and I heard the voice of many angels round about the throne and the beasts and the elders: and the number of them was ten thousand times ten thousand, and thousands of thousands; Saying with a loud voice, **Worthy is the Lamb that was slain** to receive power, and riches, and wisdom, and strength, and honour, and glory, and blessing. And every creature which is in heaven, and on the earth, and under the earth, and such as are in the sea, and all that are in them, heard I saying, **Blessing, and honour, and glory, and power, be unto him that sitteth upon the throne, and unto the Lamb for ever and ever"** (Rev 5:6-13).*

53:8a *"He was taken from prison and from **judgment** [or justice], and **who will declare His generation?"***

The Spirit led Philip to the Ethiopian eunuch as he was reading this and the previous verse in Isaiah: *"...He was led as a sheep to the slaughter; and like a lamb dumb before his shearer, so opened he not his mouth: In his humiliation his **judgment** [or justice] was taken away: and **who shall declare his generation?** for his life is taken from the earth.*

"And the eunuch answered Philip, and said, I pray thee, of whom speaketh the prophet this? of himself, or of some other man? Then Philip opened his mouth, and began at the same scripture, and preached unto him Yeshua" (Acts 8:32b-35).

53:8b *"For He was **cut off** [destroyed] from the land of the living; **for the transgressions** [rebellions] **of My people** He was stricken."*

Again we see the substitutionary atonement. The modern rabbinic argument for why this cannot refer to Yeshua says that Isaiah 53 refers to Israel as a nation. But this verse is proof that Isaiah 53 cannot be referring to the nation of Israel as a whole because they were Isaiah's/God's people for whom "He," someone else, "was stricken." Isaiah prophesies that someone will be "cut off," or die, for Israel. Daniel 9:26a is a confirmation of this verse: *"And after threescore and two weeks shall **Messiah be cut off, but not for himself**...".*

53:9 *"And they made [assigned] His grave [metaphor for death] **with the wicked** [criminals] - but [yet] **with the rich** [a rich man] at His death, because **He had done no violence** [or wrong], **nor was any deceit in His mouth**."*

Matthew 27:44; 57-60 describe in detail the fulfillment of this verse when Yeshua was crucified between two thieves yet buried in a rich man's tomb, while 1 Peter 2:22 declares that Yeshua was sinless: *"Who did no sin, neither was guile found in his mouth:"*

53:10a *"Yet it pleased* [it was the desire of, the will of] *the LORD to bruise* [crush] *Him; He* [God] *has put Him to grief* [lit: worn Him out].*"*

God the Father is the One who bears ultimate responsibility for the crucifixion of His Son, Yeshua (and our salvation). As David says in Psalm 118:22-23: *"The stone which the builders refused* [cast off, reject, refuse, despise] *is become the head stone of the corner.* ***This is the LORD's doing****; it is marvellous* [lit.: wonderful; metaphorically: accomplished or fulfilled] *in our eyes."* See again Psalm 69:26.

Yeshua understood that His death was His Father's will: *"Then said Yeshua unto Peter, Put up thy sword into the sheath: the cup which **my Father hath given me**, shall I not drink it?"* (John 18:11). This occurred after Messiah's struggle in Gethsemane to do His Father's will, to drink that cup of suffering. Because of this, and although the agents of evil were men, the death of Yeshua was in God's will, and this was eventually recognized and accepted by the apostles: *"For of a truth against thy holy child Yeshua, whom thou hast anointed, both Herod, and Pontius Pilate, with the Gentiles, and the people of Israel, were gathered together, **For to do whatsoever thy hand and thy counsel determined before to be done**"* (Acts 4:27-28).

53:10b *"When You make* [appoint] *His soul* [life] *an **offering for sin*** [lit. a sin, guilt or trespass offering], *He shall see His seed* [children], *He shall prolong His days, and the pleasure* [will] *of the LORD shall prosper* [advance, succeed] *in His hand."*

This verse points to Yeshua's death as an offering for sin, fulfilling the entire sacrificial system as the book of Hebrews declares in verses 8:1-10:18. It also hints at His resurrection, because immediately after Messiah is sacrificed, it states that *"he shall prolong his days,"* and God's pleasure, His will, shall go forward through this One.

53:11 *"He shall see the travail* [labor, trouble] *of His soul, and be satisfied. By His knowledge My righteous* [just, law abiding, obedient] *Servant shall justify many*[10] [will cause many to be accounted righteous - many, not all!], *for **He shall bear*** [carry away] ***their iniquities*** [perversity, depravity]."*

With this prophecy we again see Messiah as our substitutionary sacrifice. In Acts 13:38, Paul notes this, proclaiming the fulfillment of what Isaiah prophesied: *"Be it known unto you therefore, men and brethren, that through this man is preached unto you the forgiveness of sins:"*

53:12 *"Therefore will I divide* [issue, assign] *Him a portion with the great, and He shall divide the spoil with the strong, because* ***he poured out His soul unto death****, and He was* ***numbered with the transgressors****, and He* ***bore*** [lifted up, carried] ***the sin of many, and made intercession for the transgressors.""*[11]

Hebrews 9:28a is the New Testament verse confirming that Isaiah was speaking about Yeshua: *"So Messiah was once offered to bear the sins of many..."*

Paul may have been thinking about this verse, especially about Messiah's soul being poured out in death when he wrote to the Philippians: *"Let this mind be in you, which was also in Messiah Yeshua: Who, being in the form of God, thought it not robbery to be equal with God: But made himself of no reputation, and took upon him the form of a servant, and was made in the likeness of men: And being found in fashion as a man, he humbled himself, and* ***became obedient unto death****, even the* ***death*** *of the cross"* (Phil 2:5-8).

Mark also pointed out a fulfillment of Isaiah 53:12 when he wrote: *"And with him they crucify two thieves; the one on his right hand, and the other on his left. And the scripture was fulfilled, which saith, And he was* ***numbered with the transgressors***" (Mark 15:27-28).

Targum Jonathan also applies this verse to the Messiah, speaking about His dying and interceding for the transgressors.[12]

Conclusion

In Luke 22:37, Yeshua recognizes Isaiah 53 as a picture of His death: *"For I say unto you, that* ***this that is written must yet be accomplished in me, And he was reckoned among the transgressors*** [lawless, wicked]*: for the things concerning me have an end* [goal, purpose]*."*

> *"For even hereunto were ye called:*
> *because Messiah also suffered for us,*
> *leaving us an example, that ye should follow his steps:*
> *Who did no sin, neither was guile found in his mouth:*
> *Who, when he was reviled, reviled not again;*
> *when he suffered, he threatened not;*
> *but committed himself to him that judgeth righteously:*
> *Who his own self bare our sins in his own body on the tree,*
> *that we, being dead to sins, should live unto righteousness:*
> *by whose stripes ye were healed."*
> (1 Pet 2:21-24).

1 Verses quoted from Isaiah 53 are taken from the *New King James Version*.

2 F. Kenton Beshore, *The Messiah of the Targums, Talmuds & Rabbinical Writers*, World Bible Society, Box 1, L.A., CA 90053, Chart 15.

3 Ibid.

4 See Romans 11:11-15, 25-32.

5 See Chap. 18, section "The Mystery of Messiah".

6 *"Yeshuat"* is the feminine form of Yeshua with the possessive ending, the salvation that belongs to our God.

7 F. Kenton Beshore, *op.cit.*, Chart 21.

8 Robert R. Gorelik, *Messiah, Another Jewish View*, Eshav Books, Irvine, CA., p27.

9 F. Kenton Beshore, *op.cit.*, Chart 26.

10 Compare Proverbs 11:9 - *"An hypocrite with his mouth destroyeth his neighbour: but through knowledge shall the just be delivered."*

11 This is His present priestly role: Rom 8:34; Heb 7:25.

12 Burt Yellin, *Messiah, A Rabbinic and Scriptural Viewpoint*, Congregation Roeh Israel, Denver, p. 43, note 37.

CHAPTER 11

The Cross in the *Tanach* - Part 2

Psalm 22

Psalm 22 is another *Tanach* chapter that helps us understand the Cross and its results. Although the Gospel accounts give the disciples' view of the Cross and the events associated with it, in this psalm we hear Yeshua expressing His feelings and reaction to the Cross – while hanging on it. Dying, Yeshua declared for all who had ears to hear, that His death was fulfilling prophecy, especially this psalm.

One of the rabbinic teaching techniques of Yeshua's day was called *remez,* or hinting. Because the *Tanach* was not easily portable, large portions were committed to memory. The rabbis only needed to quote a verse or a phrase and the context would come to the minds of their disciples. David Stern points out, "In Judaism, when a Bible verse is cited its entire context is implied, if appropriate. Thus Yeshua refers all of Psalm 22 to himself..."[1] The proof for this? Yeshua quoted both the first and last lines of this psalm during His execution. Using *remez,* Yeshua implied that "this is that which was spoken by the prophet...," that is, he was referring to His crucifixion and beyond. So we will examine this psalm verse by verse as prophetic of Yeshua on the Cross.

On the Cross

22:1 *"My God, my God, why hast thou forsaken me? why art thou so far from helping* [lit. saving[2]] *me, and from the words of my roaring* [groaning]*?"*

A Jewish commentator, Rev. Dr. A. Cohen says about this verse, "He feels that he has been abandoned by God, and his faith is sorely tried."[3] A.M. Hodgkin, a Christian commentator, points out that, "The Hebrew shows not one completed sentence in the opening verses, but a series of brief ejaculations, like the gasps of a dying man whose breath and strength are failing, and who can only utter a word or two at a time."[4]

Many believers struggle with questions concerning Yeshua's crucifixion. For instance His cry, *"My God, my God, why hast thou forsaken Me?"* (Matt 27:46b). Didn't Yeshua know His Father was going to turn His back to Him?

Yeshua knew what would happen on the Cross. The separation between Him and His Father probably was the major issue He struggled with at Gethsemane. He resolved that issue, but He wanted His disciples to resolve it also. Using *remez* from the Cross, He "hints" at Psalm 22, giving a biblical perspective and foundation concerning His death.

God placed on Him the sins of the world. Yeshua understood that sin separates us from God. *"Behold, the LORD's hand is not shortened, that it cannot save; neither his ear heavy, that it cannot hear: But your iniquities have separated between you and your God, and your sins have hid his face from you, that he will not hear"* [Isa 59:1-2].

He always quoted from the Scriptures, the *Tanach*, for evidence that He was the One who was to come, the promised Messiah. And by quoting from Psalm 22, Yeshua was declaring to His disciples, and all who would ever hear or read about His death, that it was so prophesied.

Also after His resurrection He pointed, not to His resurrection in itself, but to the *Tanach* prophecies for proof of who He was.[5] To sum up, He did not say, "I am risen..." He said, "It is written..."

22:6 *"But I am a worm, and no man; a reproach of men* [Heb: *adam* = mankind], *and despised of the people* [Heb: *am* = the national group]."

Rev. Cohen writes, 'The language of this section is reminiscent of Isaiah's description of the suffering *'Servant of the Lord'*." Cohen continues concerning the phrase *"...and no man,"* "I am so disfigured by cruelty that I have not the appearance of a man, as in Isa [52]:14..." and concerning *"despised of the people"* he points to Isaiah 53:3 (see also Isa 49:7). Amazingly even rabbis tie together these two crucial chapters describing the death and resurrection of the Messiah.

Psalm 22:6 finds its fulfillment in Luke 23:35-37, *"And the people stood beholding. And the rulers also with them derided him, saying, He saved others; let him save himself, if he be Messiah, the chosen of God. And the soldiers also mocked him, coming to him, and offering him vinegar, And saying, If thou be the king of the Jews, save thyself."*

22:7-8 *"All they that see me laugh me to scorn: they shoot out the lip, they shake the head, saying, He trusted on the LORD* *that he would deliver* [rescue] *him: let him deliver him, seeing he delighted in him."*

It is easy to forget that this is a quote from the *Tanach* and not from the New Testament. The chief priests, scribes, and elders spoke these same things against Yeshua while He was hanging on the Cross. *"And they that passed by reviled* [blasphemed] *him, wagging their heads, And saying, Thou that destroyest the temple, and buildest it in three days, save thyself. If thou be the Son of God, come down from the cross. Likewise also the chief priests mocking him, with the scribes and elders, said, He saved others; himself he cannot save. If he be the King of Israel, let him now come down from the cross, and we will believe* [trust in] *him. He trusted in God; let him deliver him now, if he will have him: for he said, I am the Son of God. The thieves also, which were crucified with him, cast the same in his teeth"* (Matt 27:39-44; see also Mark 15:29).

When biblical prophecy comes to pass, we should expect to see a literal fulfillment. Although predicting *how* God will perform His Word is impossible, *after* the fact we can say with Peter *"...this is that which was spoken by the prophet..."* (Acts 2:16). The consistent literal fulfillment of God's Word allows no excuse to those who reject it! For example, what will believers say who reject the modern day nation of Israel as a fulfillment of prophecy?

22:9-10 *"But thou art he that took me out of the womb: thou didst make me hope* [trust, be bold, secure, confident (in You)] *when I was upon my mother's breasts. I was cast upon thee from the womb: thou art my God from my mother's belly* [womb]."

The psalmist mentions his mother three times, but not his earthly father. The prophetic scriptures never contradict the virgin birth.

22:12 *"Many bulls have compassed* [surrounded] *me: strong bulls of Bashan have beset me round."*

In another Jewish commentary,[6] Rabbi A. C. Feuer states that the literal interpretation of "beset me" is "they crown me!" The Roman soldiers who crowned Yeshua's head with thorns (Matt 27:29) were "strong as bulls," whether in themselves or as representatives of a conquering empire.

22:14 *"I am poured out like water, and all my bones are out of joint: my heart is like wax; it is melted in the midst of my bowels."*

This is a poetic, yet accurate, description of what a crucified person would go through. Christian doctors have written articles on the similarities of this description to actual physical events and processes which would occur in a body during crucifixion.[7]

22:15 *"My strength is dried up like a potsherd; and my tongue cleaveth* [clings] *to my jaws; and thou hast brought me into the dust of death."*

Rev. Cohen comments on *"thou hast brought me into the dust of death,"* "If his persecutors succeed in destroying his life, it must be God's will; 'for the Jew could never think of anything as happening without God'."[3] Yeshua had already expressed this thought to Peter and Pilate. *"Then said Yeshua unto Peter, Put up thy sword into the sheath: the cup which my Father hath given me, shall I not drink it?"* (John 18:11); and to Pilate, *"Yeshua answered, Thou couldest have no power at all against me, except it were given thee from above..."* (John 19:11a).

Besides this thirst described in Psalm 22, Psalm 69:21 also speaks of thirst, *"They gave me also gall for my meat; and in my thirst they gave me vinegar to drink."*

Here is the perfect New Testament fulfillment of both these verses: *"After this, Yeshua knowing that all things were now accomplished, that the scripture* [the *Tanach*] *might be fulfilled, saith, I thirst. Now there was set a vessel full of vinegar: and they filled a sponge with vinegar, and put it upon hyssop, and put it to his mouth"* (John 19:28-29; see Endnote 8 for further possible *remez*).[8]

22:16 *"For dogs have compassed* [surrounded] *me: the assembly of the wicked have inclosed me: they pierced my hands and my feet."*

Following some modern translations, Rev. Cohen has *"like a lion, they are at my hands and my feet"* as the wording for the last part of this verse. But he admits that the "Hebrew is difficult...A.V. and R.V. render *they pierce,* adopting the reading of the LXX, to accord with the Christological interpretation of the Psalm."[3] This is an amazing statement! The *Septuagint,* often designated by "LXX," is the Greek version of the *Tanach* translated by 70 Jewish scholars/rabbis around 200 BC. So, more than two centuries before Yeshua was crucified, Jewish scholars understood this verse to read "pierce"!

This is not the only place in the *Tanach* which points to Messiah being pierced. *"And I will pour upon the house of David, and upon the inhabitants of Jerusalem, the spirit of grace and of supplications: and they shall look upon* [regard with favor, consider] *me whom they have pierced, and they shall mourn for him, as one mourneth for his only son, and shall be in bitterness for him, as one that is in bitterness for his firstborn"* (Zech 12:10).

22:17 *"I may tell* [count] *all my bones: they look and stare upon me."*

Again, the first part is an accurate description of a crucified man.

22:18 *"They part* [divide] *my garments among them, and cast lots upon my vesture* [clothing].*"*

So many *Tanach* prophecies like this one were fulfilled on the day Yeshua was crucified that we can know for a fact God was in control. There was no human way Yeshua could have set up everything that happened to Him just to fulfill those scriptures. *"Then the soldiers, when they had crucified Yeshua, took his garments, and made four parts, to every soldier a part; and also his coat: now the coat was without seam, woven from the top throughout. They said therefore among themselves, Let us not rend it, but cast lots for it, whose it shall be: that the scripture might be fulfilled, which saith, They parted my raiment among them, and for my vesture they did cast lots. These things therefore the soldiers did"* (John 19:23-24; see also Matt 27:35). The literal fulfillment of Psalm 22 is another witness to the divine inspiration of the Scriptures (Isa 55:11). How else could Roman soldiers at the foot of the Cross, unknowingly accomplish what had been written a thousand years before?

Ibn Ezra, a famous 12th Century Jewish commentator makes an interesting observation about this verse, "'they are royal vestments; if he were not a king these words would make no sense'."[9]

22:20 *"Deliver my soul* [fig. my life] *from the sword; my darling* [precious life] *from the power of the dog."*

Rev. Cohen correctly points out that *"the sword"* symbolizes death by violence.

After the Resurrection

22:21b-22 *"...for thou hast heard me from the horns of the unicorns* [NKJV: *"You have answered Me."*]. *I will declare thy name* [reputation, fame] *unto my brethren: in the midst of the congregation will I praise thee.*

The declaration of triumph from this verse onward is one reason Yeshua quoted from this psalm while dying on the Cross. By doing so, He was giving His disciples "hints" that, because of His Father's faithfulness to perform His Word (Jer 1:12), He would pass through this ordeal in victory.

Quoting verse 22:22, Yeshua says that after His death He *will* declare His Father's "name," that is, His essential nature, to His disciples. This occurs in John 17:26a, in the last sentence of His last speech to His disciples before He goes to the Cross, when Yeshua says, *"And I have declared to them your name, and* ***will*** *declare it..."* He also praises the Father from within and through *"the congregation"* of His "called-out-ones," thus fulfilling the last half of verse twenty-two.

Concerning Yeshua's suffering, Hebrews 2:10-12 points to this verse to say that Messiah is one with those whom He has saved. *"For it became* [was fitting for] *him, for whom are all things, and by whom are all things, in bringing* [leading, guiding] *many sons unto glory, to make the captain* [leader] *of their salvation perfect* [complete] *through sufferings. For both he that sanctifieth* [makes holy, sets apart] *and they who are sanctified* [made holy, set apart] *are all of one: for which cause he is not ashamed to call them brethren, Saying, I will declare thy name unto my brethren, in the midst of the church* [congregation] *will I sing praise unto thee."*

Note how this psalm predicts the current work of the Holy Spirit, which is to lead us to be conformed to Yeshua's likeness, to establish the "Kingdom" - literally, the Rulership of God - in the human heart.[10]

22:23 *"Ye that fear* [lit. be afraid of; revere with trembling] *the LORD, praise him; all ye the seed* [descendants] *of Jacob, glorify him; and fear*[11] [or abide in] *him, all ye the seed of Israel."*

This verse may reflect the situation that all Israel is saved as a nation after the elect God-fearers among the gentiles enter God's Kingdom. When the *Tanach* talks about God-fearers, or *"Ye that fear the LORD,"* in context with other groups which are definitely Jews it is referring to proselytes - gentiles who have converted and become part of the community of Israel (see also Psa 115:9-13; 118:2-4). Psalm 22:23 first lists the God-fearers, then the "seed of Jacob/Israel" as those who will praise and glorify Him.

Although the early Church was almost exclusively Jewish, by the time of the Jerusalem Council in Acts 15 multitudes of non-Jews were being saved. So many were finding salvation through the Jewish Messiah that James refers to their first visitation by God, *"Simeon* [Peter] *hath declared how God at the first did visit* [inspect, attend to] *the Gentiles, to take out of them a people for his name. And to this agree the words of the prophets; as it is written, After this I will return, and will build again the tabernacle of David, which is fallen down; and I will build again the ruins thereof, and I will set it up: That the residue of men might seek after* [worship; seek to obey] *the Lord, and all the Gentiles, upon whom my name is called, saith the Lord, who doeth all these things"* (Acts 15:14-17; James is quoting from the *Tanach* - Amos 9:11-12).

God has saved a remnant mostly from among the gentiles (nations, pagans, heathens). Next He will save all Israel (*"After this I will return and will build again the tabernacle of David"* - *Amos 9:11*). In Luke 2:30-32, as the reward of his patient waiting on God, Simeon prophesies with what could be seen as the same order of events. While holding baby Yeshua he declared by the Spirit, *"For mine eyes have seen thy salvation, Which thou hast prepared before the face of all people; A light to lighten* [give understanding to] *the Gentiles, and the glory of thy people Israel."*

After Yeshua's resurrection, the early believers (the first Messianic Jews) and proselytes, God-fearers from among the nations, are the first to praise the Lord (see Acts 13:16). Even so, for almost two millennia, the good news of Yeshua has gone out mostly to the gentiles of the earth. Now, however, many Jews are having their blindness removed and receiving Yeshua as Messiah and Lord, and a time will come when *"all ye the seed of Israel"* (Ps

22:23) will be saved. This in turn will lead many more gentiles from every nation to know that the LORD God of Israel is the only true God (see Ezek 36:23; Rom 11:15). All of Jacob/Israel will join in with the elect from every nation and tongue to worship the Lord in Jerusalem!

22:25 *"My praise shall be of thee in the great congregation: I will pay my vows before them that fear him."*

Concerning this congregation Rabbi Feuer says, "This refers to all of the gentile nations who will ultimately come to fear God when they witness His salvation."[12] Amen!

22:26 *"The meek* [poor, humble] *shall eat and be satisfied: they shall praise the LORD that seek him: your heart shall live for ever."*

Rev. Cohen states, "A votive [thanksgiving] sacrifice was eaten by the offerer...and he invites the *humble* [poor] to share in it. By participating in this common meal, they become knit into a brotherhood."[13] Communion is symbolized by such a common meal. The humble eat of this grace feast – and by eating are forever satisfied. Who but *"the poor in spirit,"* knowing they are spiritual beggars before a holy God and Savior, will inherit the kingdom of heaven (Matt 5:3)?

Even some rabbis link this verse with the promised Messiah. "The most renowned commentator in Judaism, Rashi, says that this verse refers to *"the time of deliverance, to the days of the Messiah."*[14] (italics in the original)

22:27 *"All the ends of the world shall remember and turn* [return or repent] *unto the LORD: and all the kindreds* [families] *of the nations shall worship before thee."*

Rabbi Feuer continues in his commentary to say about this verse, "When the nations...see the good which will come to us [Israel] in the future they will remember our previous poverty and degradation...This will arouse them to repent and return to God."[15] Paul has already declared this in Romans 11:15: *"For if the casting away of them* [Israel] *be the reconciling* [restoration] *of the world* [lit: cosmos]*, what shall the receiving of them be, but life from the dead?"* Those who believe that what God proclaims in the *Tanach* is still applicable today, understand the enormity of what the salvation of Israel means for the world.

22:28 *"For the kingdom is the LORD's: and he is the governor* [He rules] *among the nations."*

Belief (trust) in Messiah's death and resurrection establishes God's rulership, His "Kingdom" among the nations/gentiles.

22:29b *"...all they that go down to the dust shall bow before him..."*

The psalmist says that even the dead will bow before Him. Paul agrees, stating in Philippians 2:9-11, *"Wherefore*

God also hath highly exalted him, and given him a name which is above every name: That at the name of Yeshua every knee should bow, of things in heaven, and things in earth, and things under the earth; And that every tongue should confess [acknowledge, agree fully] *that Yeshua the Messiah is Lord, to the glory of God the Father."* What total faith in God's Word Yeshua evidenced while on the Cross by referring to that *Tanach* promise!

Isaiah 45:22-23 has the same sequence as those last two verses, with all the nations coming under God's rule and all the peoples bowing before Him: *"Look* [turn] *unto me, and be ye saved, all the ends of the earth: for I am God, and there is none else. I have sworn by myself, the word is gone out of my mouth in righteousness, and shall not return, That unto me every knee shall bow, every tongue shall swear."*

James E. Smith points out that, "No Old Testament person [such as Psalm 22's author, King David] could have imagined that his personal deliverance from death could be the occasion for the world's conversion. Such a hope must be restricted to the future Redeemer. Under inspiration of the Holy Spirit, David…saw his descendent resembling, but far surpassing, himself in suffering. Furthermore, the deliverance of this descendant would have meaning for all mankind."[16]

22:30 *"A seed shall serve him; it shall be accounted to the Lord for a generation."*

"Serve" in both Hebrew and Greek can be translated "worship." To worship God we must serve Him. And this verse says Messiah will have descendants, people related to Him as in the same family, who shall worship, serving Him.[17]

22:31 *"They shall come, and shall declare his righteousness unto a people that shall be born, that he hath done this."*

These descendants of Messiah will declare "His righteousness." This is fulfilled in many New Testament epistles where the righteousness of God and His Messiah are constantly declared. For example:

"For I am not ashamed of the gospel of Messiah: for it is the power of God unto salvation to every one that believeth [trusts]*; to the Jew first, and also to the Greek. For therein is the righteousness of God revealed from faith to faith: as it is written, The just shall live by faith"* (Rom 1:16-17).

"Being justified freely by his grace through the redemption that is in Messiah Jesus: Whom God hath set forth to be a propitiation[18] *through faith* [trust] *in his blood, to declare* [demonstrate] *his righteousness for the remission of sins that are past, through the forbearance of God;"* (Rom 3:24-25).

"But of him are ye in Messiah Yeshua, who of God is made [become] *unto us wisdom, and righteousness, and sanctification, and redemption:"* (1 Cor 1:30).

"Now then we are ambassadors for the Messiah, as though God did beseech you by us: we pray you in Messiah's stead, be ye reconciled to God. For he hath made him to be sin for us, who knew no sin; that we might be made [become] *the righteousness of God in him"* (2 Cor 5:20-21).

Finally, in our verse (Psalm 22:31) the Hebrew word for "he hath done this," can also be translated, "It is finished!" In saying this, Yeshua was quoting the last line of Psalm 22 as well as having quoted the first. He thereby applied all of this psalm to Himself. Even in His agony on the Cross, Yeshua encouraged His disciples using *remez* from prophetic songs of praise to God by His ancestor, Israel's great King David.

*"And he said unto them, These are the words which I spake unto you, while I was yet with you, that all things must be fulfilled, which were written in the law of Moses, and in the prophets, and in the **psalms**, concerning me. Then opened he their understanding, that they might understand the scriptures* [the Tanach], *And said unto them, Thus it is written, and thus it behoved Messiah to suffer, and to rise from the dead the third day: And that repentance and remission* [forgiveness, pardon] *of sins should be preached in his name among all nations, beginning at Jerusalem. And ye are witnesses of these things"* (Luke 24:44-48).

---

1   David H Stern, *Jewish New Testament Commentary*, Jewish New Testament Publications, Clarksville, Maryland, 1992, p. 84.

2   From the same Hebrew root as the name *"Yeshua"*.

3   Rev. Dr. A. Cohen, *Soncino Books of the Bible, The Psalms*, The Soncino Press Ltd., New York, 1985, commentary on Psalm 22.

4   A.M. Hodgkin, *Christ in All the Scriptures*, Pickering Classic, p.117.

5   Luke 24:25-27...44-46 *"Then he said unto them, O fools, and slow of heart to believe all that the prophets have spoken: Ought not Messiah to have suffered these things, and to enter into his glory? And beginning at Moses and all the prophets, he expounded unto them in all the scriptures the things concerning himself...And he said unto them, These are the words which I spake unto you, while I was yet with you, that all things must be fulfilled, which were written in the law of Moses, and in the prophets, and in the psalms, concerning me. Then opened he their understanding, that they might understand the scriptures, And said unto them, Thus it is written, and thus it behoved Messiah to suffer, and to rise from the dead the third day."*

6 Rabbi A. C. Feuer, *The Artscroll Tanach Series, Psalms, Tehillim,* Mesorah Pub., Ltd., Brooklyn,1969, commentary on v. 13, p.276.

7 For several articles, see www.Idolphin.org/sixhours.html

8 Consider that John 19:28 explicitly links Yeshua's knowledge that He had fulfilled the Scriptures with His simple statement, *"I thirst."* Could this short phrase be another case of *remez,* or "hinting?" If so, Yeshua may have been referring to other psalms which speak of thirst - psalms which seem to emphasize His heart-breaking separation from, and His ultimate trust in, His Father. Read these psalms: 42, 63, and 143. Could Yeshua's *"I thirst"* point to the witness of these three psalms in what may be, in spite of His having hardly the strength to speak two words, His dying prayer from the Cross?

9 Risto Santala, *The Messiah in the Old Testament,* Keren Ahvah Meshihit, Jerusalem, p.130.

10 The Greek *basilea* is usually translated "kingdom" in most Bible versions. However, *PC Study Bible* (Biblesoft 1993-1998) defines this word first of all: "1) royal power, kingship, dominion, rule a) not to be confused with an actual kingdom, but rather the right or authority to rule over a kingdom." If we use a less confusing term - "rulership" for example - in many of the NT verses where "kingdom" is mentioned, the shift in meaning can be quite enlightening and makes a pro-vocative word study.

11 The two words translated "fear" in this verse are different words in Hebrew.

12 Rabbi A. C. Feuer, *op. cit.,* p.282.

13 Rev. Dr. A. Cohen, *op. cit.,* commentary on v. 27, p.65.

14 Risto Santala, *The Messiah in the New Testament,* Keren Ahvah Meshihit, Jerusalem, p.211.

15 Rabbi A. C. Feuer, *op. cit.,* commentary on v. 28, pp.283-284.

16 James E. Smith, *What the Bible Teaches About the Promised Messiah,* Thomas Nelson Pub., p. 146.

17 See comments on vv. 21b-22.

18 Propitiation is the satisfaction of divine justice. This is the same Greek word used in the Septuagint for the "mercy seat" on top of the Ark of the Covenant in the Holy of Holies. It became a "mercy seat" when the High Priest sprinkled on it the blood of the *Yom Kippur* sacrifice.

CHAPTER 12

The Cross in the *Tanach* - Part 3

We want to examine two other sections of the *Tanach* which also foreshadow the Cross of Messiah Yeshua.

The Binding of Isaac

Known as the *Akedah* in Judaism, the binding of Isaac is found in Genesis 22. In that scenario Abraham's willingness to sacrifice his son Isaac becomes a type, or foreshadow, of God the Father's willingness to sacrifice His only Son, Yeshua. As with all types, we should not expect every detail to fit the anti-type, but the similarities are amazing.

Gen. 22:1-2 *"And it came to pass after these things, that God did tempt* [test, prove] *Abraham, and said unto him, Abraham: and he said, Behold, here I am. And he said,* **Take now** *thy son,* **thine only son** *Isaac,* **whom thou lovest**, *and get thee into the land of Moriah* [Heb: "seen of God" or "chosen by God"]; **and offer him** *there for a burnt offering upon one of the mountains which I will tell thee of."*

Sometimes believers make idols out of God's gifts and promises and end up worshipping the gift more than the Giver. God tested Abraham's willingness to let go of the divine promise, and to just trust in God, so proving by his works that his faith was genuine. *"Was not Abraham our father justified by works, when he had offered Isaac his son upon the altar? Seest* [discern, understand] *thou how faith wrought* [cooperated, worked together] *with his works, and by works was faith made perfect* [brought to completion]*? And the scripture was fulfilled which saith, Abraham believed* [trusted in] *God, and it was imputed unto him for righteousness: and he was called the Friend of God"* (James 2:21-23).

Interestingly in the Hebrew, *"Take now"* is not a command from God to Abraham, but is literally, "Please take." God is making His will clear, although it is couched as a request.

Isaac is the son of the promise described in Genesis 17:15-19. *"And God said unto Abraham, As for Sarai thy wife, thou shalt not call her name Sarai, but Sarah shall her name be. And I will bless her, and give thee a son also of her: yea, I will bless her, and she shall be a mother of nations; kings of people shall be of her.*

"Then Abraham fell upon his face, and laughed, and said in his heart, Shall a child be born unto him that is an hundred years old? and shall Sarah, that is ninety years old, bear? And Abraham said unto God, O that Ishmael might live before thee!

"And God said, Sarah thy wife shall bear thee a son indeed; ***and thou shalt call his name Isaac: and I will establish my covenant with him for an everlasting covenant, and with his seed after him."***

As the promised son, Isaac is a type of Yeshua, who also is a fulfillment of a promised Son, He who was promised to King David in 2 Samuel 7:12-14. The New Testament identifies Yeshua as that One, *"He shall be great, and shall be called the Son of the Highest: and the Lord God shall give unto him the throne of his father David:"* (Luke 1:32).

In fact, the New Testament opens up by looking backwards and declaring that the promised sons of David and Abraham find their complete fulfillment in the Messiah Yeshua. *"The book of the generation* [or nature] *of Yeshua the Messiah, the son of David, the son of Abraham"* (Matt 1:1).

In Genesis 22:2, God is careful to note that Isaac is Abraham's *"only"* son (compare John 3:16). Abraham fathered Ishmael through Hagar, Sarah's servant, but that was not God's perfect will, whereas Isaac was the promised one through whom, as we have already seen in Genesis 17:19, God swore to establish His covenant.

This verse contains Scripture's first usage of the word *"love"* - *"thine only son Isaac, whom thou lovest."* Amazingly, the initial occurrence of *"love"* becomes a type for its greatest fulfillment on the Cross. Just as Yeshua is God's *"beloved Son,"*[1] so Isaac was to Abraham. But how much greater was God's sacrifice in that He gave *Himself* in human form for *us* and no one could or did stop Him! *"Greater love hath no man than this, that a man lay down his life for his friends"* (John 15:13). *"Hereby perceive* [know, understand] *we the love of God, because he laid down his life for us..."* (1 John 3:16a).

Both Judaism and ancient literature portray Isaac as fully grown, somewhere between 23 and 37 years old, causing "the realization that the sacrifice derived its full value from the fact that Isaac accepted God's will as well as his father."[2] The same can be said about Yeshua who was 33 when, accepting His Father's will, He was crucified.

God directed Abraham to the *"land of Moriah"* where Jerusalem is now located, and where the future temple of Solomon would be built. *"Then Solomon began to build the house of the LORD at Jerusalem in mount Moriah, where the LORD appeared unto David his father, in the place that David had prepared in the threshingfloor of Ornan the Jebusite"* (2 Chr 3:1). In that same geographic area, on one of Jerusalem's hills, Messiah Yeshua would lay down His life.

Isaac was to be offered as *"a burnt offering."* Yeshua's sacrifice was also a type of burnt offering. The instructions for that sacrifice, a voluntary, free will offering, are found in Leviticus 1:3-9.[3] Noting how God really asked Abraham, "Please take..." we can see that there was a voluntary aspect to it. Yeshua also stated that He was the One who decided to submit to His Father and lay down His life. *"I am the good shepherd, and know my sheep, and am known of mine. As the Father knoweth me, even so know I the Father: and **I lay down my life** for the sheep...Therefore doth my Father love me, because **I lay down my life**, that I might take it again. No man taketh it from me, but **I lay it down of myself. I have power** [of choice, liberty] **to lay it down**, and I have power to take it again. This commandment have I received of [accepted from] my Father"* (John 10:14-15,17-18).

Other instructions for the burnt offering included that it should not be killed by the priests, but by the offerer. Abraham was ready to offer Isaac, and we will see that ultimately God the Father offered His Son. Also, the sacrifice was to be totally consumed on God's altar. Isaac was willing to die, and Yeshua did die at His Father's hand (Heb 10:5-10[4]).

Finally, a burnt sacrifice made in obedient faith was a "sweet savor" pleasurable to God. What God asked both Abraham and Yeshua to do, in fact the whole system of animal sacrifices, was not the thing that God really desired, but the eventual outcome of all faithful sacrifices greatly pleased Him. As Yeshua prophetically declared, *"Sacrifice and offering thou didst not desire; mine ears hast thou opened: burnt offering and sin offering hast thou not required. Then said I, Lo, I come: in the volume of the book it is written of me, I delight to do thy will, O my God: yea, thy law is within my heart"* (Psa 40:6-8; see Heb 10:5-12).[5]

The Hebrew of Genesis 22:2 gives another hint that points to Yeshua. The original for *"offer him"* literally means "lift him up," and can also mean "exalt him."[6] Yeshua was both. He was lifted up on the Cross and exalted to the right hand of the Father.

22:3-4 *"And Abraham rose up early in the morning, and saddled his ass, and took two of his young men with him, and Isaac his son, and clave the wood for the burnt offering, and rose up, and went* *unto the place of which God had told him. Then on the third day Abraham lifted up his eyes, and saw the place afar off."*

Abraham took three days to get to where God was leading him. Undoubtedly thoughts of Isaac and death were never far away. One might say that for three days, Isaac was dead in his father's mind. Of course, Yeshua really was dead three days. *"Then opened he their understanding, that they might understand the scriptures* [the *Tanach*], *And said unto them, Thus it is written, and thus it behoved Messiah to suffer, and to rise from the dead the third day:"* (Luke 24:45-46). *"For I delivered unto you first of all that which I also received, how that Messiah died for our sins according to the scriptures* [the *Tanach*]; *And that he was buried, and that he rose again the third day according to the scriptures* [the *Tanach*]:*"* (1 Cor 15:3-4).

22:5-6 *"And Abraham said unto his young men, Abide ye here with the ass; and I and the lad will go yonder and worship* [sacrificial obedience], *and come again to you. And Abraham took the wood of the burnt offering, and laid it upon Isaac his son; and he took the fire in his hand, and a knife; and they went both of them together."*

Abraham burdened Isaac with the wood for the offering. Yeshua also bore on His back the wood of the Cross used, in a sense, to "consume" His offering (see John 19:17).

Now to answer that crucial question - Who was responsible for Yeshua's crucifixion? As can be seen from the following verses, it was God the Father:

Psalm 118:22-23 *"The stone which the builders refused* [rejected, despised] *is become the head stone of the corner. This is the LORD's doing; it is marvellous* [extraordinary, beyond understanding] *in our eyes."*[7]

Isaiah 53:6,10 *"All we like sheep have gone astray* [erred, been deceived]; *we have turned every one to his own way; and the LORD hath laid*[8] *on him the iniquity*[9] *of us all...Yet it pleased* [was willed by] *the LORD to bruise* [crush, break] *him; he hath put him to grief: when thou shalt make his soul an offering for sin, he shall see his seed, he shall prolong his days, and the pleasure* [will] *of the LORD shall prosper* [advance, succeed] *in his hand."*

John 18:11 *"Then said Yeshua unto Peter, Put up thy sword into the sheath: the cup which my Father hath given me, shall I not drink it?"*

Acts 2:23 *"Him, being delivered by the determinate* [appointed, decreed] *counsel* [purpose, intention] *and foreknowledge of God, ye have taken, and by wicked* [lawless] *hands have crucified and slain:"*

Acts 4:27-28 *"For of a truth against thy holy child Jesus, whom thou hast anointed, both Herod, and Pontius Pilate, with the Gentiles, and the people of Israel, were gathered together, For* **to do whatsoever thy hand** [power] **and thy counsel** [purpose, intention] **determined before to be done**.*"*

Continuing in Genesis 22, we see that Abraham is the active player in the drama, while Isaac is passive. So too were God the Father and His Son as we see at Gethsemane. *"And he went a little further, and fell on his face, and prayed, saying, O my Father, if it be possible, let this cup pass from me: nevertheless* **not as I will, but as thou wilt***...He went away again the second time, and prayed, saying, O my Father, if this cup may not pass away from me, except I drink it,* **thy will be done***...[He] prayed the third time, saying the same words"* (Matt. 26:39,42,44b).

22:7-8 *"And Isaac spake unto Abraham his father, and said, My father: and he said, Here am I, my son. And he said, Behold the fire and the wood: but where is the lamb for a burnt offering? And Abraham said, My son, God will provide himself a lamb for a burnt offering: so they went both of them together."*

"...but where is the lamb...?" Isaac asked. Abraham's answer is prophetic for what was about to happen that day and for what God was going to do many centuries later. *"...God will provide* [lit. see or consider] *himself a lamb..."* That statement could just as accurately be written with *"himself"* capitalized, *"...*God will provide Himself...*"*! Prophetically, this was fulfilled when John the Baptizer proclaimed about Yeshua, *"Behold the Lamb of God, which taketh away the sin of the world"* (John 1:29b).

22:9-10 *"And they came to the place which God had told him of; and Abraham built an altar there, and laid the wood in order, and bound Isaac his son, and laid him on the altar upon the wood. And Abraham stretched forth his hand, and took the knife to slay his son."*

Abraham and Isaac climbed to the top of Mount Moriah. There Abraham built the altar, placed the wood on it, bound Isaac, and took the knife to kill him. Again and again in this foreshadow of the Cross, we see God the Father, symbolized by Father Abraham, as the One in control. Isaac could have resisted. Instead he becomes a type of the Greater Son who was willing to be *"...brought as a lamb to the slaughter..."* (Isa 53:7b).

22:11-12 *"And the angel of the LORD called unto him out of heaven, and said, Abraham, Abraham: and he said, Here am I. And he said, Lay not thine hand upon the lad, neither do thou any thing unto him: for now I know that thou fearest God, seeing thou hast not withheld thy son, thine only son from me."*

Only at the last possible moment does God break in and prevent the sacrifice. The pre-incarnate Son of God speaks as *"the Angel of the LORD,"*[10] confirmed in verse 12, where the Angel identifies Himself as God when He says *"...thou hast not withheld thy son, thine only son from me."*

Dr. J. H. Hertz, the late Chief Rabbi of Britain, makes an incisive comment about the issue of human sacrifice. "In that age, it was astounding that Abraham's God should have interposed *to prevent* the sacrifice, not that He should have asked for it."[11]

"If any man come to me, and hate not his father, and mother, and wife, and children, and brethren, and sisters, yea, and his own life also, he cannot be my disciple. And whosoever doth not bear his cross, and come after me, cannot be my disciple" (Luke 14:26-27). Literal hate is not meant here, but a love that is less than that for Yeshua. Loving others more than loving God is idolatry.

22:13 *"And Abraham lifted up his eyes, and looked, and behold behind him a ram caught in a thicket by his horns: and Abraham went and took the ram, and offered him up for a burnt offering in the stead of his son."*

God miraculously provides a ram that has his horns tangled in the bushes. This becomes an example of substitutionary sacrifice. The ram died in the place of Isaac just as Yeshua died in our place. *"For when we were yet without strength, in due time Messiah died for the ungodly. For scarcely for a righteous man will one die: yet peradventure for a good man some would even dare to die. But God commendeth* [proved] *his love toward us, in that, while we were yet sinners, Messiah died for us"* (Rom 5:6-8). All of the animal sacrifices in the *Tanach* portrayed, in various ways, certain aspects of Yeshua dying for us sinners.

The Hebrew word for *"ram"* is not the same as the Hebrew word for *"lamb."* So although the ram is the God-given substitute for Isaac, it is not the fulfillment of that prophesied lamb that Abraham mentioned in verse 8 when he said that God would *"provide himself a lamb."*

22:14 *"And Abraham called the name of that place Jehovah-jireh: as it is said to this day, In the mount of the LORD it shall be seen."* Or in the NKJV, *"And Abraham called the name of the place, The-LORD-Will-Provide; as it is said...In the Mount of The LORD it shall be provided."*

That name looked forward to the day when the Lord Himself would provide the Lamb. And it was in that mountain, the mount of the Lord, that He did provide His Son. Dr. Hertz translates the end of that verse as *"where the LORD is seen"* and then comments, "i.e., where He reveals himself..."[12] God ultimately revealed Himself in the Mount of the Lord through His Son Yeshua.

"Yeshua saith unto him, I am the way, the truth, and the life: no man cometh unto the Father, but by me. If ye had known me, ye should have known my Father also: and from henceforth ye know him, and have seen [perceived, known, become acquainted with] *him.*

"Philip saith unto him, Lord, shew us the Father, and it sufficeth [is enough for] *us.*

"Yeshua saith unto him, Have I been so long time with you, and yet hast thou not known me, Philip? he that hath seen me hath seen the Father; and how sayest thou then, Shew us the Father?" (John 14:6-9).

22:15-18 *"And the angel of the LORD called unto Abraham out of heaven the second time, And said, By myself have I sworn, saith the LORD, for because thou hast done this thing, and hast not withheld thy son, thine only son: That in blessing I will bless thee, and in multiplying I will multiply thy seed as the stars of the heaven, and as the sand which is upon the sea shore; and thy seed shall possess* [inherit, occupy] *the gate of his enemies; And in thy seed shall all the nations of the earth be blessed; because thou hast obeyed my voice."*

Finally, we have from the Angel a repeat of the promise God made to Abraham in Genesis 12:3 that through his seed the blessing of the Good News would come to the gentiles, to *"all the nations of the earth."* We see this fulfilled through Yeshua, descendant of Abraham, who came through the inheritors of the promise, the Jewish people.

Paul emphasizes to the Romans that when the Son of God manifested Himself in the flesh, it was as a member of the nation of Israel. *"Concerning his Son Yeshua the Messiah our Lord, which was made of the seed of David **according to the flesh**;"* (Rom 1:3); *"Who are Israelites; to whom pertaineth the adoption, and the glory, and the covenants, and the giving of the law, and the service of God, and the promises; Whose are the fathers, and of whom as **concerning the flesh** Messiah came, who is over all, God blessed for ever. Amen"* (Rom 9:4-5).

And to the Galatians, he declares that the Gospel to the gentiles was already proclaimed to Father Abraham, *"And the scripture* [Tanach], *foreseeing that God would justify the heathen through faith, preached before the gospel unto Abraham, saying* [in Gen 12:3], *In thee shall all nations be blessed"* (Gal 3:8).

A quote from Herbert Lockyer's excellent book, *All the Messianic Prophecies of the Bible*,[13] is a good way to summarize this section on the likeness of Yeshua revealed in Isaac. "Thus, in Isaac, we have a conspicuous type of Him who was freely 'delivered up for us all' and who was received from the dead by His Father (Rom 8:32; 1 Tim 3:16)."

The Bronze Serpent

Yeshua, talking to Nicodemus about being born again, points to the bronze serpent in the *Tanach* as a type of His death on the Cross. What analogy was He making with this illustration? Look at the verses.

Yeshua said, *"And as Moses lifted up* [or exalted] *the serpent in the wilderness, even so* [in this way] *must the Son of man be lifted up: That whosoever believeth* [have faith; put confidence] *in him should not perish, but have eternal life"* (John 3:14-15).

Here is the story He was referring to: *"And the people spake against God, and against Moses, Wherefore have ye brought us up out of Egypt to die in the wilderness? for there is no bread, neither is there any water; and our soul loatheth* [hates] *this light* [contemptible, worthless] *bread.*

"And the LORD sent fiery serpents among the people, and they bit the people; and much people of Israel died. Therefore the people came to Moses, and said, We have sinned, for we have spoken against the LORD, and against thee; pray [intercede] *unto the LORD, that he take away the serpents from us. And Moses prayed* [interceded] *for the people.*

*"And the LORD said unto Moses, Make thee a fiery serpent, and set it upon a pole: and it shall come to pass, that every one that is bitten, when he **looketh** upon it, shall live. And Moses made a serpent of brass, and put it upon a pole, and it came to pass, that if a serpent had bitten any man, when he **beheld** the serpent of brass, he lived"* (Num 21:5-9).

From the *Wisdom of Solomon* Hertz quotes something that may shed light on why Yeshua related His approaching death to that incident in Israel's history. *The Wisdom of Solomon*, one of the apocryphal books written before 200 BC, says, "The brazen serpent was 'a token of salvation to put them in remembrance of the commandments of Thy Law, for he that turned toward it was not saved because of that which was beheld but because of Thee, the Savior of all'."[14]

Targum Pseudo-Jonathan, a well known Aramaic translation/ commentary of Yeshua's day, states concerning Numbers 21:8-9, "He who lifted up his heart to the name of the Memra (i.e. the Word) of Jehovah, lived."[15] Why does this commentary seem to link the serpent on the pole to the Word of God? The answer may lie in the symbolism of the serpent as a curse.

The first occurrence of the word "curse" in scripture occurs in the passage after the Fall of Man. God declares to the serpent, *"...thou art cursed..."* (Gen 3:14) The serpent has ever since been a symbol for the curse of sin. In the case of the serpent on the pole, we are reminded of the scriptures which state, *"And if a man have committed a sin worthy of death, and he be to be put to death, and thou hang him on a tree: His body shall not remain all night upon the tree, but thou shalt in any wise bury him that day;* **for he that is hanged is accursed of God***;) that thy land be not defiled, which the LORD thy God giveth thee for an inheritance"* (Deut 21:22-23). And in Galatians 3:13, Paul says, *"Messiah hath redeemed us from the curse of* [curse for breaking] *the law, being made a curse for us: for it is written,* **Cursed is every one that hangeth on a tree***:"*

We have read in Numbers 21, that God sent deadly serpents to bite the people because they loathed, they despised, His provision, calling the manna light or worthless bread (21:5). That bread was a type of Yeshua, the bread from Heaven, as we read in John 6:31-35:

"Our fathers did eat manna in the desert; as it is written, He gave them bread from heaven to eat.

"Then Yeshua said unto them, Verily, verily, I say unto you, Moses gave you not that bread from heaven; but my Father giveth you the true bread from heaven. For the bread of God is he which cometh down [descends] *from heaven, and giveth life unto the world.*

"Then said they unto him, Lord, evermore give us this bread.

"And Yeshua said unto them, I am the bread of life: he that cometh to me shall never hunger; and he that believeth on me shall never thirst."

To despise Him, which is the sin of unbelief, leads to death by God's own hand of judgment, the greatest curse, as seen in Numbers 21:6. The New Testament adds this warning, *"Neither let us tempt Messiah, as some of them also tempted, and were destroyed of serpents"* (1 Cor 10: 9). The word translated "tempt" means to entice, provoke, try to manipulate, from a root meaning "to pierce." When we entice, provoke, or try to manipulate God it is as though we are piercing Him. That is why Paul gave this serious warning.

God's swift response to His people's blasphemous remarks, withdrawing His protection, resulted in Israel's quick repentance. *"We have sinned, for we have spoken against the LORD, and against thee* [Moses]*..."* (21:7). Moses, always the compassionate leader, interceded for the people. God's answer seems strange, even to us who can now look at the anti-type of Yeshua's death. *"Make thee a fiery serpent, and set it upon a pole: and it shall come to pass, that every one that is bitten, when he looketh upon it, shall live"* (21:8).

The serpent was made of bronze, which throughout the Scriptures is symbolic of judgment. For example, the bronze altar in both the Tabernacle and the Temple was where the sacrifices for sin were offered, where judgment on sin was carried out.

The serpent was lifted up *"upon a pole."* *Nes*, the Hebrew word used here for *pole*, can also mean standard, ensign, signal, banner, something lifted up and used as a rallying point. In many *Tanach* prophecies, that is the Hebrew word that stands for the future Cross of Messiah! Here are a few examples:

*"Thou hast given a **banner** [nes] to them that fear thee, that it may be displayed because of* [in the face or presence of] *the truth. Selah"* (Psa 60:4).

*"And in that day there shall be a root of Jesse, which shall stand for an **ensign** [nes] of the people; to it shall the Gentiles seek: and his rest shall be glorious. And it shall come to pass in that day, that the Lord shall set his hand again the second time to recover* [possess] *the remnant of his people, which shall be left...And he shall set up* [lift up, exalt] *an **ensign** [nes] for the nations, and shall assemble* [gather, receive] *the outcasts of Israel, and gather together the dispersed* [scattered] *of Judah from the four corners of the earth"* (Isa 11:10, 11a,12).

*"Thus saith the Lord GOD, Behold, I will **lift up** [exalt] mine hand*[16] *to the Gentiles, and set up my **standard** [nes] to the people: and they shall bring thy sons in their arms, and thy daughters shall be **carried** upon their shoulders"* (Isa 49:22). In the Hebrew, there is a poetic repetition of the word for *"lift up"* because it is also used for *"carried."*[17]

Returning to the comparison of Yeshua's death with the bronze serpent, the Greek for *"lifted up"* in John 3:14 can, as we have indicated, also be translated as "exalted." In that verse Yeshua compares His crucifixion to the lifting up of the bronze serpent. He was certainly hinting[18] that His crucifixion would result in His exaltation.

In the wilderness the Israelites who were already bitten were dying. God did not just heal them from a sickness, He delivered them from certain death by requiring their obedient looking at the uplifted serpent. The Hebrew for *"looketh"* (Num 21:8), and *"beheld"* (21:9), although not the same word, have similar meanings. Both mean not just a physical glance, but beholding, considering, regarding. As you read these verses, all using one of these Hebrew words, you will obtain a better understanding of what the Lord desires:

Psalm 34:4-5 *"I sought the LORD, and he heard me, and delivered me from all my fears. They **looked** unto him, and were lightened: and their faces were not ashamed."*

Psalm 119:18 *"Open* [uncover] *thou mine eyes, that I may **behold** wondrous things out of thy law."*[19]

Isaiah 42:18 *"Hear,*[20] *ye deaf; and **look**, ye blind, that ye may see."*

Isaiah 51:1-2 *"Hearken to me, ye that follow after* [run after, pursue] *righteousness, ye that seek* [search out, strive after, desire] *the LORD:* **look** *unto the rock whence ye are hewn, and to the hole of the pit whence ye are digged.* **Look** *unto Abraham your father, and unto Sarah that bare you: for I called him alone, and blessed him, and increased him."*

Habakkuk 1:5 *"***Behold** *ye among the heathen, and* **regard**, *and wonder marvellously* [be amazed, astonished]*: for I will work a work in your days, which ye will not believe, though it be told you."*

Zechariah 12:10 *"And I will pour upon the house of David, and upon the inhabitants of Jerusalem, the spirit of grace and of supplications: and they shall* **look** *upon* [better: "look to"] *me whom they have pierced, and they shall mourn for him, as one mourneth for his only son, and shall be in bitterness for him, as one that is in bitterness for his firstborn."*

Of all the *Tanach* symbolism of His death and resurrection, the serpent on the pole is the only one Yeshua used to illustrate His being lifted up on a cross. We believe that another reason He used it is found in 2 Corinthians 5:21 where Paul declares, *"For he* [God] *hath made him* [Messiah Yeshua] *to be sin for us,* [Messiah] *who knew no sin; that we might be made the righteousness of God in him."* Since the Garden, the serpent has represented the Tempter, the temptation, and the curse of sin; he has become the personification of sin just as Yeshua is the personification of righteousness. We benefit from a brutal exchange on the Cross - we gain Yeshua's righteousness by His taking upon Himself the death curse for our sin.

Finally, from a 19th century commentary, "Among the Jews, the brazen serpent was considered a type of the resurrection - through it the dying lived..."[21]

"Look [Turn] *unto Me, and be ye saved, all the ends of the earth:
for I am God, and there is none else. I have sworn by Myself,
the word is gone out of My mouth in righteousness,
and shall not return,
That unto Me every knee shall bow, every tongue shall swear.
Surely, shall one say, in the LORD have I righteousness and strength:
even to Him shall men come; and all
that are incensed against Him shall be ashamed.
In the LORD shall all the seed of Israel be justified,
and shall glory* [celebrate, boast]*"* (Isaiah 45:22-25).

---

1   Matt 3:17; 2 Pet 1:17.

2   H. L. Ellison, *Fathers of the Covenant*, R. N. Haynes Publishers, Inc., 1981, p. 53.

3   *"If his offering be a burnt sacrifice of the herd, let him offer a male without blemish* [complete, whole]*: he shall offer it of his **own voluntary will** at the door of the tabernacle of the congregation before the LORD. And he shall put his hand upon the head of the burnt offering; and it shall be accepted for him to make atonement for him. And **he shall kill** the bullock before the LORD: and the priests, Aaron's sons, shall bring the blood, and sprinkle the blood round about upon the altar that is by the door of the tabernacle of the congregation. And he shall flay the burnt offering, and cut it into his pieces. And the sons of Aaron the priest shall put fire upon the altar, and lay the wood in order upon the fire: And the priests, Aaron's sons, shall lay the parts, the head, and the fat, in order upon the wood that is on the fire which is upon the altar: But his inwards and his legs shall he wash in water: and the priest shall burn all on the altar, to be a burnt sacrifice, an offering made by fire, of a sweet savour unto the LORD"* (Lev 1:3-9).

4   *"Wherefore when he cometh into the world, he saith, Sacrifice and offering thou wouldest not, but a body hast thou prepared me: In burnt offerings and sacrifices for sin thou hast had no pleasure. Then said I, Lo, I come (in the volume of the book it is written of me,) to do thy will, O God.*

*"Above when he said, Sacrifice and offering and burnt offerings and offering for sin thou wouldest not, neither hadst pleasure therein; which are offered by the law; Then said he, Lo, I come to do thy will, O God. He taketh away the first, that he may establish the second. By the which will we are sanctified **through the offering of the body of Yeshua the Messiah** once for all"* (Heb 10:5-10).

5   See also 1 Sam 15:22; Jer 7:21-23.

6   See the section on "The Bronze Serpent" following.

7   See Matt 21:42; Mark 12:10-11; Luke 20:17; and Acts 4:11 for the New Testament confirmation that this verse is pointing to Messiah Yeshua's death.

8   This same Hebrew root can mean "to intercede."

9   In Hebrew, it means not just the iniquity itself, but also the consequence and/or punishment of our iniquity.

10   See Chapter 14, section "The Angel of the LORD".

11   Dr. J. H. Hertz, *The Pentateuch and Haftorahs*, Soncino Press, 1980, p. 201.

12   Ibid., p. 75.

13   Herbert Lockyer, *All the Messianic Prophecies of the Bible*, Zondervan Pub. House, 1973, p. 221.

14   Dr. J. H. Hertz, *op. cit.*, p. 660.

15   Alfred Edersheim, *The Life and Times of Jesus the Messiah*, MacDonald Pub. Co., p. 388.

16   The hand, or right hand, of God is often used in the *Tanach* as a metaphor of the coming Messiah.

17   It is easy to see Psalm 60:4 and Isaiah 11:10 as foreshadows of the Cross, but what about the other verses from Isaiah about carrying Israel's sons and daughters? God is telling the Church that He wants them involved in regathering the Jewish people to the land of Israel. See Chapter 18, section "Mystery of Messiah" for a more detailed explanation.

18   See *remez*, Chap. 11, section "Psalm 22".

19 Here is our paraphrase from the Hebrew: *"By revelation, show me things in Your Word that cannot be understood by human knowledge alone."* Paul often talked about this - that God's revelation enabled him to understand Messiah and His Body. See Rom 16:25; Gal 1:12; 2:2; Eph 1:17; 3:3.

20 In both the Hebrew and Greek, "hear" has the meaning of listening with the intention of obeying.

21 Adam Clarke, *Clarke's Commentary, Matthew-Revelation*, Abingdon Press, p. 533.

CHAPTER 13

The Resurrection

To the apostle Paul the resurrection of Messiah Yeshua is an integral part of the Gospel. But was a resurrection by itself the proof that gave Paul and the other apostles and disciples such confidence? Did a resurrection miracle alone assure them that what they were proclaiming was from God? No, it was much more than that. Their proclamation of the Good News was based on Yeshua's resurrection as the confirmation and fulfillment of God's prophetic Word given throughout the *Tanach*. Their Good News was *"...according to the Scriptures..."*

"Moreover, brethren, I declare unto you the gospel which I preached unto you, which also ye have received, and wherein ye stand; By which also ye are saved, if ye keep in memory what I preached unto you, unless ye have believed in vain. For I delivered [committed] *unto you first of all that which I also received, how that Messiah died for our sins **according to the scriptures**; And that he was buried, and that he rose again the third day **according to the scriptures**:"* (1Cor 15:1-4).

The importance of the *Tanach* to our faith bears repeating. The New Testament calls the *Tanach* "the Holy Scriptures."[1] In the days of Yeshua, the *Tanach* was the Holy Scripture. Yeshua preached from the Word of God, but He never read a word out of New Testament texts. New Testament teaching was in the process of being written down by the Spirit of God through the early Body of Messiah. The only way these first believers knew their teaching was from God was to compare its agreement with that Word of God which they already possessed, the *Tanach*. They would have been especially mindful of *Tanach* teachings concerning resurrection.

In the *Tanach* are a number of foreshadows, types, and teachings about the resurrection of the dead. The New Testament confirms the concept of resurrection and adds that, as believers, we will have glorified bodies like our resurrected Messiah. Even this amazing truth was hinted at previously.

There are many scriptures in the *Tanach* which had to be fulfilled by the Messiah. Some await fulfillment at His return and reign, but all the *Tanach* prophecies about Messiah being resurrected have been fulfilled by Yeshua.

New Testament and *Tanach* Resurrection

Many of the New Testament writers found evidence for a resurrection in the *Tanach*. The writer to the Hebrews knew by the Holy Spirit that Abraham believed God could raise Isaac from the dead if Isaac had been sacrificed. *"By faith Abraham, when he was tried* [tested], *offered up* [lit: presented] *Isaac: and he that had received the promises offered up his only begotten son...Accounting* [reckoning, considering] *that God was able to raise him up, even from the dead; from whence also he received him in a figure* [likeness]*"* (Heb 11:17,19).

Some rabbis believe Isaac died of terror when Abraham lifted the knife and that God then raised Isaac from the dead.[2] Although not scriptural, and we do not agree with it, this interpretation implies a strong belief in the resurrection of the dead.

To us, it seems a result of God's spiritual blinding of them (Rom 11:25), that the rabbis could conceive of Isaac, but not the Messiah, raised from the dead. Isaac is a distinct type of Messiah Yeshua - the promised son whom his father loved; the son who carried his own wood on which he was to be offered; he whom his father was willing to sacrifice - and one whom some rabbis see as being resurrected![3]

Yeshua teaches about the resurrection of the dead when He speaks of Moses at the burning bush, *"Now **that the dead are raised, even Moses shewed** [intimated] at the bush, when he [God] calleth* [Himself] *the Lord the God of Abraham, and the God of Isaac, and the God of Jacob. For he is not a God of the dead, but of the living: for all live unto him"* (Luke 20:37-38). By using that *Tanach* verse, Exodus 3:6, Yeshua was stating that the forefathers were alive. Of course, their bodies were in the grave until Yeshua's resurrection, the event after which, according to Paul, Yeshua *"took captivity captive"* (Eph 4:8; cp. Mat 27:52-53).

The writer of Ecclesiastes agrees. He says that when a person dies, *"Then shall the dust return to the earth as it was: and the spirit shall return unto God who gave it"* (Ecc 12:7). And Paul in that great chapter on the resurrection, 1 Corinthians 15, also declares a similar belief.[4]

James Orr writes, 'The point to be observed is that Jesus quotes this passage, not simply in proof of the continued subsistence of the patriarchs in some state of being, but in proof of the resurrection of the dead. And how does it prove that? Only on the ground, which Jesus assumes, that the relation of the believer to God carries with it a *whole* immortality, and this...implies life in the body. If God is the God of Abraham and Isaac and Jacob, this covenant relation pledges to these patriarchs not only continuance of existence, but redemption from the power of death, i.e., resurrection."[5]

Tanach Examples of the Resurrection

In the *Tanach*, there are types but also examples of life after death, or, as in the case of Enoch and Elijah, heavenly life after earthly life. The translation from earth to heaven that these two men of God had before they died[6] can be viewed as *Tanach* examples of the first resurrection, or "rapture," referred to by Paul in 1 Corinthians 15:51-53 and 1 Thessalonians 4:13-17.

Elijah, by prayer, saw a widow's dead son restored to life. *"And he stretched himself upon the child three times, and cried unto the LORD, and said, O LORD my God, I pray thee* [please], *let this child's soul come into him again. And the LORD heard the voice of Elijah; and the soul of the child came into him again, and he revived"* (I Kings 17:21-22).

Elisha, whose many miracles often foreshadow the miracles of Yeshua (feeding the multitudes; causing an ax head to "walk on water"; healing lepers), also raised a dead boy to life and returned him to his mother (2 Kings 4:32-35). Compare that to the following miracle in the ministry of our Messiah: *"And he came and touched the bier: and they that bare him stood still. And he said, Young man, I say unto thee, Arise. And he that was dead sat up, and began to speak. And he delivered him to his mother. And there came a fear on all: and they glorified God, saying, That a great prophet is risen up among us; and, That God hath visited his people"* (Luke 7:14-16).

In 2 Kings 13:20-21, when a dead man was placed in the same cave and touched the bones of Elisha, that man came back to life. Even after death, God used this prophet to bring life. The picture is clear - all who "touch" Yeshua, the Prophet sent from God,[7] after His death also receive life.

Of course, Elisha's body remained in the grave at least until after Messiah's resurrection when many of the saints who had died were raised bodily,[8] (maybe Elisha was one of them) to ultimately ascend, following Messiah to heaven. *"Wherefore he saith, When he ascended up on high, he led captivity captive, and gave gifts unto men"* (Eph 4:8).

Tanach Teaching on the Resurrection

The book of Job contains a number of references to life after death. Believing that Job lived at the time of Abraham, many scholars think the book to be one of the oldest in the Scriptures.

If any saint needed assurance of a better life to come it was Job. He makes some of the strongest *Tanach* statements about resurrection, even applying it to himself, *"For I know that my redeemer* [kinsman-redeemer] *liveth, and that he shall stand* [rise] *at the latter day* [or "the last days"] *upon the earth: And though after my skin* [mortality[9]] *worms destroy this body, yet in my flesh shall I see God: Whom I shall see for myself, and mine eyes shall behold, and not another; though my reins* [mind] *be consumed within me"* (Job 19:25-27). Job is speaking about a bodily resurrection from the dead. Although the Hebrew of this passage is difficult, there is no doubt that he is stating a belief in life after death and that he has a Redeemer who will vindicate and save him.

Earlier, Job had already referred to his being changed in the resurrection, *"If a man die, shall he live again? all the days of my appointed time* [lit: warfare; army service!] *will I wait* [hope, expect], *till my change* [renewal] *come"* (Job 14:14).

Paul agrees in 1 Corinthians 15:35-44, saying that our resurrected bodies will not be the same as our current bodies. Not only does the Bible give us these two voices, but here is a third witness to this truth - King David. *"As for me, I will behold thy face in righteousness: I shall be satisfied, when I awake, with thy likeness"* (Psa 17:15). This affirms a resurrection with glorified bodies like Yeshua's.

On *Shavuot* the Spirit of God was poured out on the disciples who were waiting in obedience to the Lord's last command. Then Peter proclaimed the Gospel with power to the Jewish multitudes by using many *Tanach* verses. Referring to the resurrection, he quoted Psalm 16:9-11 (Acts 2:29-32), *"Therefore my heart* [inner man] *is glad, and my glory rejoiceth: my flesh* [body] *also shall rest* [abide, dwell] *in hope* [lit: safety, security]. *For thou wilt not leave my soul* [nephesh - life, that which breathes] *in hell* [sheol = grave, pit; metaphor for death]; *neither wilt thou suffer* [permit] *thine Holy One to see corruption* [pit, animal trap; metaphor for destruction]. *Thou wilt shew me the path of life: in thy presence is fulness of joy; at thy right hand there are pleasures for evermore."* After three days a dead body has begun to stink with decay, of which Martha tries to remind Yeshua in John 11:39. But Yeshua Himself was raised at or before dawn of the third day. In truth God did not allow His *"...Holy One to see corruption."*

Other places in the Psalms also refer to resurrection. David wrote, *"O LORD, thou hast brought up my soul* [nephesh = life, being] *from the grave [Sheol = fig. death]: thou hast kept me alive, that I should not go down to the pit"* (Psa 30:3). Though David was speaking figuratively about death, since the context is his healing, his mind was dwelling on resurrection.

Here are several other verses:

"But God will redeem [ransom, rescue, deliver] *my soul* [life, being] *from the power of the grave: for he shall receive* [take] *me. Selah"* (Psa 49:15).

"Thou, which hast shewed me great and sore troubles, shalt quicken me again [return me to life], *and shalt bring me up again from the depths of the earth"* (Psa 71:20).

"Thou shalt guide me with thy counsel, and afterward receive [take] *me to glory"* (Psa 73:24).

The prophets make some strong declarations about the resurrection. For example, Isaiah says, *"Thy dead men shall live, together with my dead body shall they arise. Awake and sing* [shout for joy], *ye that dwell in dust: for thy dew is as the dew of herbs, and the earth shall cast out the dead"* (Isa 26:19). Kimchi, a noted Jewish commentator states that these words concern the days of the Messiah.[10]

Revelation 20:5-6 indicates that there will be two resurrections, *"But the rest of the dead lived not again until the thousand years were finished. This is the first resurrection. Blessed and holy is he that hath part in the first resurrection: on such the second death hath no power, but they shall be priests of God and of Messiah, and shall reign with him a thousand years."* But does the idea of two resurrections have support in the *Tanach*?

Daniel also refers to the concept of a double resurrection, *"And many of them that sleep in the dust of the earth shall awake, some to everlasting life, and some to shame and everlasting contempt"* (Dan 12:2). The New Testament confirms this. Yeshua speaking about the "sheep" and "goats" before His throne of judgment says, *"And these shall go away into everlasting punishment: but the righteous into life eternal"* (Matt 25:46).

Proclamations and Prophecies of Resurrection[11]

Maimonides' thirteen principles of faith are the closest thing Judaism has to a creed. The final one is, "I believe with perfect faith that there will be a revival of the dead at the time when it shall please the Creator..."[12]

We have already mentioned that some rabbis believe Isaac died and was resurrected when Abraham was willing to sacrifice him. They also hint at Jonah being resurrected.[13] Jonah cried out to God from his "grave," at least figuratively in the as-good-as-dead sense. *"Then Jonah prayed unto the LORD his God out of the fish's belly, And said, I cried by reason of mine affliction unto the LORD, and he heard me; out of the belly of hell [Sheol* = grave, death] *cried I, and thou heardest my voice...I went down to the bottoms of the mountains; the earth with her bars was about me for ever: yet hast thou brought up my life from corruption* [the pit, grave, fig. destruction], *O LORD my God"* (Jonah 2:1-2,6).

Why did Yeshua say Jonah's three days in the *"fish"* would be the only confirming sign given to His generation? Because it pointed to His resurrection. *"But he answered and said unto them, An evil and adulterous generation seeketh after* [desires] *a sign* [token, miracle - here and following]; *and there shall no sign be given to it, but the sign of the prophet* [Jonah]: *For as* [Jonah] *was three days and three nights in the whale's belly; so shall the Son of man be three days and three nights in the heart of the earth"* (Matt 12:39-40; see Jon 1:17). Was the rabbinical belief in Jonah's resurrection current in Yeshua's day? We don't know for sure, but if it was, then His use of Jonah was directly to the point.

Ezekiel's vision of the valley of dry bones (Ezk 37:7-10) points to a resurrection of the whole house of Israel. Whether that passage is meant to be taken literally, figuratively, or both ways, it proclaims an understanding of God's ability by His Spirit to raise the dead to life.

The same chapter of Ezekiel contains the Passover week *Shabbat Haftorah* portion, a selection from the Prophets which is read with the weekly *Torah* portion in synagogues. These *Haftorah* selections were first developed before Yeshua's day, during the time of the *Maccabbees*, when Jews were not allowed to read the "Law." These same readings were probably in use during Yeshua's day.[14] Where was Yeshua after His crucifixion during the *Shabbat* of the Passover week? In the grave. So on the yearly *Shabbat* of the Hebrew calendar when the Messiah was in the grave, Jewish people are reading Ezekiel 37 and thinking about resurrection!

Yeshua's resurrection fulfilled a Jewish holy day, a day that the Lord proclaimed as His *moed,*[15] a feast of the Lord. This specific feast is called the "Firstfruits" of the barley harvest (see Lev 23:9-14). Paul refers to this in 1 Corinthians 15, where he calls Messiah *"the firstfruits"* twice, *"But now is Messiah risen from the dead, and become* **the firstfruits** *of them that slept. For since by man came death, by man came also the resurrection of the dead. For as in Adam all die, even so in Messiah shall all be made alive. But every man in his own order:* **Messiah the firstfruits***; afterward they that are Messiah's at his coming"* (1 Cor 15:20-23).

Finally, we see two powerful verses on resurrection in the book of the prophet Hosea. Chapter 6 has a reference to being raised from the dead on the third day. *"Come, and let us return unto the*

LORD: for he hath torn, and he will heal us; he hath smitten, and he will bind us up. After two days will he revive us: in the third day he will raise us up, and we shall live in his sight [lit. to His face; fig. in His presence]*"* (Hos 6:1-2).

In Hosea 13:14a we have one of God's most far-reaching promises concerning His ultimate victory over the last enemy – death[16], *"I will ransom* [lit. sever; fig. rescue, deliver] *them from the power of the grave; I will redeem them* [as a kinsman-redeemer] *from death: O death, I will be thy plagues; O grave, I will be thy destruction:...."*

"Why should it be thought a thing incredible with you,
that God should raise the dead?" (Acts 26:8)

---

1   See the following verses to confirm this fact: Matthew 21:42; 22:29; Luke 24:27; 44-46; John 5:39; 19:36-37; Acts 8:32-35; 17:10-11; Romans 1:1-2; 16:25-26; Galatians 3:8; 2 Timothy 3:15-17. (see Chapter 1 on the *Tanach's* relation to the New Testament.

2   *Legends of the Bible*, Louis Ginzberg, Jewish Publication Society of America, Abridged Ed., 1909, p. 133.

3   See Chap. 13 section "The Binding of Isaac".

4   See 1 Cor 15:20-24, 35-38, 42-44, 51-54.

5   *Classical Evangelical Essays in OT Interpretation*, "Immortality in the Old Testament" by James Orr, ed. by Walter C Kaiser, Jr., Baker Book House Co., 1972, pp. 258-259.

6   See Genesis 5:22-24 and 2 Kings 2:11.

7   See Chap. 8, "A Prophet Like Moses".

8   Matt 27:52-53 *"And the graves were opened; and many bodies of the saints which slept arose, And came out of the graves after his resurrection, and went into the holy city, and appeared unto many."*

9   Skin in Scripture is often used as a symbol for mortality. God "covered" Adam and Eve with mortality, represented by the skins of dead animals (Gen 3:21). The animal skins were to signify Adam's and Eve's own sure death as well as to remind them of the efficacy of blood sacrifice. God killed the animals, shedding blood, then used their skins as a covering (the literal meaning of atonement). Thus our first parents lived for many more years before death took its toll.

10   *Clarke's Commentary*, Vol. IV, Abingdon Press, Nashville, pg. 118,.

11   In Chap. 10 and 11, we examined the resurrection of Israel's Messiah as prophesied in Isaiah 53 and Psalm 22.

12   *The Authorised Daily Prayer Book*, by Dr. Joseph H. Hertz, NY Bloch Pub. Co. 1948, p. 255.

13   *The Twelve Prophets*, ed. by Rev. Dr. A Cohen, Soncino Press, 1948, pp. 144-145.

14   Some scholars think that Luke 4 could be an example of this.

15 *Moed* is the Hebrew word translated in Leviticus 23 as "feast." It is more than a holiday. It is a time divinely appointed by God during which He meets with His people.

16 See 1 Cor 15:26

CHAPTER 14

The Deity of Messiah

It is difficult to comprehend the New Testament claim that God came in the flesh as Yeshua our Messiah. This chapter, while not an attempt to scientifically explain the Incarnation, will show that the *Tanach* points to a divine, as well as human, Messiah.

I and the Father are One

Yeshua is not the Father, but as the promised Messiah He *must be* Deity - God in the flesh. He authoritatively declares in John 14:9b, *"...he that hath seen*[1] *me hath seen the Father..."* He had previously stated in John 10:30, *"I and my Father are one,"* and repeats that claim in His prayer in John 17:11, 21-22. There can be no doubt that Yeshua knew Himself to be *one* with the Father. Since most of the formal education of Yeshua and his audience centered on the *Tanach*, we must understand the concept of "one" within that framework.

Two biblical Hebrew words can be translated as "one" in English. *Yachid* means "one" in the sense of singular, indivisible, the only one (Gen 22:2 and Judg 11:34: "only"), and is not used often in Scripture. The other word translated as "one," *echad,* "stresses unity while recognizing diversity within that oneness,"[2] and is an important word/concept throughout the *Tanach*.

Here are several examples in which the word translated "one," *echad,* indicates the concept of diversity in unity.

One "day" includes both day and night. *"And God called the light Day, and the darkness he called Night. And the evening and the morning were the **first** [one] day"* (Gen 1:5).

Marriage joins two people in a relationship so close that God says they are one flesh. *"Therefore shall a man leave his father and his mother, and shall cleave unto* [join closely with] *his wife: and they shall be* **one** *flesh"* (Gen 2:24).

When the numerous people of Israel were united, they spoke with "one voice." *"And Moses came and told the people all the words of the LORD, and all the judgments: and all the people answered with* **one** *voice, and said, All the words which the LORD hath said will we do"* (Exo 24:3).[3]

Considering that definition of *echad*, look at the most important commandment in both Judaism and Christianity, the *Sh'ma* ("Hear!"), *"Hear, O Israel: The LORD our God is* **one** *LORD* [lit: LORD is one/*echad*]: *And thou shalt love the LORD thy God with all thine heart, and with all thy soul, and with all thy might."* (Deut 6:4-5; cp. Mark 12:28-30). Moses, inspired by God's Spirit, used *echad* to describe God's nature in the *Sh'ma* as a diversity in unity.

Yeshua, speaking according to *Tanach* Hebraic thought, said *"I and my Father are* **one** *"* (John 10:30). Yeshua is not the Father, but is one with the Father in a unique way. If the Father is God, can Yeshua, who claims unity with Him, be less than divine? The Jews rightly understood His statement as a claim to Deity. *"Then the Jews took up stones again to stone him. Yeshua answered them, Many good works have I shewed you from my Father; for which of those works do ye stone me? The Jews answered him, saying, For a good work we stone thee not; but for blasphemy; and because that* **thou, being a man, makest thyself God** *"* (John 10:31-33). And if Yeshua is not God in the flesh, then according to God's law, He should have been stoned to death.

The Angel of the LORD

John 1:18 states, *"No man hath seen God at any time;* **the only begotten Son**, *which is in the bosom of the Father, he* **hath declared him**.*"* It is clear from this verse and others, for example, Exodus 33:20b, in which God says to Moses, *"...Thou canst not see my face: for there shall no man see me, and live,"* that *no man has ever seen God* with his physical eyes. But we have many recorded appearances of God in the *Tanach*. Who did those Old Testament saints see? According to John's statements in 1:1 and 1:18, it must have been the pre-incarnate Son/Word of God declaring or revealing Him.

Yeshua seemed to appear as a different person to some of his followers after assuming His glorified state.[4] This was nothing new, since He had appeared in different manifestations before the Incarnation. One of the most frequent was as "The Angel [lit: Messenger] of the LORD." In the Bible, in both the Hebrew and the Greek, the word translated "angel" is also translated "messenger." Scriptures show that this Angel explicitly identifies Himself with, and was called by, God's personal name (see below - The Name of God). He was also recognized by people as divine and received worship. This particular Angel carried the authority of God into the world of men, yet was inseparable from God in Heaven. The following scriptures, among others, identify this Angel as God.

Genesis 32:4 relates that Jacob wrestled with a "Man" whom he identified as God in 32:30, *"And Jacob called the name of the place Peniel: for I have seen God face to face, and my life is preserved."* Later, the prophet Hosea identifies this Man/God as the Angel. *"He took his brother by the heel in the womb, and by his strength he* [Jacob] *had power* [prevailed] *with God: Yea, he had power over **the angel**, and prevailed: he wept, and made supplication unto him: he found him in Bethel, and there he spake with us;"* (Hos 12:3-4). Hosea goes on to proclaim in 12:5 that this God/Angel is *"Even the LORD God of hosts; the LORD* [personal name of God] *is his memorial."*

In Genesis 48:15-16, Jacob on his deathbed makes a comparison between God and the Angel, stating that they are one. Although he starts with God, he ends asking that "The Angel"[5] would bless his grandsons in a way that only God would be able to do. *"And he* [Jacob] *blessed Joseph, and said, God, before whom my fathers Abraham and Isaac did walk, the God which fed* [shepherded] *me all my life long unto this day, **The Angel** which redeemed me from all evil, bless the lads; and let my name be named on them, and the name of my fathers Abraham and Isaac; and let them grow into a multitude in the midst of the earth."*

In describing his encounter with God, Moses wrote in Exodus 3:2a, *"And **the angel** of the LORD appeared unto him in a flame of fire out of the midst of a bush:..."* Then in verse 4b, he said, *"...God called unto him out of the midst of the bush."* He who was originally called "the angel of the LORD" goes on to identify Himself in verse 6b declaring *"...I am the God of thy father, the God of Abraham, the God of Isaac, and the God of Jacob..."*

When reading Exodus 23:20-23, it is important to understand that in biblical Hebraic thought "the name was considered to be a description of the essential nature of the person or thing..."[6] God says that He is sending an angel before Israel to guard them as they travel and bring them to the land He has promised to give them. But in verse 21, God declares, *"Beware of* [Give heed to] *him* [the Angel], *and obey his voice, provoke him not; for he will not pardon your transgressions* [rebellions]: *for **my name is in him**."* One could say that the essential nature of this Angel was the Name of the Lord. This Angel had God's Name, His *"essential nature,"* in Him.

In a beautiful portion of Isaiah, the prophet portrays this Angel as Israel's Savior, Redeemer, and Shepherd, the One who carried them through life. *"For he said, Surely they are my people, children that will not lie* [deal falsely]*: so he was their Saviour. In all their affliction* [trouble] *he was afflicted, and **the angel** [messenger] **of his presence** saved them: in his love and in his pity* [mercy] *he redeemed them; and he bare them, and carried them all the days of old"* (Isaiah 63:8-9).

One final example is found in Malachi 3:1. *"Behold, I will send my **messenger** [or angel], and he shall prepare the way before me: and the Lord, whom ye seek, shall suddenly come to his temple, even **the messenger** [or the Angel] of the covenant, whom ye delight in: behold, he shall come, saith the LORD of hosts."* Notice that the temple is "his", the Lord's/Angel's, temple.

The Angel of the Lord revealed God to many *Tanach* saints. They saw, touched and talked with Him. According to John 1:18, this Angel must have been the pre-incarnate Son/Word of God who finally entered the world as Yeshua.

The Name of God

We want to emphasize again what "name" in biblical Hebraic thinking means. "The concept of personal names in the OT often included existence, character and reputation (1 Sam 25:25)."[8] "Declaring one's name was a chief means of revealing or manifesting oneself."[9]

Here are two of many examples. Through Moses, God states to Pharaoh, *"And in very deed for this cause have I raised thee up, for to shew in thee my power; and that **my name** may be declared throughout all the earth"* (Exo 9:16).

In fear the Hivites lied to Joshua about their home territory. As God said in the verse quoted above, fear of Him had fallen on them because they heard what He had done in Egypt. *"And they said unto him, From a very far country thy servants are come because of the **name** of the LORD thy God: for we have heard the **fame** of him, and all that he did in Egypt,"* (Josh 9:9). Their declaration concerning God's name is true, and note the conceptual parallel[10] between "name" and "fame."

The meaning of "name" in Hebrew is another strong proof of the divinity of the promised Messiah. In Isaiah 9:6b Messiah is prophesied to be more than a man because His name – that which He will be – shall be proclaimed as, *"Wonderful, Counsellor, The mighty God, The everlasting Father, The Prince of Peace."* Also Isaiah 7:14b informs us that the name of the virgin's Son would be called *"Immanuel,"* which means His essential nature would be "God with us" as Matthew 1:23 confirms.

YHWH – God's Personal Name

Some believers do not know that God constantly uses His personal name in the *Tanach*. "One of the most fundamental and essential features of the biblical revelation is the fact that God ...has a personal name...."[11] His name of four letters, the tetragrammaton, is composed of the four Hebrew letters - *yod, hay, vav* and *hay*. In some translations and commentaries it is written *Yahweh* or YHWH. However in most Bible versions God's Name in Hebrew is translated "LORD" (infrequently "Jehovah" or "Yah" or "GOD").

Most of the following verses use *"the LORD."* We have eliminated the added "the" because it is not found in the original Scriptures. Doing so gives a much better sense of God revealing His personal name. So you will see just "LORD" instead of "the LORD" in these verses.

Genesis 12:7-8 is one of the foundational scriptures concerning the promise of the Land of Israel to Abraham's descendents. *"And LORD appeared unto Abram, and said, Unto thy seed* [offspring] *will I give this land: and there builded he an altar unto LORD, who appeared unto him. And he removed* [moved on] *from thence unto a mountain on the east of Bethel...and there he builded an altar unto LORD, and called upon the name of LORD."*

In Exodus 33:18, Moses begged God to show him His glory. God said Moses would have to be satisfied with having Him proclaim His name (33:19) because no one could see His glory and live (33:20-22). Exodus 34:5-6 describes what happened. *"And LORD descended in the cloud, and stood with him there, and proclaimed the name of LORD. And LORD passed by before him, and proclaimed, LORD, LORD God, merciful and gracious, longsuffering, and abundant in goodness* [chesed] *and truth."* Note how God proclaims His name as His nature.

Throughout Leviticus 18:1-22, God's reason for expecting Israel to obey His commands is based on who He is. In that short section, He states *thirty-two times* that *"I am LORD."*

The Aaronic benediction found in Numbers 6:22-27 is one of the more traditional blessings heard in both church and synagogue. Reread it here with the concept of God's name in mind. *"And LORD spake unto Moses, saying, Speak unto Aaron and unto his sons, saying, On this wise ye shall bless the children of Israel, saying unto them, LORD bless thee, and keep* [guard] *thee: LORD make his face shine upon thee, and be gracious unto thee: LORD lift up his countenance* [face] *upon thee, and give thee peace.[12] And they shall put **my name** upon the children of Israel; and I will bless them."*

Look at the *Sh'ma* again and focus on the use of "LORD." *"Hear, O Israel: LORD our God is one LORD: And thou shalt love LORD thy God with all thine heart, and with all thy soul, and with all thy might"* (Deut 6:4-5).

One of the best examples of the use of God's proper name is Elijah's challenge to the people of Israel and their response once the fire of LORD fell. *"And Elijah came unto all the people, and said, How long halt* [hop; skip] *ye between two opinions? if LORD be God, follow him: but if Baal, then follow him. And the people answered him not a word...Then the fire of LORD fell, and consumed the burnt sacrifice, and the wood, and the stones, and the dust, and licked up the water that was in the trench. And when all the people saw it, they fell on their faces: and they said, LORD, he is the God; LORD, he is the God"* (1 Kings 18:21,38-39). Is it not appropriate that Elijah's name means "My God is YHWH?"

The Psalms contain many excellent examples of the use of God's personal name. See this endnote for some of the more pertinent verses.[13]

Through His *Tanach* prophets God uses His personal name consistently to make sure that everyone understands that He is the only true and living God. *'I am LORD, that is my name; and my glory will I not give to another..."* (Isa 42:8a); *"Therefore, behold, I will this once cause them to know, I will cause them to know mine hand and my might; and they shall know that my name is LORD"* (Jer 16:21); *"Thus saith LORD the maker thereof, LORD that formed it, to establish it; LORD is his name;"* (Jer 33:2); *"So will I make my holy name known in the midst of my people Israel; and I will not let them pollute* [profane; defile] *my holy name any more: and the heathen* [gentiles] *shall know that I am LORD, the Holy One in Israel"* (Ezek 39:7); *"And I will bring the third part through the fire, and will refine them as silver is refined, and will try* [test; prove] *them as gold is tried: they shall call on my name, and I will hear them: I will say, It is my people: and they shall say, LORD is my God"* (Zech 13:9).

Elohim is another Hebrew word for "God." It literally means "mighty ones", and is usually translated as "God," "gods" or "judges," but the Hebrew word YHWH, or "LORD," is never used for anyone other than God. How many times does the *Tanach* use God's personal name, "YHWH?" According to the *Logos Bible Software Program,* a total of 6668 times!

YHWH – The Name of God's Son

The use of "LORD" in the following verses applies to God the Father but can also be linked to God the Son, in essence declaring that the nature of the pre-incarnate Son is the same as the nature of His Father. Genesis 18:1a says, *"And LORD appeared unto* [Abraham]...;" v 22b, *"...Abraham stood yet before LORD."* Again, according to John 1:18 which states that no one can see God and live, the only "LORD" with whom Abraham could have had a face-to-face encounter is the Son, the pre-incarnate Word of God.

The Good Shepherd

The Jewish apostle Peter[14] writes to believers that Yeshua is *"the Shepherd and Bishop* [Overseer] *of your souls"* (1 Pet 2:25b). In John 10:11 and 14 Yeshua Himself proclaims that He is the Good Shepherd. *'I am the good shepherd: the good shepherd giveth his life for the sheep...I am the good shepherd, and know my sheep, and am known of mine."* What does the *Tanach* say about this Shepherd?

Psalm 23:1 is the best known verse for the *Tanach* identification of Israel's Shepherd as "LORD." *'LORD is my shepherd; I shall not want."*

Isaiah 40:10-11 comes within the context of a prophecy of Messiah Yeshua's first coming. Verses 1 and 2 command "comfort" to Jerusalem because her iniquity is forgiven; verse 3 prophesies of John the Baptist as the voice in the wilderness; verses 6 to 8 proclaim that only God's Word endures forever; verse 9 says to Judah, *"Behold your God!."* And then verses 10-11 identify this One as Israel's Shepherd. *"Behold, the Lord* **GOD** [YHWH] *will come with strong hand, and his arm shall rule for him: behold, his reward is with him, and his work before him. He shall feed his flock like a* **shepherd***: he shall gather the lambs with his arm, and carry them in his bosom, and shall gently lead those that are with young."* Note that Israel's Shepherd is identified here as Lord GOD [YHWH].[15]

Asaph, the author of Psalm 80 calls on the "Shepherd of Israel" in verse 1, *"Give ear, O* **Shepherd** *of Israel, thou that leadest Joseph like a flock; thou that dwellest between the cherubims, shine forth."* He identifies this One as YHWH God in verse 4, *'O LORD God of hosts, how long wilt thou be angry against the prayer of thy people?"* Asaph presents this image in Psalm 78:52 as well.

Seeing the unity between Israel's Shepherd and Israel's God helps us as we read John 10:24-33. Now we can grasp the instant reaction of the religious leaders to Yeshua's declaration that, because He is that Shepherd, He and the Father are one. *"Then came the Jews...and said unto him, How long dost thou make us to doubt? If thou be the Messiah, tell us plainly." "Yeshua answered them, I told you, and ye believed not: the works that I do in my Father's* **name***, they bear witness of me. But ye believe not, because ye are not of* **my sheep**...**My sheep** *hear my voice, and I know them, and they follow me: And I give unto them eternal life; and they shall never perish, neither shall any man pluck* [seize by force] *them out of my hand. My Father, which gave me them, is* *greater than all; and no man is able to pluck them out of my Father's hand.* **I and my Father are one***."*

"Then the Jews took up stones again to stone him."

"Yeshua answered them, Many good works have I shewed you from my Father; for which of those works do ye stone me?"

"The Jews answered him, saying, For a good work we stone thee not; but for blasphemy...because that **thou, being a man, makest thyself God***."*

The King

The New Testament declares that Yeshua is King of the Jews and of the world. *"Where is he that is born* **King of the Jews?***..."* (Matt 2:2a); *"Then shall* **the King** *say unto them on his right hand, Come, ye blessed of my Father..."* (Matt 25:34a); *"Nathanael answered and saith unto him, Rabbi, thou art the Son of God;* **thou art the King of Israel***"* (John 1:49); *"On the next day much people that were come to the feast* [Passover], *when they heard that Yeshua was coming to Jerusalem, Took branches of palm trees, and went forth to meet him, and cried, Hosanna* [lit: Save now!]: *Blessed is* **the King of Israel** *that cometh* **in the name of the Lord** [from Psa 118:25-26]. *And Yeshua, when he had found a young ass, sat thereon; as it is written, Fear not, daughter of Sion: behold,* **thy King cometh***, sitting on an ass's colt* [from Zech 9:9]*"* (John 12:12-15); *"These shall make war with the Lamb, and the Lamb shall overcome them: for he is Lord of lords, and* **King of kings***: and they that are with him are called, and chosen, and faithful"* (Rev 17:14). But who is the King of Israel in the *Tanach*?

In Isaiah 44:6 God describes Himself as the **King of Israel**. *"Thus saith LORD the* **King of Israel***, and his redeemer LORD of hosts* [armies]*; I am the first, and I am the last; and beside me there is no God."* We will explore this verse in depth in the next two sections. It is a key scripture for understanding Yeshua's divinity.

First and Last

In our key verse from the *Tanach*, Isaiah 44:6, quoted above, God also calls Himself "the first" and "the last." He uses the same phrases in Isaiah 48:12, *"Hearken unto me, O Jacob and Israel, my called; I am he;* **I am the first, I also am the last.***"*

In the New Testament book of Revelation Yeshua calls Himself by the title of "the first and the last" at least four times, *"I am Alpha and Omega,* **the first and the last***..."* (Rev 1:11a); *"And when I saw him, I fell at his feet as dead. And he laid his right hand upon me, saying unto me, Fear not;* **I am the first and the last***:"* (Rev 1:17); *"And unto the angel of the church in Smyrna write; These things saith* **the first and the last***, which was dead,* *and is alive;"* (Rev 2:8); *"I am Alpha and Omega, the beginning and the end, **the first and the last**"* (Rev 22:13). If He is the first *and* the last, He must also be eternal. By using the same title found in that key scripture from Isaiah, *"Thus saith LORD the King of Israel, and his redeemer LORD of hosts; I am the first, and I am the last;"* Yeshua is proclaiming His deity through *remez*/hinting, for the verse ends with, *"and beside me there is no God."*

LORD of Hosts

Our key verse from Isaiah includes the title "LORD of hosts." Zechariah 2:8-12 contains some verses that might cause one to believe that there are two LORDs of Hosts! In verse 2:8, LORD of Hosts says to Israel that Someone else has sent Him to the gentiles, *"For **thus saith LORD of hosts**; After the glory **hath he sent me** unto the nations* [or gentiles] *which spoiled you: for he that toucheth* [strikes] *you toucheth the apple* [pupil] *of **his** eye."* The same LORD of Hosts goes on to say, *"For, behold, I will shake mine hand upon them, and they shall be a spoil to their servants: and ye shall know that **LORD of hosts hath sent me**. Sing* [Shout] *and rejoice, O daughter of Zion: for, lo, I come, and I will dwell in the midst of thee, saith LORD. And many **nations** [gentiles] **shall be joined** [united] **to LORD** in that day, and shall be my people: and I will dwell in the midst of thee, and thou shalt know that **LORD of hosts hath sent me** unto thee. And LORD shall inherit Judah his portion in the holy land, and shall choose Jerusalem again"* (Zech 2:9-12).

How many "LORD of Hosts" are there? Yeshua is LORD of Hosts who is speaking because he repeatedly states in the gospels that God has sent Him[16] and He is also the One who has enabled many gentiles to become part of God's family, Israel's Olive Tree (Rom 11:17-18).[17] Yeshua is God and LORD of Hosts, but He is not identical to His Father, who sent Him, who is also God and LORD of Hosts.[18] This is why Yeshua could say, *"...for my Father is greater than I,"* and still not deny His own deity (John 14:28b).

Zechariah 14:16 ends with a vision of God's kingdom on earth. *"And it shall come to pass, that every one that is left of all **the nations** which came against Jerusalem shall even go up from year to year to **worship the King, LORD of hosts**, and to keep the feast of tabernacles."*

The book of Revelation identifies this King as *"King of saints"* and *"Lord God Almighty"*: *"And they sing the song of Moses the servant of God, and the song of the Lamb, saying, Great and marvellous are thy works, **Lord God Almighty**; just and true are thy ways, thou **King of saints** [lit: ethnos, gentiles/nations]. Who shall not fear thee, O Lord, and glorify* *thy name? for thou only art holy: **for all nations** [ethnos] **shall come and worship before thee**; for thy judgments are made manifest* [revealed]*"* (Rev 15:3-4). A few chapters later, in Revelation 17:14 and 19:16, the *"King of Kings and Lord of Lords"* is identified as Yeshua, our Messiah.

From our key verse, Isaiah 44:6 quoted in the previous two sections, Yeshua must be *"LORD of Hosts."* To grasp this, first read what the apostle Peter says about Yeshua, *"Unto you therefore which believe he is precious: but unto them which be disobedient* [lit: unbelieving]*, the stone which the builders disallowed, the same is made the head of the corner, And **a stone of stumbling, and a rock of offence**, even to them which stumble at the word, being disobedient: whereunto also they were appointed"* (1 Pet 2:7-8, cp. Rom 9:32-33; 1 Cor 1:23).

When Peter and Paul speak of Messiah Yeshua as *"a stone of stumbling, and a rock of offence,"* they are referring to Isaiah 8:14. Now read the context of the original quote in Isaiah. *"Sanctify **LORD of hosts himself**; and let him be your fear, and let him be your dread. And **he shall be** for a sanctuary; but **for a stone of stumbling and for a rock of offence** to both the houses of Israel, for a gin* [trap] *and for a snare to the inhabitants of Jerusalem"* (Isa 8:13-14). So Peter and Paul are equating Messiah Yeshua with "LORD of Hosts."

These and many *Tanach* scriptures call the pre-incarnate Son/ Word of God by the name "LORD" (YHWH), God's personal name.

The Savior

In looking at God as "the Savior" in the *Tanach*, we will find another "root" supporting the New Testament proclamation that Messiah Yeshua is *"God...manifest* [revealed] *in the flesh..."* (1 Tim 3:16b).

"Savior...used frequently of God [in the *Tanach*]...emphasizes a quality and initiative in *Yahweh* as fundamental as creatorhood, sovereignty, and [is] unique in ancient religion."[19] "In the OT [savior or deliverer] is used of men...(Jud 2:16; 3:9; 12:3; 2 Kin 13:5; Neh 9:27) in the sense that these men were instruments of God for salvation. Otherwise, the OT is emphatic that God is the only Savior... and salvation by man is vain (Psa 60:11 - *"Give us help from trouble: for vain is the help* [salvation; deliverance] *of man."*)."[20] Here are some of the many references in the *Tanach* which declare that the God of Israel is the only Savior.

God says that He created Israel (Isa 43:1,7,21), redeemed her from Egypt and her other enemies, and will continue to redeem her (43:3-4), to be His witness - the same reason He created and redeemed gentile believers. *"For I am LORD thy God, the Holy*

One of Israel, *thy Saviour...I, even I, am LORD; and **beside me there is no saviour**. I have declared, and have saved, and I have shewed, when there was no strange god among you: therefore ye are my witnesses, saith LORD, that I am God. Yea, before the day was I am he; and there is none that can deliver out of my hand: I will work, and who shall let* [undo] *it?"* (Isa 43:3a,11-13).

In the following verses from Isaiah, God challenges the futile worship of idols, pleading with idol worshippers to come to Him to be saved. Many such *Tanach* verses appeal to both Jews and gentiles to recognize the true and living God and to claim Him as their Savior. *"Tell ye, and bring them near; yea, let them take counsel together: who hath declared this from ancient time? who hath told it from that time? have not I LORD? and there is no God else beside me; a just* [or righteous] *God and a **Saviour**; there is **none beside me**. Look* [Turn] *unto me, and be ye saved, **all the ends of the earth**: for I am God, and there is none else"* (Isa 45:21-22).

God pleads with Israel in Hosea 13:4 to avert His judgment by returning to Him, *"Yet I am LORD thy God from the land of Egypt, and thou shalt know no god but me: for **there is no saviour beside me**."*

The *Tanach* is emphatic on this point – the God of Israel is the only Savior. The following verses differ from the previous verses only in that they do not explicitly state that He is the *only* Savior, although this is assumed in all of Scripture.

In David's great psalm of praise to God for delivering him from his enemies, he declares, *"The God of my rock; in him will I trust* [seek refuge]*: he is my shield, and the horn of my salvation, my high tower, and my refuge, **my saviour; thou savest** me from violence"* (2 Sam 22:3). In Psalm 27:1a, he states, *"...**LORD is** my light and **my salvation**; whom shall I fear?..."* Again we are faced with the straightforward declaration that *"LORD,"* Yahweh, is our salvation.

The Psalmist states that Israel made and worshipped the golden calf because, *"They forgat* [or ignored] *God their **saviour**, which had done great things in Egypt;"* (Psa 106:21; see 19-20 for the context).

Isaiah cries out to His God, *"Verily thou art a God that hidest thyself, O God of Israel, **the Saviour**"* (Isa 45:15).

Nevertheless, the New Testament proclaims without compromising that Yeshua is the world's Savior. First look at these verses.

The angels announced this good news to the shepherds in the fields around Bethlehem, *"And the angel said unto them, Fear not: for, behold, I bring you good tidings of great joy, which shall be to all people. For unto you is born this day in the city of David a **Saviour, which is Messiah the Lord**"* (Luke 2:10-11).

Yeshua's encounter with the Samaritan woman at the well led her to return to her city to tell her neighbors about Him. After spending some time with Yeshua, they say, *"...Now we believe, not because of thy saying: for we have heard him ourselves, and know that this is indeed **the Messiah, the Saviour of the world**"* (John 4:42b).

In Acts 5:29b Peter and the other apostles have disobeyed the ruling Jewish council in Jerusalem by continuing to proclaim Yeshua as Messiah and Lord, saying, *"We ought to obey God rather than men."* Then they boldly declare to these same rulers, *"Him* [Yeshua] *hath God exalted with his right hand to be a Prince and a **Saviour**, for to give repentance to Israel, and forgiveness of sins"* (Acts 5:31).

Paul declared in a synagogue in Antioch, *"Of this man's* [David's] *seed hath God according to his promise raised unto Israel a **Saviour, Yeshua:**"* (Acts 13:23). Then writing to the Philippians, Paul stated, *"For our conversation* [community; citizenship] *is in heaven; from whence also we look for* [with expectation] ***the Saviour, the Lord Yeshua the Messiah:***" (Phil 3:20).

Paul also encourages Timothy to trust *"God our Saviour...God our Saviour...we trust* [hope] *in the living God, who is the Saviour of all men, specially of those that believe"* (1 Tim 1:1b, 2:3b, 4:10b).

Finally, the beloved apostle John writes a word of assurance to his family in the faith, *"And we have seen and do testify that the Father sent **the Son to be the Saviour of the world**"* (1 John 4:14).[21]

We must ask ourselves whether these New Testament statements contradict the *Tanach* which, as already seen, asserts that only God is the Savior of the world. Are they talking about the same Savior? Is there any proof in the *Tanach* that the coming Messiah would also be the Savior and therefore God?

First consider that Yeshua's name itself means salvation. "It is the oldest name containing the divine name Yahweh, and means 'Yahweh is help' or 'Yahweh is salvation'."[22] Its Hebrew root means wide, spacious, free from constraint. Other Hebrew words derived from the same root mean deliverance, salvation, help, victory, and preservation.

Concerning this name, Matthew recounts what the angel said to Joseph, *"And she shall bring forth a son, and **thou shalt call his name** [nature; character] **Yeshua: for he shall save** his people from their sins"* (Matt 1:21).[23] Matthew proceeds to root that revelation in the *Tanach*, *"Now all this was done, that it might be fulfilled which was spoken of the Lord by the prophet , saying, Behold, **a virgin**[24] shall be with child, **and shall bring forth a son**, and they shall call his name* [character] *Emmanuel, which being interpreted is, **God with us**"* (Matt 1:22-23; see Isa 7:14). So this child, this savior is none other than God in the flesh, *"Emmanuel...God with us."*

Does the *Tanach* prophesy elsewhere that the coming Messiah will be the instrument, better – the embodiment, of God's salvation? Yes. The *Tanach* declares three times in the next passage that the Messiah comes as a human servant! In Isaiah 49:5-6 the pre-incarnate Son of God talks about what His Father said to Him. *"And now, saith LORD* [the Father] *that formed me* [the Messiah] *from the womb to be his servant, to bring Jacob again to him, Though Israel be not gathered, yet shall I* [Messiah] *be glorious in the eyes of LORD* [the Father], *and my God* [the Father] *shall be my strength. And he* [the Father] *said, It is a light thing that thou* [Messiah] *shouldest be my servant to raise up the tribes of Jacob, and to restore the preserved of Israel: I* [the Father] *will also give thee* [Messiah] *for a light to the Gentiles, that thou mayest be my salvation* [*yeshuah* – the feminine of the word Yeshua] *unto the end* [farthest part] *of the earth."* Obviously the **servant** addressed here is not Jacob or Israel because they are the ones needing to be raised up and restored.

In Zechariah 9:9, the prophet points to salvation residing in the King Messiah who is to come, *"Rejoice greatly, O daughter of Zion; shout, O daughter of Jerusalem: behold, thy King cometh unto thee: he is just* [or righteous], *and having salvation; lowly* [humble like a servant], *and riding upon an ass, and upon a colt the foal of an ass."*[25] Once again the *Tanach* portrays the King Messiah as a servant, yet having salvation.

What does Yeshua say about Himself? In His High Priestly prayer from John 17:6a Yeshua says to the Father, *"I have manifested thy name unto the men which thou gavest me out of the world..."* Here the Word witnesses that **Yeshua carries the personal name** [character] **of God.**[26]

The apostle Paul absolutely believed that although Yeshua is not the Father, He is our Savior and God manifest in the flesh. Notice how he goes back and forth in his letter to Titus, proclaiming both God and Yeshua as our Savior.

Titus 1:3b *"...the commandment of **God our Saviour**;"*

Titus 1:4b *"...God the Father and the **Lord Yeshua the Messiah our Saviour**."*

Titus 2:10b *"...the doctrine* [instruction; teaching] *of **God our Saviour**..."*

Titus 2:13 *"Looking for that blessed hope, and the glorious appearing of the great God and **Saviour Yeshua the Messiah**;"*

Titus 3:4b *"...the kindness and love of **God our Saviour** toward man appeared,"*

Titus 3:6b *"...through Yeshua the Messiah our Saviour;"*

Paul based all of his theology on God's Word, the *Tanach*, as it was revealed to him by the Holy Spirit of truth, and he was always bold to declare that Yeshua is God, our Savior!

*"For the LORD is our judge, the LORD is our lawgiver, the LORD is our king; **he will save us**"* (Isa 33:22).

The Redeemer

The primary Hebrew root *goel* means to perform the role of a kinsman who redeems his kin from difficulty and danger or avenges their blood. "The essential meaning of *goel* is 'kinsman-redeemer'. [His] functions...include all kinds of actions whereby persons or properties were brought back or restored from alienation to their proper position and relationship."[27] The word is translated into English as "redeem" or "redeemer" and underlies other biblical Hebrew words translated as "redemption" and "ransom." "Though closely allied to salvation, redemption is more specific, for it denotes the means by which salvation is achieved...by the payment of a ransom."[28]

The sacrificial system in the *Tanach* provided a type and picture of redemption. By "picture," we do not mean to imply that actual redemption was not accomplished by it. In offering the sacrifices ordained by God, one was able to obtain forgiveness from sin and iniquity through the death of a substitute life. Although the animal sacrifices could not deal with our basic sin nature, there was still forgiveness for sins through them.

Even the New Testament recognizes this fact. Hebrews 9:13 says, *"...the blood of bulls and of goats, and the ashes of an heifer sprinkling the unclean* [defiled; profane]*, sanctifieth* [purified; made holy] *to the purifying of the flesh:"* The *Tanach* sacrifices were a type of the ultimate fulfillment in Messiah's death which the writer of Hebrews points out in the next verse, *"How much more shall the blood of Messiah, who through the eternal Spirit offered himself without spot* [faultless] *to God, purge* [cleanse] *your conscience from dead works to serve the living God?"*

God states that He is our Redeemer, and He has established rules about who may redeem another person. These are found in Leviticus 25:47-54. Look at how they define and limit the relationship of a legitimate *goel*, a kinsman-redeemer, for a poverty-stricken Jew who sold himself to a gentile. *"After that he is sold he may be redeemed again; **one of his brethren** may redeem him: Either his uncle, or his uncle's son, may redeem him, or **any that is nigh of kin unto him of his family may redeem him**; or if he be able, he may redeem himself"* (Lev 25:48-49). Accordingly, the *goel* is also known as the kinsman-redeemer.

Because of these limitations, God could accomplish His redemptive role as our kinsman-redeemer only by coming in the flesh as part of the human family. Recognizing this, the author of

156

Hebrews stated, *"Forasmuch then as the children are partakers of flesh and blood, he* [Yeshua] *also himself likewise took part of the same; that through death he might destroy* [render useless] *him that had the power of death, that is, the devil; And deliver* [release] *them who through fear of death were all their lifetime subject to bondage* [slavery]. *For verily he took not on him the nature of angels; but he took on him the seed of Abraham. Wherefore in all things it behoved him* [He was under obligation] *to be made like unto his brethren, that he might be a merciful and faithful high priest in things pertaining to God, to make reconciliation* [atone] *for the sins of the people."* (Heb 2:14-17).

Yeshua is our redemption price as well as our Redeemer, as He declared, *"For even the Son of man came not to be ministered unto, but to minister, and to give his life a ransom* [redemption price] *for many"* (Mark 10:45). John states it in this way, *"For God so loved the world, that he gave his only begotten Son..."* (John 3:16a). Of course, we should expect this pattern for it says in the *Tanach, "For thus saith LORD, Ye have sold yourselves for nought; and ye shall be redeemed without money"* (Isa 52:3).

In Egypt the blood of the Passover lamb physically saved the children of Israel, while the sudden death of Egypt's cherished heirs, their population of firstborns became Israel's ransom. God states in Isaiah 43:3, *"For I am LORD thy God, the Holy One of Israel, thy Saviour: I gave Egypt for thy ransom, Ethiopia and Seba for thee."* God paid the price; He takes no pleasure in the death of unbelievers.

The biblical declaration that God is our Redeemer gives much weight to the argument that Yeshua, in order to be our Redeemer, had to be God in the flesh. With this in mind, let's look at the following verses from the *Tanach*:

In Exodus 6:6-7, God commands Moses, *"Wherefore say unto the children of Israel, I am LORD, and I will bring you out from under the burdens of the Egyptians, and I will rid* [deliver; rescue] *you out of their bondage, and I will redeem you with a stretched out arm, and with great judgments: And I will take* [also acquire, marry] *you to me for a people, and I will be to you a God: and ye shall know that I am LORD your God, which bringeth you out from under the burdens of the Egyptians."* Phrases from those two important verses give a particular structure to the Passover feast. The rabbis use those verses to explain why we drink wine four times at the Passover *seder* [order]. First is the cup of sanctification, from v6 *"bring you out";* second is the cup of praise, from v6 *"rid you out of their bondage";* third is the cup of **redemption**, from v6 *"redeem you";* fourth is the cup of acceptance, from v7 *"I will take you to me for a people."*

At His last Passover supper Yeshua took what today is called the Third Cup, the Cup of Redemption, the cup after the meal (1 Cor 11:25), and said that it represents His blood which would be shed to make the New Covenant.

Yeshua was saying this cup would now also symbolize His saving blood, the blood of the Lamb of God. At the same time, being the Cup of Redemption, it would recall the means which redeemed Israel. Is there a symbolic connection between Egypt's firstborn and the fact that Yeshua was God's firstborn and lived for some time in Egypt? In Ex 4:22 and Hos 11:1 God describes the people of Israel as His firstborn son who was in Egypt, but this verse is also quoted in Matthew 2:15 as a prophecy of Yeshua. Ransomed by the blood of the firstborn in Egypt might not seem fair to today's humanistic, peace-and-unity establishment, but the Lord knew it was for His glory and best for mankind.

The song of newly redeemed Israel on the shores of the Red Sea included these verses, *"Thou in thy mercy [chesed] hast led forth the people which thou hast **redeemed**...till thy people pass over, O LORD, till the people pass over, which thou hast **purchased**"* (Exo 15:13a,16b). Compare this with what Paul states in Acts 20:28b, *"...the **church of God**, which he hath **purchased with** [by means of] **his own blood**."* Paul is declaring that with His own blood God bought us from sin's slavery (Rom 6:18,22) as our kinsman redeemer. That is a strong New Testament statement that Yeshua must be God. John 4:24a says, *"God [the Father, in context; see v23] is a Spirit,"* and a spirit by definition has no blood. But Paul says that God's own blood (it is definite in the Greek) was our redemption price, a powerful reason why God had to come in the flesh to redeem us.

Asaph writes in Psalm 77:15, *"Thou hast with thine arm **redeemed** thy people, the sons of Jacob and Joseph. Selah."* If you trace all verses about "the arm of" or "the right hand of the LORD/ God" in the *Tanach*, it soon becomes apparent that this phrase is a metaphor for the pre-incarnate Son of God.

In Psalm 130, one of the Psalms of Ascent,[29] the Psalmist encourages his nation with these words, *"Let Israel hope in LORD: for with LORD there is mercy [chesed], and with him is plenteous **redemption**. And **he shall redeem Israel** from all his iniquities"* (Psa 130:7-8). The only One who is able to redeem Israel is "LORD" – *YHWH*, in whose name [character] is mercy and redemption. Psalm 20:7 has, *"Some trust in chariots, and some in horses: but we will remember the **name of** LORD our God."*

God promises by Isaiah that He will fight for Israel and defeat her enemies, with the result that *"...all flesh shall know that I LORD am **thy Saviour** and **thy Redeemer**, the mighty One of Jacob"* (Isaiah 49:26b). God also states through the prophet that the oppressors and despisers of Israel (historically "Christendom") will finally serve and help her, so that Israel *"...shalt know that I LORD am **thy Saviour** and **thy Redeemer**, the mighty One of Jacob"* (Isa 60:16b). In these quotes from Isaiah we see LORD God of Israel claiming as His own, two of the various roles we have studied to show the Deity of Messiah Yeshua, the roles of Savior and Redeemer.

Finally, in the little book of Ruth, we find in Boaz the perfect *Tanach* example of a kinsman-redeemer, and a beautiful type of the Messiah Yeshua. Boaz's name means "strength"; he is a man of wealth/property (2:3); he comes from Bethlehem, the "house of bread" (2:4); he is the lord of the harvest (2:4-9); he is a man obedient to God's Law (3:12-13; 4:1-10); he is an advocate for His non-Jewish bride (4:5); as kinsman-redeemer he redeems a wife (4:9-10). As a result, Ruth, a gentile, lived with and blessed God's people, and God used her faithfulness to contribute to the Messianic lineage destined to bring salvation to the world (4:17; Matt 1:5-6). For every aspect of that description of Boaz we find its perfect anti-type in Yeshua.

The New Testament proclaims Yeshua as our Redeemer because through Him God ransoms fallen man. *"Being justified freely* [undeservedly] *by his grace through the **redemption** that is in Messiah Yeshua:"* (Rom 3:24); *"But of him are ye in Messiah Yeshua, who of God is made* [become] *unto us wisdom, and righteousness, and sanctification, and **redemption**:"* (1 Cor 1:30); *"In whom we have **redemption** through his blood, the forgiveness* [pardon] *of sins, according to the riches of his grace;"* (Eph 1:7; cp. Col 1:14); *"Who gave himself for us, that he might **redeem*** [liberate by payment of a ransom] *us from all iniquity, and purify unto himself a peculiar people, zealous of good works"* (Titus 2:14); *"Neither by the blood of goats and calves, but by his own blood he entered in once into the holy place, having obtained **eternal redemption** for us"* (Heb 9:12); *"And they sung a new song, saying, Thou* [the Lamb] *art worthy to take the book, and to open the seals thereof: for thou wast slain, and **hast redeemed us** to God by thy blood out of every kindred, and tongue, and people, and nation;"* (Rev 5:9). Hallelujah!

God's Son

Yeshua is often called God's Son in the New Testament and Yeshua declares that truth, *"The hour is coming, and now is, when the dead shall hear the voice of **the Son of God**: and they that hear shall live"* (John 5:25b); *"...This sickness is not unto death, but for the glory of God, that **the Son of God** might be glorified* [honored] *thereby"* (John 11:4b); *"These things saith **the Son of God**..."* (Rev 2:18b).

Many others in the New Testament also bear witness that Yeshua is the Son of God.

Angels say, *"He shall be great, and shall be called **the Son of the Highest**...And the angel answered...her, The Holy Ghost shall come upon thee, and the power of the Highest shall overshadow thee: therefore also that holy* [lit. set apart] *thing which shall be born of thee shall be called **the Son of God** "* (Luke 1:32a,35).

Demons say, *"...What have we to do with thee, Yeshua, thou **Son of God**? art thou come hither* [here] *to torment us before the time?"* (Matt 8:29b).

John the Baptist says, *"And I saw* [perceived; knew], *and bare record* [witnessed] *that this is **the Son of God** "* (John 1:34).

His disciples *"...came and worshipped* [prostrated themselves before] *him, saying, Of a truth* [Most certainly] *thou art **the Son of God** "* (Matt 14:33); *"And Simon Peter answered and said, Thou art **the Messiah, the Son of the living God** "* (Matt 16:16) and *"Unto you* [the Jewish nation] *first God, having raised up **his Son** Yeshua, sent him to bless you, in turning away every one of you from his iniquities"* (Acts 3:26).

Martha says, *"...Yea, Lord: I believe that thou art **the Messiah, the Son of God**, which should come into the world"* (John 11:27b).

Paul says, *"...that he is **the Son of God** "* (Acts 9:20b); *"Concerning **his Son Messiah** Yeshua our Lord, which was made of the seed of David according to the flesh; And declared to be **the Son of God** with power, according to the spirit of holiness, by the resurrection from the dead:"* (Rom 1:3-4); *"God is faithful, by whom ye were called unto the fellowship of **his Son** Yeshua the Messiah our Lord"* (1Cor 1:9).

The writer of Hebrews said, *"Seeing then that we have a great high priest, that is passed into the heavens, Yeshua **the Son of God**, let us hold fast* [seize or retain] *our profession* [confession]*"* (Heb 4:14).

Other New Testament writers said, *"The beginning of the gospel of Yeshua **the Messiah, the Son of God**;"* (Mark 1:1); *"No man hath seen God at any time; **the only begotten Son**, which is in the bosom of the Father, he hath declared him"* (John 1:18); *"But these are written, that ye might believe that Yeshua is **the Messiah, the Son of God**; and that believing ye might have life through his name"* (John 20:31).

Notice the significant link between Yeshua proclaimed as Messiah and also as the Son of God. For Yeshua to be Israel's Messiah He must be the only begotten Son of God, and conversely, if we deny His Deity as Son – then He cannot be the promised Messiah nor the Savior of the world.

The Messiah was (and still is) expected to be the "Son of David," but Yeshua challenged the limitations of that, showing that the *Tanach* declared the Messiah to be more than David's Son. *"While the Pharisees were gathered together, Yeshua asked them, Saying, What think ye* [your opinion] *of Messiah? whose son is he? They say unto him, The Son* [descendant] *of David. He saith unto them, How then doth David in spirit call him Lord, saying, LORD said unto my Lord, Sit thou on my right hand, till I make thine enemies thy footstool? If David then call him Lord, how is he his son?"* (Matt 22:41-45; cp. Psa 110:1). Without denying that Messiah is the Son of David, He used the authority of Scripture to make an even greater claim for the Messiah as David's Lord.

Nonetheless, on many occasions He was receptive to the title "Son of David". For example: Matthew 21:9, *"And the multitudes that went before, and that followed, cried, saying, Hosanna* [lit: Please save us!] *to the **Son of David**: Blessed is he that cometh in the name of the Lord* [Psa 118:25-26]; *Hosanna in the highest,"* and Luke 18:38-39, *"And he* [a blind man] *cried, saying, Yeshua, thou **Son of David**, have mercy on me. And they which went before rebuked him, that he should hold his peace* [be silent]: *but he cried* [shouted] *so much the more, Thou **Son of David**, have mercy on me."*

The title comes from the *Tanach*. In 2 Samuel 7:12-16, God makes an everlasting covenant with David and his son Solomon. *"He shall build an house* [also means "family"] *for my name, and I will stablish* [establish] *the throne of his kingdom for ever...And thine house and thy kingdom shall be established for ever before thee: thy throne shall be established for ever"* (2 Sam 7:13,16).[30] Although Solomon is the natural fulfillment of the covenant (as Solomon states in 1 Kings 8:13-20), God makes promises in the covenant that point to another "Son" [Heb: can mean "descendant"] who is to reign forever, indicating this Son's divine nature.

Up to a point, Solomon is a beautiful type of the Messiah – the son of Israel's greatest king; a man of peace (his name in Hebrew; 1 Chr 22:9); a man beloved by the Lord, as his God-given name, *Jedidiah*, indicates (2 Sam 12:24-25); a builder of God's temple (1 Chr 22:10-11); and the wisest man ever (1 Kin 3:11-12; 4:29-34). As with all Bible types, one should not expect everything to correlate with the anti-type – and so with Solomon.

That the meaning of "the Son of God" goes far beyond that of "the Son of David" is apparent. In fact, several *Tanach* verses indicate that the God of Israel has a unique Son. For instance, God's ultimate answer to the global rebellion against His rightful rule is to remind the world of His Ruler, *"Yet have I set* [anointed] ***my king*** [the king of My choosing] *upon my holy hill of Zion. I will declare the decree: LORD hath said unto me, **Thou art my Son**; this day have I begotten* *thee...**Kiss the Son**, lest he be angry, and ye perish from the way, when his wrath is kindled but a little. Blessed are all they that put their trust in him"* (Psa 2:6-7,12). God is stating that this **King is His Son.** All people are encouraged to put their trust in the King/ Son. Since the *Tanach* often warns about trusting in man,[31] the One in whom God exhorts us to trust, has to be more than a man.

In Proverbs 30:4 there is a question which is part of the "utterance," or "oracle" (the literal translation of the KJV's "prophecy" in v1), of Agur, *"Who hath ascended up into heaven, or descended? who hath gathered the wind in his fists? who hath bound the waters in a garment? who hath established all the ends of the earth? **what is his name**, and **what is his son's name**, if thou canst tell?"* In reply, the Creator, LORD God of Israel, has given (revealed) His name to His people. And He has also given the name of His Son.

A familiar prophecy found in Isaiah also indicates that God has a unique Son, *"For unto us a child is born, unto us **a son is given**: and the government [rule; dominion] shall be upon his shoulder: and his name shall be called Wonderful, Counsellor, The mighty God, The everlasting Father, The Prince [Ruler; Captain] of Peace. Of the increase of his government and peace there shall be no end, **upon the throne of David**, and upon his kingdom, to order it, and to establish it with judgment and with justice [or justice and righteousness] from henceforth **even for ever**. The zeal of LORD of hosts will perform this"* (Isa 9:6-7).

That prophecy reveals much about the coming Messiah, who will sit on the throne of David forever, fulfilling the criteria of being David's Son. A *"child is born"* is a normal way of talking about a birth, but why add *"a son is given?"* John 3:16a shows why, *"For God so loved the world, that he **gave** his only begotten son...."* Looking back, the unusual combination of terms Isaiah uses gives a fairly strong hint of the human and divine natures of the Messiah and of His sacrifice.

We repeat, a name in Hebraic thinking is more than just a label; it often indicates the essential nature of the thing named. What is the essential nature of this Son? Look again at the verse, *"...and His name* (His essential nature) *shall be called...The mighty God, The everlasting Father..."* Can there be any doubt that this points to One who is more than a mortal man?

Further evidence of Yeshua's divine nature comes from a Jew who, without ever having read the New Testament, believed Yeshua to be the Son of God. Why did Paul, an observant Jew before and after meeting Yeshua, say that he, Paul, was a blasphemer before he was saved? *"And I thank Messiah Yeshua our Lord, who hath enabled me, for that he counted me faithful,* *putting me into the ministry; Who was before a **blasphemer**, and a persecutor, and injurious: but I obtained mercy, because I did it ignorantly in unbelief"* (1 Tim 1:12-13). Blasphemy is slander against God. Paul had blasphemed Yeshua.

Why did Paul confess that he compelled other believers to blaspheme? *"I verily thought with myself, that I ought to do many things contrary to the name of Yeshua of Nazareth. Which thing I also did in Jerusalem: and many of the saints did I shut up in prison, having received authority from the chief priests; and when they were put to death, I gave my voice* [voted] *against them. And I punished them oft in every synagogue, and compelled them to **blaspheme**…"* (Acts 26:9-11b)? We know that Paul would never have blasphemed, or have forced others to blaspheme, the God of Israel. In fact, that is why he was so zealous to persecute this new way, because he believed its adherents were blaspheming God. But as Paul later came to the realization that Yeshua is the Son of God, then without hesitation he could confess that, before he met his Lord, he had blasphemed and caused others to blaspheme.

The Eternal God

More evidence for the Deity of the prophesied Messiah is seen in verses stating that the One to come is eternal. God proclaims in Micah 5:2 that His Messiah, who will come from Bethlehem (Hebrew for "house of bread"!), will be the *"…ruler in Israel; whose goings forth* [origin] *have been from of old, from everlasting."* The word used for everlasting, *olam*, is the same word used to describe God as everlasting,[32] and means eternal.

The Spirit of God is referring to Messiah Yeshua when He declares in Psalm 45:6, *'**Thy throne, O God**, is for ever and ever: the sceptre of thy kingdom is a right* [just] *sceptre."* Why do we say that verse refers to Yeshua and not God the Father? Read verse 7. The Psalmist says this God has been anointed by God. Remember, "Messiah" means "Anointed One." (Both verses are quoted in Heb 1:8-9.) So the *Tanach*, besides identifying this Anointed One as "God," also attributes eternal duration to His throne, His kingdom rule.

The Creator

John begins his Gospel, *"In the beginning was the Word, and the Word was with God, and the Word was God. The same was in the beginning with God. All things were made by him; and without him was not any thing made that was made"* (John 1:1-3). John's prologue calls Yeshua not only the Word of God but also describes Him as the Creator. There are other places where different New Testament writers call Yeshua the Creator.

In Ephesians, Paul writes that he received grace so that he could preach to the gentiles the *"unsearchable riches"* (3:8) of Israel's Messiah, in order to *"...make all men see what is the fellowship of the mystery, which from the beginning of the world hath been hid in **God, who created all things by Yeshua the Messiah**:"* (Eph 3:9).

In Colossians 1:16-17 Paul repeats the truth that God created all things through His Son, *"**For by him** [Messiah Yeshua] **were all things created**, that are in heaven, and that are in earth, visible and invisible, whether they be thrones, or dominions, or principalities, or powers: all things were created by him, and for him: And he is before all things, and by him all things consist."* Paul includes all things in what Yeshua has created, both in heaven and on earth, both visible and invisible things. There is nothing left out except God.

The writer to the Hebrews begins his letter with this truth, saying that God, *"Hath in these last days spoken unto us by **his Son**, whom he hath appointed heir of all things, **by whom also he made the worlds**;"* (Heb 1:2).

While the New Testament abundantly proclaims Messiah Yeshua as the Creator, the *Tanach* plainly states that God, LORD, is the Creator.

Isaiah 40:28b links the creative and eternal aspects of God that we have discussed, *"...the **everlasting God**, LORD, the **Creator** of the ends of the earth* [all the earth defined by its "boundaries"]...*"* Initially Genesis 1:1, the most important of verses because it is the foundation upon which all rests, states, *"In the beginning **God created** the heaven and the earth."*[33]

Can we reconcile the seeming dilemma of two Creators? We know that God created by His Word, as stated in Psalm 33:6, *"By the **word of LORD** were the heavens made; and all the host of them by the breath* [Heb: *ruach,* which can also be translated as "spirit"] *of his mouth."* God the Father created everything through His Word, later manifested in the flesh as Messiah Yeshua (John 1:14), who also possessed the fullness of the Spirit (John 3:34).

The Word of God

The apostle John uses "the Word" as a title for Messiah Yeshua in all his writings. In the prologue of his gospel John says, *"In the beginning was **the Word**, and **the Word** was with God, and **the Word was God**"* (1:1) and a few verses later, he says that this same *"**Word was made flesh**, and dwelt among us..."* (1:14a).

John affirms even more strongly that he and the other original disciples were personal witnesses of, *"That which was from the beginning, which we have heard, which we have seen with our eyes, which we have looked upon* [contemplated], *and our hands have handled, of the Word of life;"* (1 John 1:1).

At the end of his life, while caught up in a God-given vision, John "sees" the return of Yeshua. He describes Yeshua this way, *"And he was clothed with a vesture* [garment or cloak] *dipped* [lit: "baptized," immersed] *in blood: and his name is called The Word of God "* (Rev 19:13).[34]

The roots of that title are found in the *Tanach. "He sent his word, and healed them, and delivered them from their destructions"* (Psa 107:20). *"So shall my word be that goeth forth out of my mouth: it shall not return unto me void* [in vain], *but it shall accomplish that which I please, and it shall prosper in the thing whereto I sent it"* (Isa 55:11). John not only stated, *"And the Word was made flesh, and dwelt among us..."* (John 1:14a), but he also emphasized forty times in his gospel that Yeshua was **sent** by the Father, just as God declares in Isaiah 55:11 quoted above.

We mentioned at the end of the last section that the *Tanach* says Creation was accomplished by the Word of LORD (Psa 33:6). Psalm 119:89 states, *"For ever, O LORD, thy word is settled in heaven."* These verses are saying that the Word was the creating agent and has existed for eternity, both descriptions of God.

Psalm 119, is a beautiful psalm speaking of the great riches and glory of God's Word, or Law (*Torah* in Hebrew, which is usually translated "Law" in English, but means "teaching" and "instruction"). We do not want to lessen the importance of the literal meaning of the text, but if we temporarily substitute the word "Yeshua" as the antitype for "word," "law," "commandments," etc., it is easy for believers to see that He is the ultimate fulfillment of many of these verses.

For example, the following verses proclaim benefits of God's "Law," "Word," etc., and can also point to what we have obtained in Messiah Yeshua: vv 41,123,174 (salvation); 50,93,116 (life); 74,116,147 (hope); 105,130 (light); 133 (leading); 137-138 (righteousness); 140 (purity); 140,165,174 (love of God's Word); 142,160 (truth); 162 (great treasure); 165 (great peace); 170 (deliverance).[35]

Other Titles

Psalm 146:5-10 extols the praises of "LORD." It proclaims Him to be the Creator (v6), the Deliverer (v7), the Healer (v8), and the One who reigns forever (v10). The New Testament also uses all these descriptions for Messiah Yeshua,[36] implying that the nature of the Messiah is the same as the nature of His Father and that Messiah Yeshua is God in the flesh, revealing the Father.

Finally, Jeremiah 23:5-6 declares that the Messiah is LORD our righteousness. *"Behold, the days come, saith LORD, that I will raise unto David a righteous Branch, and a King shall reign and prosper, and shall execute judgment and justice in the earth. In his days* [as King] *Judah shall be saved, and Israel shall dwell safely: and this is **his name** whereby he shall be called, **LORD OUR RIGHTEOUSNESS**."* Rabbinic scholars and Christian theologians alike say this refers to the Messiah, the Righteous Branch of David. Note that His name, His essential nature, is LORD [*YHWH*] OUR RIGHTEOUSNESS. That is the name of God's Messiah, Yeshua!

Paul, probably thinking of this verse, wrote in 2 Corinthians 5:21, *"For he hath made him to be sin for us, who knew no sin; that we might be made the **righteousness of God in him**."*[37] This agrees with a powerful verse in the *Tanach, "No weapon that is formed against thee shall prosper; and every tongue that shall rise against thee in judgment thou shalt condemn. This is the heritage of the servants of LORD, **and their righteousness is of me, saith LORD**"* (Isa 54:17).

Concluding Thoughts

God declares in Isaiah 45:22-23, *"Look* [lit: Turn] *unto me, and be ye saved, all the ends of the earth: for I am God, and there is none else. I have sworn by myself, **the word** is gone out of my mouth in righteousness, and shall not return, **That unto me every knee shall bow, every tongue shall swear**."*

Under the inspiration of the Holy Spirit, Paul sees that declaration fulfilled in Yeshua, its final goal being the Father's glory, *"Wherefore God also hath highly exalted him, and given him a name which is above every name: **That at the name of Yeshua every knee should bow**, of things in heaven, and things in earth, and things under the earth; **And that every tongue should confess that Yeshua the Messiah is Lord, to the glory of God the Father**"* (Phil 2:9-11).

Those two verses together reveal that Yeshua must be *"God...manifest in the flesh"* (1 Tim 3:16b). The only way to avoid that conclusion is to say God changed His Plan, or found a mere man with whom He could trust all His glory. Since neither of these scenarios is possible, we must rest on the transcendent but revealed reality that Yeshua is God.

We need to make firm our commitment to "keep the Word of God," to guard its use and protect it from abuse, to depend finally not on our limited logic and world-view, but on the divinely inspired Scriptures. Usually there is no mystery, but at other times, such as with the Deity of the Messiah Yeshua, we must recognize that *"without controversy great is the mystery of godliness: God was manifest* [revealed] *in the flesh..."* (1Tim 3:16a)

Lon Roberts, Bible teacher, author, and friend, explained Yeshua's deity like this, "The less divine you make Him, the more you have two gods." [38] If we believers see Yeshua as God, as one with the Father, then we are monotheists, worshipping one God. If we call ourselves believers in Yeshua but do not see Yeshua as God and one with the Father, then we are polytheists, worshipping two gods.

It need not discourage us if we find it difficult to grasp Yeshua's Man/God nature. On the contrary, we should rejoice, for of all the miracles of God, the Incarnation is the greatest wonder of all.

"The word which God sent unto the children of Israel,
preaching peace by Yeshua the Messiah:
(he is Lord of all:)" (Acts 10:36).

"I am Alpha and Omega,
the beginning and the ending, saith the Lord,
which is, and which was, and which is to come,
the Almighty" (Rev 1:8).

---

1   The Greek word for "seen" includes the figurative meanings of perceived, known, heeded; been acquainted with by experience.

2   *Theological Wordbook of the Old Testament*, Harris, Archer, Waltke, Vol. 1, pg. 30.

3   Other examples: Gen 11:6 (*"the people is one…one language"*); 34:16 (*"one people"*); Ex 26:6 (*"one tabernacle"*); Judg 20:1,8,11 (*"one man"*).

4   Mark 16:12; Luke 24:16,31; John 20:14,15.

5   The definite article is in the original text. Jacob is referring to a specific angel, "the" Angel.

6   *Wycliffe Bible Encyclopedia*, Moody Press Vol. 2, p. 1174.

7   For other examples, see the stories of Hagar (Gen 16:10-11,13), Gideon (Judg 6:11-23) and the parents of Samson (Judg 13:2-23).

8   *Theological Wordbook of the Old Testament*, Vol. 2, p. 934.

9   *Wycliffe Bible Encyclopedia*, Vol. 2, p. 1174.

10   In Hebrew, parallel thoughts confirm and explain one another, as here where "name" is parallel to "fame."

11   *Dictionary of New Testament Theology*, Colin Brown, Ed., Vol. 2, p. 649.

12   "Shalom" includes physical, emotional, mental and spiritual wholeness.

13   For example, Psalms 7:17; 20:1,7,9; 54:6; 99:6; 113:1-5; 118:26; 135:13.

14   All the original apostles, including Paul, are Jewish.

15   See also Ezekiel 34:11-13, which identifies Israel's Shepherd as YHWH in a prophecy we see coming to pass now.

16   Matt 10:40; 15:24; 21:37; Mark 9:37; 12:6; Luke 4:18,43; 10:16; John 3:17,34; 4:34; 5:23-24,30,36-38; 6:29,38-40,57; 7:16,28-29; 8:16-

18,26,29,42; 10:36; 11:42, 17:3,21 etc.

17 Matt 12:18-21; Luke 2:30-32; Acts 11:17-18; 13:36-48; 26:22-23; Rom 15:8-12,16; Gal 3:14; Eph 3:6-8; Col 1:27; 1 Tim 3:16;

18 Here is another verse that seems to talk about more than one LORD, *"Then **LORD** rained upon Sodom and upon Gomorrah brimstone and fire from **LORD** out of heaven;"* (Gen 19:24).

19 *Evangelical Dictionary of Theology*, Elwell, Ed., p 975.

20 *Wycliffe Bible Encyclopedia*, Pfeiffer, Vos, Rea, Eds., p 1531.

21 There are more New Testament verses which declare the same thing about Messiah Yeshua, i.e. Eph 5:23; 2 Tim 1:10; 2 Pet 1:1,11; 2:20; 3:18.

22 *Dictionary of New Testament Theology*, Vol. 2, p 331.

23 Note that the angel says *"...his people,"* - Israel in this context.

24 Many Jewish commentators say that the word in this *Tanach* verse is not translated "virgin," but just "young woman." However, if that dubious assertion were true, it would turn the "sign" which the previous verse in Isaiah speaks of, into an everyday occurrence.

25 The New Testament uses this verse, or references to it, in each of the four gospels to establish the link between Yeshua and the humble King who brings salvation: Matt 21:4-5; Mark 11:7-10; Luke 19:29-38; John 12:12-16.

26 Remember, we believe that Yeshua is Lord and God, but He is not the Father, although one with Him. See the first section of this chapter (14).

27 *Wycliffe Bible Encyclopedia*, Pfeiffer, Vos, Rea, eds., Vol. 2, p 1447.

28 *Evangelical Dictionary of Theology*, Elwell, ed., p 918.

29 Apparently, Israelis sang the "Psalms of Ascent" (Psa 120-134) also known as "Songs of Degrees" as they ascended to Jerusalem to celebrate each of the three pilgrim feasts – *Pesach* (Passover), *Shavuot* (Weeks or Pentecost) and *Succot* (Booths or Tabernacles).

30 Yeshua's human descent is traced through his mother back to Solomon's brother Nathan, another son of David, in Luke 3:31. But Yeshua's legal claim to the throne of David came through his step-father Joseph traced back to Solomon as listed in Matt 1:6,7.

31 Here are three verses warning us against trusting in man: *"Some trust in chariots, and some in horses: but we will remember the name of the LORD our God"* (Psa 20:7); *"Woe to the rebellious children, saith the LORD, that take counsel, but not of me; and that cover with a covering* [or anoint with an anointing], *but not of my spirit, that they may add sin to sin: That walk to go down into Egypt, and have not asked at my mouth; to strengthen themselves in the strength of Pharaoh, and to trust in the shadow of Egypt!"* (Isa 30:1-2); *"Thus saith the LORD; Cursed be the man that trusteth in man, and maketh flesh his arm, and whose heart departeth from the LORD"* (Jer 17:5).

32 For example, see Gen 21:33; Isa 40:28; Jer 10:10.

33 In Isaiah 45:17, God states, *"But Israel shall be saved in the LORD with an everlasting salvation: ye shall not be ashamed nor confounded world without end* [ever again]. *"* Since this seemed so impossible in Israel's then current situation, God immediately reminds His readers who He is, *"For thus saith the **LORD that created** the heavens; **God himself that formed** the earth and made it; he hath **established** it, he **created** it not in vain, he **formed** it to be inhabited: I am the*

LORD*; and there is none else."* If God had a calling card the main title would be, "I am the LORD, your Creator." In the *Tanach* He usually presents His calling card just before or after He states that He will do something we would find difficult to believe. By this He reminds us who He is, as if to say, "If I created all this universe, I can and will do whatever I say."

34   The writings of John may be the most "Hebraic" in the New Testament. For example, the book of Revelation is incomprehensible without understanding the various images it draws from the *Tanach*. The picture presented in the first half of the verse just quoted (Rev 19:13) is taken from Isaiah 63:1-6.

35   Of course, David was describing the benefits of studying the written Word of God – at least the parts then extant, the first five books of Moses and maybe a few of the other earlier books. If this is how he and the Spirit of God (who inspired him to write this psalm), described parts of the *Tanach,* shouldn't we Bible-believers let the Old Testament have its God-ordained place in our lives as a source of correction and instruction in righteousness (2 Tim 3:16-17)? Moses urges the children of Israel to recognize that *."..the word is very nigh unto thee, in thy mouth, and in thy heart...,"* so that they can perform what God desires (Deut 30:14b). Even so, our Messiah Yeshua is near by His Spirit, dwelling in our hearts by faith and bringing to our remembrance all that He commanded us.

36   Yeshua as Healer is quite obvious from the gospels. Here are references to Him as the Creator - John 1:1-3,10; Eph 3:9; Col 1:16. The Deliverer - Luke 4:18; Rom 11:26; Gal 1:4; Heb 2:14-15. Reigning forever - 2 Sam 7:13,16; Psa 45:6-7; Isa 9:6-7; Luke 1:31-33; Rev 1:5-6; 5:13; 11:15.

37   See also Rom 4:5.

38   Lon Roberts, *A Stone in Zion,* p 4.

CHAPTER 15

The Holy Spirit in the
Tanach - Part 1

Have you noticed that when Yeshua talked about the Holy
Spirit, no one in the gospels ever asked, "What is this new doctrine
He declares?" It is because the work of the Holy Spirit was part of
the revelation given in the *Tanach*. Although the full revelation of
the personal relationship between the Holy Spirit and the believer
is stated most clearly in the New Testament, there are many
examples and promises of it in the *Tanach*. The New Testament
doctrine surrounding God's Spirit was not completely new.[1]

God's Spirit Reveals God

Yeshua's declarative statement about the relationship between
God and His worshippers is found in John 4:24, *"**God is a Spirit:**[2]
and they that worship him must **worship him in spirit and in
truth**."* This fact has crucial implications for how we relate to
and understand our God. Paul states that we understand the
things of God only by the Holy Spirit, *"For what man knoweth
the things of a man, save* [except] *the spirit of man which is in
him? even so the things of God knoweth* [are understood, perceived
by] *no man, but* [by] *the Spirit of God...But the natural* [sensual[3]]
*man receiveth not the things of the Spirit of God: for they are
foolishness unto him: neither can he know them, because they are
spiritually discerned* [examined, judged]*"* (1 Cor 2:11,14 see
context vv. 9-14).

The New Testament explicitly teaches that to understand who
Yeshua is requires revelation by the Holy Spirit, *"But when the
Comforter*[4] *is come, whom I will send unto you from the Father,
even the Spirit of truth, which proceedeth from the Father, **he shall
testify** [witness] **of me:**"* (John 15:26).

"Wherefore I give you to understand, that no man speaking by the Spirit of God calleth Yeshua accursed [Gk: *anathema]: and that no man can* [has the power or ability to] *say* [truthfully] *that Yeshua is the Lord, but by* [through] *the Holy Ghost* [Spirit]*"* (1 Cor 12:3).

The Holy Spirit and Creation

"In the beginning God created the heaven and the earth. And the earth was without form, and void; and darkness was upon the face of the deep. And the Spirit of God moved upon [brooded or hovered over] *the face of the waters"* (Gen 1:1-2). The Holy Spirit was active in creation. God's Spirit can be seen as that "part" of the Godhead (Father, Son, and Holy Spirit) carrying out the plan of God. Such is not an inferior position, as we would understand it in talking about the things of man. Scriptures show interrelationship in the workings of the Godhead, but there is no rigid separation. At times, what the Father does is also attributed to His Son or His Spirit. Often we realize that what we see Yeshua do is done through the agency of the Holy Spirit.

Although we are studying the teaching on God's Spirit, it is important not to separate the various aspects of God that are revealed to us. The more we separate them, the less we have only One God! We must always remember that *Elohim,*[5] the Godhead, is a mystery we cannot hope to understand with our finite minds, except in those areas God has chosen to reveal in His Word. *"And without controversy great is the mystery of godliness: God was manifest in the flesh, justified in the Spirit, seen of angels, preached unto the Gentiles, believed on in the world, received up into glory"* (1 Tim 3:16).

Concerning God's activity in creation, we read in Psalm 33:6, *"By the word of the LORD were the heavens made; and all the host of them by the breath* [lit: *ruach,* or Spirit] *of his mouth."* This *Tanach* verse shows God's Son, *"the word of the LORD"* (see John 1:1-3), and God's Spirit, *"the breath* [or spirit] *of his mouth,"* acting together from *"the beginning."*

Yeshua Creates

Many New Testament verses confirm that God created everything by Messiah Yeshua.

"And to make all men see what is the fellowship of the mystery, which from the beginning of the world [eternity] *hath been hid in God, who created all things by Messiah Yeshua:"* (Eph 3:9).

"All things were made by him; and without him was not any thing made that was made...He was in the world, and the world was made by him, and the world knew him not" (John 1:3,10).

*"But to us there is but one God, the Father, of whom are all things, and we in him; and one **Lord Yeshua the Messiah, by whom are all things**, and we by him"* (1 Cor 8:6).

"For by him were all things created, that are in heaven, and that are in earth, visible and invisible, whether they be thrones, or dominions, or principalities, or powers [authorities]: **all things were created by him, and for him**: *And he is before all things, and by him all things consist"* (Col 1:16-17).

*'[God] Hath in these last days spoken unto us by **his Son**, whom he hath appointed heir of all things, **by whom also he made the worlds**...But unto the Son he saith...Thou, Lord* [YHWH][6], *in the beginning hast laid the foundation of the earth; and the heavens are the works of thine hands:"* (Heb 1:2,8a,10 - quoting Psa 102:25).

The Holy Spirit Creates

The Holy Spirit is revealed as one through whom God creates. For example, look at these *Tanach* verses:

*"The **Spirit** of God hath made me, and the breath* [neshamah - breath, spirit] *of the Almighty hath given me life."* (Job 33:4).

*"Thou hidest thy face, they are troubled: thou takest away their **breath*** [lit: ruach – spirit], *they die, and return to their dust. Thou sendest forth thy **spirit*** [ruach], *they are created* [Heb: bara]: *and thou renewest the face of the earth"* (Psa 104:29-30). The Hebrew word *bara* means to create from nothing. It is only used in the *Tanach* when God is the active agent, as in Genesis 1:1.

The word King David used in Psalm 51:10 is the same word, *bara*. *"Create* [bara] *in me a clean* [pure] *heart, O God; and renew* [make new, renew, repair] *a right* [firm, stable, steadfast] *spirit within me. Cast me not away from thy presence; and take not **thy holy spirit** from me. Restore unto me the joy of thy salvation; and uphold me with thy free* [generous] *spirit."* (Psa 51:10-12).

Nathan the prophet had just confronted David with his sins in the Bathsheba affair. Instead of getting angry or making excuses, David, the man after God's heart, deeply repents. He comes to an understanding that in his flesh dwells no good thing and asks God to have mercy on him and restore him. That is a *Tanach* example of a convicted backslider recognizing that he needs to be remade a new creation. Although not stated in those words in the psalm, the theological concept is the same.

Many years later, during the Babylonian exile, the Lord revealed through the prophet Ezekiel that a new creation is what He has planned, *"A new heart* [inner man] *also will I give you, and a new **spirit** will I put within you: and I will take away the stony heart out of your flesh, and I will give you an heart of flesh"* (Ezek 36:26).

The Promise of the Spirit

Yeshua said that one of the reasons for His return to the Father was so He could pour out the promise of His Father, the baptism, the immersion into, the Holy Spirit, *"And, behold, I send **the promise of my Father** upon you: but tarry ye in the city of Jerusalem, until ye be endued* [clothed] *with power* [also ability] *from on high"* (Luke 24:49, cp. Acts 1:4). The fulfillment was confirmed by Peter, *"Therefore* [Yeshua] *being by the right hand of God exalted, and having received of the Father **the promise**[7] of the Holy Ghost, he hath shed forth this, which ye now see and hear"* (Acts 2:33).

This promise fulfilled in the New Testament had been given by God in the *Tanach*. The main reference is Joel 2:28-29, *"And it shall come to pass afterward, that I will pour out **my spirit** upon all flesh; and your sons and your daughters shall prophesy, your old men shall dream dreams, your young men shall see visions: And also upon the servants and upon the handmaids in those days will I pour out **my spirit**."* Peter certainly tied the outpouring of the Spirit on *Shavuot*/Pentecost (Acts 2:16-18) to that *Tanach* promise.

Here are several other verses that can be seen as part of this promise of the Father.

In Numbers 11:29 Moses expresses a prophetic desire that begins its New Testament fulfillment when Yeshua pours out Holy Spirit on His Body, *"And Moses said unto him, Enviest thou for my sake? would God that all the LORD's people were prophets, and that the LORD would put **his spirit** upon them!"*

Isaiah 32:15-17 prophesies what will happen when God's people in the nation of Israel receive His Spirit, *"Until **the spirit** be poured upon us from on high, and the wilderness be a fruitful field, and the fruitful field be counted for a forest* [wild place]. *Then judgment* [or justice] *shall dwell in the wilderness, and righteousness remain* [dwell] *in the fruitful field. And the work of righteousness shall be peace; and the effect of righteousness quietness and assurance* [safety] *for ever"* (cp. Isa 44:3-5). This outpouring also now applies to the redeemed from all nations.

What Scripture calls "fruit" or "fruitful" accompanying the outpouring of the Spirit is not defined by signs and miracles, although signs and miracles often do accompany an outpouring of God's Spirit. But the "fruit" which God promises is righteousness, peace, joy, and confidence (or faith), which are "fruits" of the Holy Spirit. Paul could easily have been thinking about that verse in Isaiah when he said *"For the kingdom* [rulership] *of God is not meat and drink; but righteousness, and peace, and joy in the Holy Ghost"* (Rom 14:17; see also Gal 5:22-23 – the fruit of the Spirit).

Here is something else to consider when reading Isaiah 32:15. In the *Tanach,* "forest" represents a type of wilderness, a fruitless place. In ancient Israel a forest was not a pleasant picnic spot; it was a frightening abode of dangerous animals. So in verse 15 Isaiah is using different words to say, *"Every valley shall be exalted, and every mountain and hill shall be made low..."* (Isa 40:4a). God's Spirit will turn everything upside down – making things right, beginning to return the world and mankind to God's order.

In Ezekiel 39:29 the Lord says, *"Neither will I hide my face any more from them: for I have* [will have] *poured out **my spirit** upon the house of Israel, saith the Lord GOD."* This *Tanach* verse is a root of Paul's Spirit-directed declaration in Romans 11:26a, *"And so all Israel shall be saved..."*

Born Again by the Spirit

Sin separates us from God as Isaiah 59:1-2 plainly says, *"Behold, the LORD's hand is not shortened, that it cannot save; neither his ear heavy, that it cannot hear: But your iniquities* [perversity, depravity, guilt] *have separated between you and your God, and your sins* [offences] *have hid his face from you, that he will not hear"* (Isa 59:1-2).

Some of the events that usually comprise the born-again experience are: the Father draws us to Yeshua; we receive the revelation - the "seed" of faith - that Yeshua is the *"way, the truth and the life";* the Holy Spirit revives our dead spirits and begins to convict us of sin; God gives us a spirit of repentance, and freely forgives us.[8] Yeshua is then always with us by His Spirit, enabling us to walk in obedience to His Word. All this is accomplished by His grace, and in His order and timing, which is different for everyone.[9]

In Ezekiel 36:25-27 we find one of the best descriptions of what it means to be "born again" in all of Scripture. *"Then will I sprinkle clean* [pure] *water upon you, and ye shall be clean* [pure]: *from all your filthiness, and from all your idols, will I cleanse* [purify] *you. A new heart also will I give you, and **a new spirit will I put within you***: *and I will take away the stony heart out of your flesh, and I will give you an heart of flesh. And **I will put my spirit within you**, and cause you to walk in my statutes, and ye shall keep my judgments, and do them."* Yeshua's imparting His Holy Spirit is integral to this experience.

Israel Redeemed

God's order in the redemption of His people means a regathering of the Jewish people, most in unbelief. Although many Jews are being redeemed in exile, when all Israel is saved, it will occur in the physical land of Israel. First God says that He will bring them back from all the nations to which He scattered them (Jer 31:10), settling them in the land of Israel (see Ezek 36 in context). Hallelujah! We see this happening today! Then, through a spirit of grace (favor), He gives them faith to believe so that they cry out for Him and He cleanses them. To some extent this also is happening today.

How will the Lord accomplish this? Zechariah 12:10 describes this event. Notice how it involves an outpouring of God's Spirit. *"And I will pour upon the house of David, and upon the inhabitants of Jerusalem, **the spirit of grace**[10] **and of supplications:**[11] and they shall look upon me whom they have pierced,[12] and they shall mourn for him, as one mourneth for his only son, and shall be in bitterness for him, as one that is in bitterness for his firstborn."*

With that verse in mind, we believe Yeshua is probably talking about the tribes of Israel in the following verse when he speaks of His coming again, *"And then shall appear the sign of the Son of man in heaven: and then shall all the **tribes of the earth** [or land] mourn, and they shall see the Son of man coming in the clouds of heaven with power and great glory"* (Matt 24:30). We think it a possibility because in Hebrew the word for either "land" or "earth" is the same word – *eretz*. The choice in translation then depends on the context, and often in Scripture it refers specifically to the land of Israel.

Here is another verse which may refer specifically to the people of Israel in regards to the Second Coming, *"Behold, he cometh with clouds; and every eye shall see him, **and they also which pierced him**: and all kindreds [**tribes**][13] of the earth [or **land**] shall wail because of him. Even so, Amen"* (Rev 1:7).

God is Faithful!

The New Testament recognizes that the Holy Spirit is given to gentile believers because, as seen above, God is faithful to His *Tanach* promises *to the Jewish people!*

*"That the blessing of Abraham might come on the Gentiles through Yeshua the Messiah; that we might **receive the promise of the Spirit** through faith"* (Gal 3:14).

*"In whom ye also trusted, after that ye heard the word of truth, the gospel of your salvation: in whom also after that ye believed, ye were sealed with that **holy Spirit of promise**"* (Eph 1:13).

"Teach me to do thy will; for thou art my God:
thy spirit is good*; lead me into the land of uprightness"*
(Psa 143:10).

---

1   The Hebrew word for "spirit" is *ruach*. It is also the word for "wind" or "breath."

2   In Greek this is literally "Spirit, the God," or "God is spirit." Just like in Hebrew, the Greek word for "spirit" (*pneuma)* can also mean "wind" or "breath."

3   This does not mean sexual; it means judging only by the carnal senses and mind, making man the center of all things. This is humanism. Secular humanism manifests as materialism and atheism. Religious humanism seeks spiritual experiences, thinking only how to benefit from them, easily falling prey to demonic influence.

4   Greek: *parakletos* – one called alongside for help; one who pleads the case of another before a judge, an advocate; also an intercessor.

5   This common Hebrew word for God is always in a plural form.

6   In Chapter 14 we learned that Yeshua is called, or identified as YHWH manifested to man (e.g. Isa 40:3 and Matt 3:3).

7   The "promise" in these two verses refers to the time of *fulfillment* of the promise.

8   The first instruction Yeshua gave His disciples after imparting the Holy Spirit to them was concerning forgiveness of sins. *"And when he had said this, he breathed on them, and saith unto them, Receive ye the Holy Ghost: Whose soever sins ye remit* [forgive], *they are remitted unto* [forgiven] *them; and whose soever sins ye retain, they are retained"* (John 20:22-23). They were then responsible to forgive and to seek forgiveness whenever necessary.

9   Sanctification is progress in faith and works. The Holy Spirit gives us a desire to know the Word of God and to please Him.

10   Heb 10:29 states that everyone gets saved by *"the Spirit of grace."*

11   Compare this with Romans 8:26: *"Likewise the Spirit also helpeth our infirmities [weaknesses]: for we know not what we should pray for as we ought: but the Spirit itself maketh intercession for us with groanings which cannot be uttered"*

12   John 19:34-37: *"But one of the soldiers with a spear pierced his side, and forthwith* [immediately] *came there out blood and water. And he that saw it bare record, and his record is true: and he knoweth that he saith true, that ye might believe. For these things were done, that the scripture should be fulfilled, A bone of him shall not be broken. And again another scripture saith,* **They shall look on him whom they pierced**.*"*

13   This same word is translated "tribes' in the verse quoted in the previous paragraph, Matt 24:30. It can also be translated as nations, or peoples.

CHAPTER 16

The Holy Spirit in the
Tanach – Part 2

Spirit-anointed Believers in the *Tanach*

Next let's consider from the *Tanach,* examples of the Holy Spirit working with and through God's people. Although the Holy Spirit's permanent dwelling in believers occurs after the Lord Yeshua's death and resurrection, the *Tanach* contains examples of many temporarily Spirit-filled children of God.

The Call of Israel

Joseph and Daniel were recognized even by gentile rulers to have an anointing, which we know was God's Spirit fulfilling the reason God chose Israel – to bring the knowledge of Himself to the nations/ gentiles.[1] *"And Pharaoh said unto his servants, Can we find such a one as this is, [Joseph] a man in whom the Spirit of God is?"* (Gen 41:38); *"I have even heard of thee* [Daniel]*, that the spirit of the gods is in thee, and that light and understanding and excellent wisdom is found in thee"* (Dan 5:14; see also 4:8-9,18; 5:11,14).

How were gentiles to gain knowledge of God? It happened when gentiles saw that God was with His people! As Moses expressed it, *"For wherein shall it be known here that I and thy people have found grace in thy sight? is it not in that thou goest with us? so shall we be separated* [distinct, marked out]*, I and thy people, from all the people that are upon the face of the earth"* (Exo 33:16. See the context: vv. 12-17).

The Ability to Obey

God's Spirit equips His children to do what He commands, as the Lord points out in Zechariah 4:6b, *"Not by might, nor by power, but **by my spirit, saith the LORD** of hosts"* (Zech 4:6b).

An example of this happened when God anointed men among the children of Israel to construct the Tabernacle in the wilderness. The Lord said to Moses, *"And **I have filled him** [Bezalel] **with the spirit of God**, in wisdom, and in understanding, and in knowledge, and in all manner of workmanship"* (Exo 31:3; see also 28:3; 35:31).

The New Testament indicates that Yeshua was able to do what His Father wanted because He had the fullness of God's Spirit, *"For he whom God hath sent speaketh the words of God: for **God giveth not the Spirit by measure** [not just partially] **unto him"*** (John 3:34); *"How **God anointed Yeshua of Nazareth with the Holy Ghost** and with power: who went about doing good, and healing all that were oppressed of the devil; for God was with him"* (Acts 10:38). Though not the hoped for political deliverance, Yeshua's anointed works did fulfill what the *Tanach* prophesied about the coming Messiah.[2]

The Biblical Response

When the Holy Spirit comes on a person, the typical response is a verbal one, whether tongues, prophesying, confession of sins, or praising God. When God raised up seventy elders in Israel to aid Moses, He placed His Spirit on them. This resulted in the elders breaking forth in prophecy. *"And the LORD came down in a cloud, and spake unto him, and took of the **spirit** that was upon him [Moses], and gave it unto the seventy elders: and it came to pass, that, **when the spirit rested upon them, they prophesied**, and did not cease"* (Num 11:25).

And in the New Testament, *"While Peter yet spake these words, **the Holy Ghost fell** on all them which heard the word. And they of the circumcision which believed were astonished, as many as came with Peter, because that on the Gentiles also was poured out **the gift of the Holy Ghost**. For they heard them **speak with tongues**, and **magnify God**. Then answered Peter, 'Can any man forbid water, that these should not be baptized, which have **received the Holy Ghost** as well as we?'"* (Acts 10:44-47).

God's Deliverers/Judges

The men and women whom God used as His representatives to deliver and judge His people were empowered to accomplish the task because the Spirit of God was on them. Many examples are brought out in the *Tanach*:

*"And when the children of Israel cried unto the LORD, the LORD raised up a deliverer [moshiah – savior] to the children of Israel, who delivered [saved] them, even Othniel...Caleb's younger brother. And **the Spirit of the LORD came upon him**, and he judged*

Israel, and went out to war: and the LORD delivered...[the] *king of Mesopotamia into his hand...*" (Jud 3:9-10a).

The Holy Spirit also came on the following judges of Israel. *"But the Spirit of the LORD came upon* [clothed Himself with!] *Gideon, and he blew a trumpet..."* (Jud 6:34). *"Then the Spirit of the LORD came* [was] *upon Jephthah, and he passed over Gilead..."* (Jud 11:29a). *"And the woman bare a son, and called his name Samson: and the child grew, and the LORD blessed him. And the Spirit of the LORD began to move* [push, impel] *him at times in the camp of Dan..."* (Jud 13:24-25); *"And the Spirit of the LORD came mightily upon* [rushed on, pushed] *him, and he rent* [the lion] *as he would have rent a kid, and he had nothing in his hand..."* (Jud 14:6a); *"And the Spirit of the LORD came upon* [see 14:6a] *him, and he went down to Ashkelon, and slew thirty men..."* (Jud 14:19a); *"...the Philistines shouted against him: and the Spirit of the LORD came mightily upon him* [see 14:6a], *and the cords that were upon his arms became as flax that was burnt with fire, and his bands loosed from off his hands"* (Jud 15:14). *"And the Spirit of God came upon* [see 14:6a] *Saul when he heard those tidings, and his anger was kindled greatly"* (1 Sam 11:6).

In all these instances God's Spirit filled His chosen deliverer/ savior, leading and empowering each one to perform God's works (cp. 1 Sam 11:6; Acts 10:38).

Spirit's Work in Salvation

The prophet Samuel declared to King Saul, *"And the Spirit of the LORD will come upon* [rush on, push] *thee, and thou shalt prophesy with them, and shalt be turned* [changed, transformed] *into another man. And let it be, when these signs are come unto thee, that thou do as occasion serve thee; for God is with thee...behold, a company of prophets met him; and the Spirit of God came upon* [rushed on, pushed] *him, and he prophesied among them"* (1 Sam 10:6-7,10b). Although not salvation, and only temporary, this episode can be seen as a foreshadow of salvation, or being "born again," because it connects the Spirit of God coming on someone with that particular someone changing into a new person.[3] *"Therefore if any man be in Messiah, he is a new creature* [creation]: *old things are passed away; behold, all things are become new"* (2 Cor 5:17).

"Yeshua answered, Verily, verily [Truly], *I say unto thee, Except a man be born of water and of the Spirit, he cannot* [does not have the power or ability to] *enter into the kingdom* [rulership] *of God. That which is born of the flesh is flesh; and that which is born of the Spirit is spirit. Marvel not that I said unto thee, Ye must be born again* [or from above]. *The wind* [ruach, spirit] *bloweth* [or breathes]

where it listeth [wants, desires], *and thou hearest the sound* [or voice] *thereof, but canst not tell whence it cometh, and whither it goeth: so is every one that is **born of the Spirit** "* (John 3:5-8).

As mature believers, we know we don't have the power to change ourselves. *Tanach* saints were also aware of their need and cried out for God to save them. For example:

"Turn us again [Help us to repent], *O God, and cause thy face to shine; and we shall be saved"* (Psa 80:3; see vv. 7,19).

"Turn thou us unto thee [same as above], *O LORD, and we shall be turned; renew our days as of old"* (Lam 5:21).[4]

Here is a wonderful verse showing how the Spirit of God is needed to accept and submit to God's Anointed One. *"Then the **spirit** came upon* [clothed Himself with] *Amasai, who was chief of the captains, and he said, Thine are we, David, and on thy side, thou son of Jesse..."* (1 Chr 12:18a).

The analogy is simple. If it took the Spirit of God coming on Amasai for him to join with David, God's anointed king, how much more does it take the Holy Spirit to enable us to confess that *"Yeshua is Lord?"* As it says in 1 Corinthians 12:3, *"Wherefore I give you to understand* [I want you to know], *that no man speaking by the Spirit of God calleth* [affirms or teaches] *Yeshua accursed: and that **no man can** [has the power or ability to] **say that Yeshua is the Lord, but by the Holy Ghost.** "*

Godly Conviction

It takes the Spirit's power to convict us of sin so we can lovingly and fruitfully, from a humbled heart, show others their sins. We are commanded to do this.[5] Too easily we speak of other people's faults as though we were immune. The necessary thing is to speak in love and humility in the power of the Holy Spirit. All godly and effective correction will be motivated by love, a fruit of the Spirit.

Yeshua said the Holy Spirit is the convictor of sin, *"Nevertheless I tell you the truth; It is expedient* [profitable] *for you that I go away: for if I go not away, the Comforter* [Advocate, Helper, Intercessor] *will not come unto you; but if I depart, I will send him unto you. And when he is come, **he will reprove** [convict] the world of [concerning] sin, and of righteousness, and of judgment:"* (John 16:7-8; cp. Acts 4:8-14).

The *Tanach* prophets could say in truth, *"But truly I am full of power by the spirit of the LORD, and of judgment, and of might, **to declare unto Jacob his transgression** [lit: rebellion], and to Israel his sin"* (Mic 3:8).

One of Messiah Yeshua's divine characteristics was His ability, by the Spirit, to know a person's real intent. The rich young ruler, Mary Magdalene, Peter and the other disciples are examples of how Yeshua judged impartially and not by appearances. This was prophesied of the coming Messiah in a riddle, *"Who is blind, but my servant? or deaf, as my messenger that I sent? who is blind as he that is perfect* [complete, mature]*, and blind as the LORD's servant? Seeing* [perceiving, considering] *many things, but thou observest not; opening the ears, but he heareth not. The LORD is well pleased for his righteousness' sake; he will magnify* [honor] *the law, and make it honourable"* (Isa 42:19-21; cp. 11:3). The interpretation cannot, as some say, be a condemnation of Israel, because God commends this servant in these verses. Only Yeshua's likeness fits here. Only He is truly righteous[6] and only He truly honors God's Law.[7]

The Anointed One

There are many *Tanach* types of the coming Messiah. The root word for Messiah means to be smeared (anointed) with oil. "Messiah" literally means "Anointed One." King David, in particular, is a wonderful type of Yeshua as the anointed King of Israel.

"Then Samuel took the horn of oil, and anointed him in the midst of his brethren: and the Spirit of the LORD came [rushed] upon David from that day forward..." (1 Sam 16:13). This verse links the Spirit of God with being anointed by oil. For this reason oil is sometimes used as a symbol of God's Spirit.[8]

David understood the deep connection between the Spirit of God and His Word. *"Now these be the last words of David. David the son of Jesse said, and the man who was raised up on high,* **the anointed** [Heb: *mashiach* – messiah] *of the God of Jacob, and the sweet psalmist of Israel, said,* **The Spirit of the LORD spake by** [or "in"] **me, and his word was in my tongue**...*"* (2 Sam 23:1-2).[9]

The prime example of this connection occurs in King David's greater Son, Messiah Yeshua, who declared the Word of God in the fullness of the Spirit, *'**The Spirit of the Lord is upon me**, because **he hath anointed me to preach** the gospel to the poor; he hath sent me to heal the brokenhearted,* **to preach** [proclaim] *deliverance to the captives, and recovering of sight to the blind, to set at liberty them that are bruised,* **To preach** [proclaim] *the acceptable year of the Lord...This day is this scripture fulfilled in your ears"* (Luke 4:18-19,21b). In that one verse, half the things Yeshua did concerned healing and the other half involved proclaiming God's Word - all by the Holy Spirit.

Just as God gave directions for the pattern of the Tabernacle to Moses (see Heb 8:5), so God's expanded sanctuary built by Solomon also followed a pattern revealed to David by the Spirit. *"Then David gave to Solomon...the pattern of all that he had* **by the spirit***, of the courts of the house of the LORD..."* (1 Chr 28:11-12a). Just so, declaring

God's Word, as Moses and David did under the anointing, builds God's House. The Body of Messiah, a geographically unconfined spiritual Temple built by the Holy Spirit's directions given to the apostles and prophets, allows whosoever will to worship God in spirit and in truth at any time and in any place. *"Now therefore ye are no more strangers and foreigners, but fellowcitizens with the saints, and of the household [family] of God; And are built upon the foundation of the apostles and prophets, Yeshua the Messiah himself being the chief corner stone; In whom all the building fitly framed together groweth unto* **an holy temple in the Lord***: In whom ye also are builded together for* **an habitation** *[dwelling-place]* **of God through** *[by]* **the Spirit** *"* (Eph 2:19-22).

Yeshua haMashiach, Jesus the Messiah

The New Testament witnessed of Yeshua that He had the fullness of the Holy Spirit.[10] *"And John bare record, saying, I saw* **the Spirit** *descending from heaven like a dove, and it* **abode upon him**. *And I knew him not: but he that sent me to baptize with water, the same said unto me,* **Upon whom thou shalt see the Spirit descending, and remaining on him***, the same is he which baptizeth with the Holy Ghost. And I saw, and bare record that* **this is the Son of God** *"* (John 1:32-34, cp. 3:34; 20:21).

The *Tanach* had prophesied that the coming Messiah would have the Holy Spirit in fullness. *"And there shall come forth a rod out of the stem of Jesse, and a Branch shall grow* [lit: bear fruit] *out of his roots: And* **the spirit of the LORD shall rest** *[settle down, remain]* **upon him***, the spirit of wisdom and understanding, the spirit of counsel and might, the spirit of knowledge and of the fear of the LORD; And shall make him of quick understanding* [sensitive, discerning] *in the fear of the LORD: and he shall not judge after the sight of his eyes* [not just by appearances][11]*, neither reprove after the hearing of his ears: But with righteousness shall he judge the poor* [weak, lowly]*, and reprove with equity for the meek* [humble] *of the earth: and he shall smite the earth with the rod of his mouth, and with the breath* [lit: spirit/*ruach*] *of his lips shall he slay the wicked"* (Isa 11:1-4).

Please note the following points about that portion of Scripture:

This prophecy, which was given after David's son Solomon died, must refer to David's promised son, the Messiah.

These verses explain Revelation 1:4, 3:1, 4:5 and 5:6 which mention *"the seven Spirits of God."* Isaiah describes the Holy Spirit using seven terms: the Spirit of the LORD; of wisdom, understanding, counsel, might, knowledge and fear of the LORD. The number seven in Scripture is often symbolic of completion or perfection. Just as we can be filled with the Spirit of the Lord without diminishing that

Spirit, so the Holy Spirit can operate in these seven aspects of His power as He did in Yeshua and remain as "one Spirit."[12]

Yeshua amazed people by striking at the heart of every issue and judging with righteousness and equity. Toward the end of the portion under consideration, Isaiah (Chpt. 11) talks about the Second Coming, when God's Anointed One, Messiah Yeshua, comes as the Judge of the earth.[13]

The next verse was used in Matthew 12:17-21, to prove that Yeshua is Messiah and Savior of not just the Jewish people, but of the gentiles as well. *"Behold my servant, whom I uphold; mine elect* [chosen], *in whom my soul delighteth* [is completely satisfied]; *I have put **my spirit upon him**: he shall bring forth judgment* [also justice] *to the Gentiles"* (Isa 42:1).

To announce His commission, Yeshua read part of the following passage in the synagogue in His home town of Nazareth, *"The **Spirit of the Lord GOD is upon me**; because **the LORD hath anointed me** to preach good tidings unto the meek* [poor, humble, afflicted]; *he hath sent me to bind up the brokenhearted, to proclaim liberty to the captives, and the opening of the prison to them that are bound; To proclaim the acceptable year of the LORD, and the day of vengeance of our God;* [14] *to comfort all that mourn; To appoint unto them that mourn in Zion, to give unto them beauty for* [instead of] *ashes, the oil of joy for mourning, the garment of praise for the spirit of heaviness; that they might be called trees of righteousness, the planting of the LORD, that he might be glorified"* (Isa.61:1-3; quoted in Luke 4:18-21). Many understand that Yeshua stopped quoting half way through verse two, just before *"the day of vengeance,"* because the rest of the text describes the "day of the Lord," when Yeshua will come the second time to set up His rulership on earth. Although the Second Coming will involve great judgment, it will also bring great joy to those who believe in Him.

Conclusion

Simeon was what we would call a *Tanach* saint because he was led by the Holy Spirit decades before Yeshua started His ministry. Simeon's Holy Spirit-led declaration becomes a bridge between the promise of the expected Messiah and the promise fulfilled.

> *"And, behold, there was a man in Jerusalem,*
> *whose name was Simeon;*
> *and the same man was just* [righteous] *and devout,*
> *waiting for the consolation* [or comfort, advocate] *of Israel:*
> *and **the Holy Ghost was upon him**.*
> *And it was **revealed unto him by the Holy Ghost**,*

*that he should not see death, before he had seen the Lord's
Messiah.
And **he came by the Spirit** into the temple:
and when the parents brought in the child Yeshua,
to do for him after the custom of the law,
Then took he him up in his arms, and blessed* [or praised] *God,
and said, Lord, now lettest thou thy servant depart in peace,
according to thy word:
For mine eyes have seen thy salvation,
Which thou hast prepared before the face of all people;
A light to lighten* [enlighten] *the Gentiles,
and the glory* [honor, praise] *of thy people Israel"*
(Luke 2:25-32).

---

1   See Deut 4:6-8; Ex 19:4-6a; cp. 1 Pet 2:9.

2   Isaiah 61:1, 2.

3   For Saul it was only temporary and probably a warning from God.

4   See also Psa 31:16; 85:4; 109:26; Isa 25:9; Jer 31:7.

5   See Galatians 6:1.

6   Rom 3:25; 2 Cor 5:21; 1 John 2:1.

7   Matt 5:17-19; 23:23; Luke 24:44; Rom 7:12-14; 8:4.

8   See Psa 45:7; Zech 4:11ff.

9   See Matt 22:43 and Acts 4:24-25 for the New Testament witness that the Holy Spirit spoke through David.

10   *"For he whom God hath sent* [Yeshua] *speaketh the words of God: for God giveth not the Spirit by measure unto him"* (John 3:34).

11   Cp. John 7:24; 8:15-16.

12   See Ephesians 4:4; 1 Corinthians 12:13.

13   See Acts 10:40-43; 17:31; Rom 2:16; 2 Tim 4:1; Rev 19:11-16.

14   Note that the time in which God's grace is available is stated as a year while, in comparison, the time of His judgment is described only as a day! See Isaiah 63:4 as well.

CHAPTER 17

The Holy Spirit in the *Tanach* – Part 3

Let's look at some other aspects of the Spirit of God which were taught by the *Tanach* before the first coming of Messiah Yeshua.

Salvation and God's Spirit

In John 3, Yeshua declared to Nicodemus, *"Except a man be born again, he cannot see the kingdom of God"* (v3).[1] Nicodemus was not able to follow His thinking, asking *"How can these things be?"* (v9). Yeshua responded, *"Art thou a* [the] *master* [teacher] *of Israel, and knowest not these things?"* (v10).

As we explored in Chapter 7, Messiah Yeshua is implying that the concept of being born from above was already revealed in the *Tanach*. Ezekiel 36:25-27 is one of the most comprehensive descriptions in all of Scripture for this doctrine and connects salvation with the indwelling of the Holy Spirit.

God is gathering the scattered Jewish people to the land of Israel (36:24). He states to them, *"Then will I sprinkle clean* [pure] *water upon you, and ye shall be clean* [purified]*: from all your filthiness* [impurity]*, and from all your idols, will I cleanse you. A new heart* [mind, inner man] *also will I give you, and a **new spirit** will I put within you: and I will take away the stony heart out of your flesh, and I will give you an heart of flesh. And **I will put my spirit within you**, and cause you to walk in my statutes, and ye shall keep* [observe] *my judgments, and do them"* (Ezek 36: 25-27; see also 11:19-20). Please note that God's Spirit enables obedience.

Although its literal, final fulfillment awaits Israel's salvation, this prophecy's continuing fulfillment establishes the true Church. The Holy Spirit placed inside us when we become believers enables us to obey God's Word. Look at how the New Testament declares it: *"But ye are not in the flesh, but in the Spirit, if so be that the **Spirit of God dwell in you**. Now if any man have not **the Spirit of Messiah**, he is none of his"* (Rom 8:9).[2] We have God's Holy Spirit dwelling inside of us.

The Holy Spirit justifies and sanctifies us in the name (nature) of Yeshua. *"And such were some of you: but ye are washed, but ye are sanctified* [made holy – separated from the world to God], *but ye are justified* [declared righteous] *in the name of the Lord Yeshua, and **by the Spirit of our God** "* (1 Cor 6:11).[3]

We are made new creations in Messiah. *"Therefore if any man be in Messiah, he is a new creature: old things are passed away; behold, all things are become new"* (2 Cor 5:17).[4]

We have received God's Spirit who causes us to know God's will and enables us to obey His Word. *"For the law of **the Spirit** of life in Messiah Yeshua hath made me free* [liberated] *from the law of sin and death. For what the law could not do, in that it was weak through the flesh,[5] God sending his own Son in the likeness of sinful flesh, and for sin, condemned sin in the flesh: That the righteousness of the law might be fulfilled* [accomplished; realized] *in us, who walk* [i.e., live] *not after* [according to] *the flesh, but after **the Spirit** "* (Rom 8:2-4).[6]

God's Spirit is God's Presence

Often in the *Tanach*, God's Spirit and His presence are paralleled, which means that they indicate the same thing.

*"Whither shall I go from **thy spirit**? or whither shall I flee from **thy presence*** [lit: face]*?"* (Psa 139:7).

*"Neither will I hide **my face** any more from them: for I have poured out **my spirit** upon the house of Israel, saith the Lord GOD"* (Ezek 39:29). "Face" is to be taken figuratively and signifies His presence by His Spirit. No man can literally "see God," that is, experience the fulness of God through his physical senses, and live. As the New Testament makes abundantly clear, if we have His Spirit, we have His presence.

"And I will pray [request of] *the Father, and he shall give you another Comforter* [intercessor, advocate, helper]*, that he may abide with you for ever; Even the **Spirit of truth**; whom **the world cannot*** [does not have the power or ability to] *receive, because it seeth him not, neither knoweth him: but ye know him; for he dwelleth with you, and shall be in you. I will not leave you comfortless* [lit: orphaned]*: I will come to you"* (John 14:16-18).

"Know [Perceive] *ye not that ye are the temple of God, and that **the Spirit of God dwelleth in you**?"* (1 Cor 3:16).

The Blood and the Spirit

We have already mentioned that at times in Scripture, oil can be symbolic of God's Spirit. The following passage is taken from the procedure for the leper's cleansing, which was necessary so that he could re-enter the community of Israel and worship his God.

"And the priest shall take some of the **blood** *of the trespass offering, and the priest shall put it* **upon** *the tip of the right* **ear** *of him that is to be cleansed* [purified], *and upon the thumb of his right* **hand**, *and upon the great toe of his right* **foot**: *And the priest shall take some of the log* [a measure] *of* **oil** *and ...put* **upon** *the tip of the right* **ear** *of him that is to be cleansed, and upon the thumb of his right* **hand**, *and upon the great toe of his right* **foot**, **upon the blood** *of the trespass offering:"* (Lev 14:14-15a,17).

Notice how the oil was placed on top of the blood and not on uncovered flesh. This teaches that God's Spirit will not rest on unconsecrated flesh but only on the one whose life is hid in the Messiah (Col 3:3). Hidden in Yeshua, *"The LORD our righteousness"* (Jer 33:16),[7] we can expect the Spirit to quicken our "ear," that is our mind's perception of the things of God (1 Cor 2:9-16[8]), to empower our "hands" to obey God's will,[9] and to guide our feet, representing our lifestyle choices, on His Way.[10]

The Spirit as Teacher

The following verses confirm what was pointed out in the previous section, that we need God's Spirit to understand the things of God.

"Thou gavest also **thy good spirit to instruct them**, *and withheldest not thy manna from their mouth, and gavest them water for their thirst"* (Neh 9:20).

*'***Teach me to do thy will** [that which delights You]*; for thou art my God;* **thy spirit is good***; lead me into the land of uprightness"* (Psa 143:10).

Messiah Yeshua declares the same thing about God's Spirit, *"But the Comforter* [Advocate, Intercessor, Helper], *which is* **the Holy Ghost**, *whom the Father will send in my name, he* **shall teach you** *all things, and bring all things to your remembrance, whatsoever I have said unto you"* (John 14:26).

"Howbeit **when he, the Spirit of truth, is come, he will guide** [or teach] **you into all truth**: *for* **he shall not speak of himself***; but whatsoever he shall hear, that shall he speak: and he will shew* [announce, make known to] *you things to come. He shall glorify me: for he shall receive of mine, and shall shew it unto you"* (John 16:13-14). Yeshua always speaks the truth, so we must understand that the job of the Holy Spirit is not to bring attention to Himself as Spirit. He comes to glorify

189

Yeshua, to focus us on the Son of God, and to teach and remind us what Yeshua said.

If we find ourselves concentrating on the Holy Spirit, we are not being led by the Holy Spirit! Any Spirit-led meeting, or prayer, or church, or believer – will exalt the Lord Yeshua by name. Search the Scriptures – you will not find, except in Ezekiel 37 when the prophet is specifically commanded by the Lord to do so, one example of a saint speaking or praying directly to the Holy Spirit.

Here are a couple of further points on the Holy Spirit as God's teacher for His children. The will to repent and to seek righteousness is produced by a heart submitted to the Lord's discipline, and is a heart ready to receive God's teaching. The book of Proverbs says, *"**Turn** [repent] you at my reproof [rebuke, correction, chastisement]: behold, I will pour out **my spirit** unto you, I will **make known my words** unto you"* (Prov 1:23). This verse makes a repentant heart the condition for receiving God's teaching by His Spirit.

Peter also links together repentance and receiving God's Spirit, *"Then Peter said unto them, **Repent**, and be baptized every one of you in the name of Yeshua the Messiah for the remission [forgiveness, pardon, release from the bondage] of sins, and ye shall **receive the gift of the Holy Ghost**"* (Acts 2:38).

A final note to always have in mind, especially during prayer, is that we are never to command God's Spirit or angels. *"Who hath directed **the Spirit of the LORD**, or being his counselor hath taught him?"* (Isa 40:13). The biblical approach to prayer is to let the Lord work out the answers to our requests in His way and timing.

The Spirit and God's Punishment or Judgment

God is patient even if we spurn His discipline, but eventually a lack of repentance will result in our punishment. Nehemiah proclaims that by the Spirit of God, God's prophets warned disobedient Israel of danger, *"Yet many years didst thou forbear them, and **testifiedst against them by thy spirit** in thy prophets: yet would they not give ear: therefore gavest thou them into the hand of the people of the lands"* (Neh 9:30).

Here is an example. Through the prophet Isaiah God warns His stubborn children not to partake of an anointing that is of a different spirit from the Holy Spirit, *"Woe to the rebellious [and/or stubborn] children, saith the LORD, that take counsel [make plans], but not of me; and that cover with a covering [lit.: anoint with an anointing], **but not of my spirit**, that they may add sin to sin:"* (Isa 30:1). The result of this rebellion is that dependence on Egypt brings Israel's downfall (see vv. 2-3).

In that familiar passage of John 16:8, Yeshua assures us that the Holy Spirit will convict the world concerning sin, righteousness, and justice, *"And when he is come, **he will reprove** [convict] the world of [concerning] sin, and of [concerning] righteousness, and of [concerning] judgment [justice]:"*

Finally, Stephen links Israel's rebellion, especially that of her leadership, to resisting the influence of God's Spirit. *"Ye stiffnecked [stubborn] and uncircumcised in heart and ears, ye do always **resist the Holy Ghost**: as your fathers did, so do ye"* (Acts 7:51). Of course this verse implies what we have been stating, that the Spirit of God was at work in the lives of God's people even before Yeshua came.

God's Redeemer and the Holy Spirit

In the Old Testament avenging the shedding of innocent blood is part of the job description of a redeemer. Isaiah 59:19b-21 ties together the coming of God's Redeemer with the Spirit of God fighting against the enemy, *"When the enemy shall come in like a flood, **the Spirit of the LORD** shall lift up a standard against [to attack, put to flight] him.[11] And the **Redeemer** [or Avenger] shall come to Zion, and unto them that turn [repent] from transgression [rebellion] in Jacob, saith the LORD.[12] As for me, this is my covenant with them,[13] saith the LORD; **My spirit** that is upon thee, **and my words** which I have put in thy mouth, shall not depart out of thy mouth, nor out of the mouth of thy seed, nor out of the mouth of thy seed's seed, saith the LORD, from henceforth and for ever."[14]*

According to that prophecy, after the Redeemer comes, God's Spirit is promised to be on or in the remnant of Israel forever. Also note that the Spirit's coming on someone anoints their "mouth," the spoken word, so that by His Spirit we can proclaim the Good News. As Yeshua said to His disciples, *"But ye shall **receive power** [or ability], **after that the Holy Ghost is come upon** [overtakes] **you: and ye shall be witnesses unto me** both in Jerusalem, and in all Judaea, and in Samaria, and unto the uttermost part of the earth"* (Acts 1:8).

Isaiah 63:9-14 - God's Spirit in Redemption

This meaty portion of Isaiah has a number of points we want to explore and confirm from elsewhere in the Scriptures. First, here is the entire passage of Isaiah 63:9-14 with verse numbering and some Hebrew word meanings:

9. *"In all their affliction [trouble] he was afflicted, and the angel of his presence [lit. face] saved[15] them: in his love and in his pity [or mercy] he redeemed [ransomed] them; and he bare them, and carried them all the days of old.* **10.** *But they rebelled, and vexed [hurt, grieved] **his holy Spirit**: therefore he was turned to be [transformed into] their enemy, and he fought against them.* **11.** *Then he remembered the days of old, Moses, and his people, saying, Where is*

*he that brought them up out of the sea with the shepherd of his flock?
where is he that put **his holy Spirit** within* [or, in the midst of] *him?*
12. *That led them by the right hand of Moses with his glorious arm,
dividing the water before them, to make himself an everlasting name?*
13. *That led them through the deep, as an horse in the wilderness,
that they should not stumble?* **14**. *As a beast goeth down into the
valley,* **the Spirit of the LORD** *caused him to rest* [settle]*: so didst
thou lead thy people, to make thyself a glorious name."*

Let's study parts of this passage more closely.

v9 – God is afflicted when His people suffer, whether Israel or
the Church. Here is another *Tanach* verse that agrees with this.
*"And the children of Israel said unto the LORD, We have sinned: do
thou unto us whatsoever seemeth good unto thee; deliver* [rescue] *us
only, we pray thee, this day. And they put away the strange* [foreign]
*gods from among them, and served the LORD: and **his** [God's] **soul
was grieved for the misery of Israel**"* (Jud 10:15-16).

The New Testament also contains a confirming passage. *"And
as he* [Saul] *journeyed, he came near Damascus: and suddenly
there shined round about him a light from heaven: And he fell to
the earth, and heard a voice saying unto him, Saul, Saul, why
persecutest thou me? And he said, Who art thou, Lord? And the Lord
said,* **I am Yeshua whom thou persecutest***: it is hard for thee to
kick against the pricks"*[16] (Acts 9:3-5). When the Lord's people
were persecuted, He was persecuted.

vv9,13 – After redemption, God still needs to "carry" us to the
"promised land." It is still His work of grace - working with our
faith in that grace - to see us all the way home. *"Ye have seen what
I did unto the Egyptians, and how **I bare you** on eagles' wings,
and brought you unto myself"* (Exo 19:4). Though God carries us
as He did Israel, we still must walk. *"Come unto me, all ye that
labour and are heavy laden, and **I will give you rest**. Take my
yoke upon you, and learn of me; for I am meek and lowly* [humble]
in heart: and ye shall find [obtain] *rest unto your souls. For my
yoke is easy, and my burden is light"* (Matt 11:28-30). Though we
rest in Him, we still must serve. *"Wherefore, my beloved...work
out your own salvation with fear and trembling. For it is **God which
worketh** [is active] **in you** both to will and to do* [for the sake] *of
his good pleasure"* (Phil 2:12-13). Though God works in us, we
still must choose.

v10 – After redemption we (just like Israel) can grieve His
Spirit, turning God into an adversary who resists what we want
to do, or who even afflicts us! *"And **grieve** [offend] **not the
holy Spirit of God**, whereby ye are sealed unto the day of
redemption* [i.e., full deliverance]*"* (Eph 4:30; cp. Heb 3:7-15;
12:22-29). *"Ye adulterers and adulteresses* [fig: apostates]*, know*

ye not that the friendship of the world is **enmity** [conflict] **with God**? *whosoever therefore will* [deliberately desire to] *be a friend of the world is* [declares or shows himself] *the enemy* [adversary] *of God"* (James 4:4).

v11 – Even in the *Tanach,* God's Holy Spirit was in the midst of His people. *"Yet now be strong* [and/or courageous], *O Zerubbabel, saith the LORD; and be strong, O Joshua...the high priest; and be strong, all ye people of the land, saith the LORD, and work: for I am with you, saith the LORD of hosts: According to the word that I covenanted with you when ye came out of Egypt, so* **my spirit remaineth among you***: fear ye not"* (Hag 2:4-5).

v14 – The Holy Spirit causes us to enter into God's rest, the *Shabbat* rest of redemption, which has been promised to God's people. Through ongoing repentance and obedience we enter God's rest. But, we are only able to enter Yeshua's rest with the Holy Spirit's help in convicting us of sin, leading us to repent, and enabling us to declare truthfully that *"Yeshua is Lord"* (1 Cor 12:3): *"And in that day there shall be a root of Jesse* [David's Son – Yeshua], *which shall stand for an ensign of the people; to it shall the Gentiles seek: and* **his rest** *shall be glorious"* (Isa 11:10).

Yeshua declares the fulfillment, *"Come unto me, all ye that labour and are heavy laden, and* **I will give you rest***. Take my yoke upon you, and learn of me; for I am meek and lowly in heart: and* **ye shall find rest** *unto your souls"* (Matt 11:28-29).[17] Another spirit will not lead us into rest in Yeshua. *"Arise ye, and depart; for* **this is not your rest***: because* **it is polluted***, it shall destroy you, even with a sore destruction. If a man walking in the spirit and falsehood* [NKJV- in a false spirit] *do lie, saying, I will prophesy unto thee of wine and of strong drink; he shall even be the prophet of this people"* (Micah 2:10-11).

vv12,14 – God's purpose in all of salvation history is to glorify His name, in His Son through His Spirit, so that the world will know the real Creator and Father, the God of Israel. When God says that He will sanctify His name through Israel, He specifies that it will happen when Israel is regathered and then redeemed. *"And* **I will sanctify my great name** [character, reputation, glory], *which was profaned* [defiled, polluted] *among the heathen* [nations, gentiles]...*and the heathen shall know that I am the LORD, saith the LORD God, when* **I shall be sanctified** *in you* [Israel] *before their eyes. For I will...gather you out of all countries, and will bring you into your own land.* **Then** *will I sprinkle clean* [pure] *water upon you, and ye shall be clean* [purified]*: from all your filthiness, and from all your idols, will I cleanse you. A new heart* [inner man] *also will I give you, and a new spirit will I put within you...And* **I will put my spirit within**

you, and cause you to walk in my statutes, and ye shall keep [guard, observe] *my judgments, and do them"* (Ezek 36:23-27).

Yeshua tells us that sanctifying God's name should be our number one priority when we pray, *"After this manner therefore pray ye: Our Father which art in heaven,* **Hallowed** [holy, sanctified] **be thy name**. *Thy kingdom come. Thy will be done in earth, as it is in heaven"* (Matt 6:9-10). Sanctifying His name will be the final result of God's making history – His story. *"Who shall not fear thee, O Lord, and* **glorify** [magnify, praise, celebrate] **thy name?** *for thou only art holy: for all nations shall come and worship before thee; for thy judgments are made manifest"* (Rev 15:4).[18]

God Speaks by His Spirit

The Holy Spirit is the One enabling Ezekiel to speak the word of the Lord. *"Therefore prophesy against them, prophesy, O son of man. And* **the Spirit of the LORD** *fell upon me, and said unto me, Speak; Thus saith the LORD; Thus have ye said, O house of Israel: for I know the things that come into your mind* [ruach – spirit], *every one of them"* (Ezek 11:4-5).

God also spoke by His Spirit in the New Testament,[19] and He is still speaking by His Spirit to and through the Church today. But we are cautioned not to be deceived. The Spirit of God will only speak that which agrees with the Word of God. Because He is called *"the Spirit of truth"* (John 14:17; 16:13), we must expect Him to bear witness to God's truth, which is in the Scripture. *"Sanctify them through thy truth: thy word is truth"* (John 17:17). Yeshua is praying that God will sanctify us – keep us separated from the world and for Himself, for His purposes - inasmuch as His Word finds a home in us.

We all need the Holy Spirit's power to fulfill the Great Commission. That is why Satan counterfeits that power by causing excitement or a deceptive appearance of godliness. Yeshua spoke strongly on this subject in the context of the end times, *"For there shall arise false Messiahs* [false anointed ones], *and false prophets, and shall shew* **great signs and wonders**; *insomuch that, if possible, they shall deceive the very elect. Behold, I have told you before"* (Matt 24:24-25).

Ezekiel 37:1-14 – The Spirit of Life is Restoring Now!

The following prophecy is being fulfilled today in the modern nation of Israel through the power of God's Spirit. The words in **bold** are the same Hebrew word, *ruach*. Depending on context it is translated either "spirit," "breath" or "wind":

"The hand of the LORD was upon me, and carried me out in the **spirit** *of the LORD, and set me down in the midst of the valley*

which was full of bones...and, lo, they were very dry. And he said unto me, Son of man, can these bones live? And I answered, O Lord GOD, thou knowest. Again he said unto me, Prophesy...unto them, O ye dry bones, hear the word of the LORD. Thus saith the Lord GOD...Behold, I will cause **breath** *to enter into you, and ye shall live: And I will lay sinews upon you, and will bring up flesh upon you, and cover you with skin, and put* **breath** *in you, and ye shall live; and ye shall know* [by experience conforming to God's Word] *that I am the LORD. So I prophesied as I was commanded: and as I prophesied, there was a noise* [or voice], *and behold a shaking, and the bones came together...the sinews and the flesh came up upon them, and the skin covered them above: but there was no* **breath** *in them. Then said he unto me, Prophesy unto the* **wind**... *and say to the* **wind**, *Thus saith the Lord GOD; Come from the four* **winds**, *O* **breath**, *and breathe upon these slain, that they may live. So I prophesied as he commanded me, and the* **breath** *came into them, and they lived, and stood up upon their feet, an exceeding great army. Then he said unto me, Son of man, these bones are the whole house of Israel: behold, they say, Our bones are dried, and our hope is lost: we are cut off for our parts* [divided from each other]. *Therefore prophesy and say unto them, Thus saith the Lord GOD; Behold, O my people, I will open your graves, and cause you to come up*[20] *out of your graves, and bring you into the land of Israel. And ye shall know that I am the LORD, when I have opened your graves, O my people, and brought you up*[21] *out of your graves, And shall put my* **spirit** *in you, and ye shall live, and I shall place you* [settle you permanently] *in your own land: then shall ye know that I the LORD have spoken it, and performed it, saith the LORD"* (Ezek 37:1-14).

In this portion the *ruach,* or spirit, is associated with life. A number of times here it is prophesied that the dead will be resurrected when touched by the *ruach,* the Spirit of the Lord. Although by analogy this section can apply to being born from above, the plain meaning, especially from the context (Ezekiel 34-39), points to the current resurrection of the nation of Israel out of the grave of the Holocaust. Very many *"dry bones,"* having *"our hope...lost,"* and being *"cut off"* one from another describe the Holocaust, while *"an exceeding great army"* and settling us in our *"own land"* describe current events in Israel.

A Closing Thought

God's word to Zerubbabel is relevant to all of God's people. When it comes to doing His work, we must always remember that it is *"...Not by might, nor by power, but by* **my spirit**, *saith the LORD of hosts"* (Zech 4:6).

1 Here is an alternative rendering of the Greek: "Unless a man is born from above, he cannot know the rulership of God."

2 See also Rom 8:11,14-16; Eph 1:13-14; 1 John 3:24.

3 See also 2 Cor 5:21; 1 Pet 1:22; Rev 19:8.

4 See also Matt 9:16-17; 1 Cor 5:7.

5 Paul often uses "flesh" to mean man's earthly nature (mind and body apart from divine influence) which is predisposed to sin and opposed to God.

6 See also Acts 2:16-17; Rom 8:13-14; Heb 8:10; 1 John 3:24.

7 Cp. Psa 24:5; 31:1; Isa 45:24; 54:17; 1 Cor 1:30; 2 Cor 5:21.

8 *"But as it is written, Eye hath not seen, nor ear heard, neither have entered into the heart* [soul, mind] *of man, the things which God hath prepared for them that love him.* **But God hath revealed them unto us by his Spirit**: *for the Spirit searcheth* [investigates] *all things, yea, the deep things of God. For what man knoweth* [understands] *the things of a man, save the spirit of man which is in him? even so* **the things of God knoweth no man, but the Spirit of God**. *Now we* **have received**, *not the spirit of the world, but* **the spirit which is of** [from] **God; that we might know the things that are freely given to us of God**. *Which things also we speak, not in the words which man's wisdom teacheth, but which* **the Holy Ghost teacheth**; *comparing* [or interpreting] *spiritual things with spiritual. But the natural man receiveth not the things of the Spirit of God: for they are foolishness* [absurd] *unto him: neither can he know* [able to perceive, understand] *them, because they are spiritually discerned* [examined, judged]. *But he that is spiritual judgeth all things, yet he himself is judged of no man. For who hath known the mind* [thoughts, purposes, counsel] *of the Lord, that he may instruct him? But* **we have the mind of Messiah**" (1 Cor 2:9-16).

9 See Deut 14:28-29; Psa 90:17; Matt 7:21,24; 1 Cor 4:12; Eph 6:8; 1 John 3:7.

10 See Deut 10:12; Psa 86:11; Prov 3:5-6; Rom 6:4; 8:4; 2 Cor 5:7; Eph 5:8.

11 Cp. 2 Thes 2:8, *"And then shall that Wicked* [lit: lawless] *be revealed, whom the Lord shall consume* [abolish, destroy] *with the spirit of his mouth, and shall destroy with the brightness* [appearance] *of his coming:"*

12 *"And so all Israel shall be saved: as it is written, There shall come out of Sion the Deliverer, and shall turn away* [remove] *ungodliness from Jacob:"* (Rom 11:26; cp. Acts 3:19,26).

13 See Jer 31:31-34; Ezek 36:26-27; Heb 8:6-13.

14 See John 7:37-39; Rom 8:9.

15 *Hoshea* comes from the same root word as Yeshua.

16 According to Thayer's definition (*PC Study Bible*, Biblesoft Co.) *"to kick against the pricks"* is an idiomatic saying that means "to offer vain and perilous or ruinous resistance."

17 In Hebrews 3:11-4:11 the word "rest" occurs eleven times.

18 See also John 12:28; 17:6,26; Rom 9:17.

19 See Acts 1:2,16; 8:29; 10:19; 21:11; 28:25.

20 This is from the same Hebrew root word as *aliyah,* the word used today for Jews immigrating to Israel. It literally means to go up, since Jerusalem, with the location of God's Temple on top of a ridge, was always the ultimate goal for returning Jews. From whatever the direction of approach, it was necessary to go up.

21 See previous endnote.

PART THREE

Taught Ones

Israel's Olive Tree has a healthy *Tanach* rootstock, but many of the natural branches are weak or broken. The Gardener prunes the weak branches to strengthen them. He also grafts in many branches taken from wild olive trees. The two kinds of branches joined in one tree, bear spiritual fruit for the glory of God.

CHAPTER 18

The Bride in the *Tanach*

The Mystery of Messiah

Have you ever read Ephesians 3:3-6 and considered what Paul, as a Jewish believer, must have been thinking? *"How that by revelation he made known unto me the **mystery**; (as I wrote afore in few words, Whereby, when ye read, ye may understand my knowledge in the **mystery** of Messiah) Which in other ages was not made known unto the sons of men, as it is now revealed unto his holy apostles and prophets by the Spirit; **That the Gentiles should be fellowheirs** [with whom? with the Jews!], and **of the same body** [again, with the Jews], and **partakers** [once more, with the Jews] **of his promise in Christ** [the Jewish Messiah] **by the gospel**."* Paul was declaring that the mystery which God revealed to him and the other apostles was the extraordinary inclusion of gentiles, *uncircumcised in flesh*, with Jews[1] in God's plan of salvation!

Let's explore the *Tanach* roots of gentile salvation, as well as the concept of a global body of believers, the Bride. First we need to understand that the New Testament word "mystery" means ."..a divine truth, formerly hidden, but now supernaturally revealed to men, which can be fully understood only by the saved individual though the illumination of the Holy Spirit."[2]

The most surprising act of God in the life of the early "Church"[3] was not Jewish salvation, but that He had *"also to the Gentiles granted repentance unto life"* through Yeshua, the Jewish Messiah (Acts 11:18b). Can you hear Rabbi Saul's (Paul's) delight and joy, even amazement, when he proclaims in Colossians 1:25-27, *"Whereof I am made a minister [servant], according to the dispensation [stewardship] of God which is given to me for you, to* *fulfil the word of God; Even **the mystery** which hath been hid from ages and from generations, but now is made manifest* [revealed] *to his saints: To whom God would make known what is the riches of the glory of **this mystery among the Gentiles; which is Christ** [the Jewish Messiah] **in you, the hope of glory**:."* Through the Messiah promised to Israel, Jews and gentiles now have equal access to God. And, although like male and female they are not identical, they are one in Messiah Yeshua.

Now, where was this mystery "formerly hidden?" It was hidden in the *Tanach*.

Prophecies of Gentile Salvation

The New Testament declares that the universal Gospel was proclaimed before the birth of the Messiah. *"And the scripture* [the *Tanach*], *foreseeing that God would justify the **heathen**[4] through faith, preached* [announced] *before* [beforehand] *the gospel unto Abraham, saying, In thee shall **all nations** be blessed"* (Gal 3:8).

That part where Paul quotes from the *Tanach*, *"In thee shall all nations be blessed,"* is found in Genesis 12:3, and confirmed to Abraham twice, in Genesis 18:18 and 22:17-18. The Lord proclaimed that same "Gospel" to Isaac in Genesis 26:3-4 and to Jacob in Genesis 28:13-14. God thereby prophesied that all nations/gentiles would be blessed through the *seed*, or line, of Abraham, Isaac and ultimately Jacob (the children of Israel - the Jewish people).[5]

Looking back through the filter of the New Testament, we see the ultimate Seed to be Yeshua, the perfect representative of Israel. He was the One who accomplished Israel's task completely, bringing gentiles to a saving knowledge of the God of Israel. In fact one of His prophesied names is "Israel." *"Listen, O isles, unto me; and hearken, ye people, from far; The LORD hath called me from the womb; from the bowels of my mother hath he made mention of my name...And said unto me, **Thou art my servant, O Israel** [lit: Prince with God], **in whom I will be glorified**"* (Isa 49:1,3).[6]

As you read these other verses concerning gentile salvation in the *Tanach*, remember that the Hebrew word *"goyim"* can be translated "nations," "heathen," or "gentiles."

In the midst of apparent end time upheavals, God says to Israel through the psalmist, *"Be still, and know that I am God; I will be exalted among the **heathen**, I will be exalted in the earth* [or land]*"* (Psa 46:10). God declares He will be exalted in defending His people against the world's persecution. A theme that occurs often in the *Tanach* is God's reputation and glory increasing among the gentiles because of what He does in and through Israel in the last days.[7]

These next two quotes relate to the gentiles under God's coming Messianic kingdom. In Psalm 72 the author, although writing specifically about King Solomon, prophesies about the ultimate King, *"Yea, all kings shall fall down* [bow down in worship] *before him: all nations shall serve him"* (Psa 72:11, cp. Rev 11:15).

Isaiah, whose prophecies often touch on Messiah's kingdom, states in 2:2, *"And it shall come to pass in the last days, that the mountain of the LORD's house shall be established in the top of the mountains, and shall be exalted above the hills; and all nations shall flow unto it."*

Based on "even" gentiles being saved through Yeshua's sacrifice for their sins, we can apply to the present day the following Scripture promises. [Following each quotation and its Tanach reference are superscript numbers referring to endnotes which give some New Testament verses showing the fulfillment of these *Tanach* promises.]

"And in that day there shall be a root of Jesse, which shall stand for an ensign [banner, sign] *of the people; to it shall the **Gentiles** seek: and his rest shall be glorious"* (Isa 11:10).[8]

"Behold my servant, whom I uphold; mine elect [chosen One], *in whom my soul delighteth; I have put my spirit upon him: he shall bring forth judgment* [and/or justice] *to the **Gentiles**...I the LORD have called thee in righteousness, and will hold* [strengthen] *thine hand, and will keep* [sustain; guard over] *thee, and give thee for a covenant of the people, for a light of the **Gentiles**..."* (Isa 42:1,6; see the context, vv 1-12).[9]

*"Also the **sons of the stranger**, that join themselves to the LORD, to serve* [or obey] *him, and to love the name* [nature; character] *of the LORD, to be his servants, every one that keepeth the sabbath from polluting* [profaning; desecrating] *it, and taketh hold of my covenant; Even them will I bring to my holy mountain, and make them joyful in my house of prayer: their burnt offerings and their sacrifices shall be accepted upon mine altar; **for mine house shall be called an house of prayer for all people**. The Lord GOD which gathereth the outcasts of Israel saith, Yet will I gather **others** to him, beside those that are gathered unto him"* (Isa 56:6-8; see the context, vv 3-8).[10]

Here are several verses that apply to the end of this current period, the end of the time of the gentiles.[11] The following verse from Jeremiah occurs in the context of God sending fishers and hunters to gather His people back to their land (16:16). One of the results of this final regathering of Israel is a revelation among the gentiles that God is still the God of Israel. Or as Jeremiah says, *"O LORD, my strength, and my fortress, and my refuge in the day of affliction* [distress], *the **Gentiles** shall come unto thee from the ends of the earth, and shall say, Surely our fathers have inherited* *lies* [also deceptions], *vanity* [emptiness], *and things wherein there is no profit"* (Jer 16:19).[12]

At some time during that same period,[13] God defends Israel from the invasion of Gog and Magog, not because Israel is sinless, but to fulfill His Word for His glory. *"Thus will I magnify myself, and sanctify myself; and I will be known in the eyes of **many nations**, and they shall know that I am the LORD"* (Ezek 38:23; cp. Rev 15:3-4).

Finally a verse that applies to that timeframe as well as to the millennium reign of Messiah Yeshua, *"For from the rising of the sun even unto the going down of the same my name* [reputation; fame] *shall be great among the **Gentiles**; and in every place incense shall be offered unto my name, and a pure offering: for my name shall be great among the **heathen**, saith the LORD of hosts"* (Mal 1:11).[14]

Many other verses point to believing gentiles having a part in the Messiah of Israel. We list more of these in this endnote.[15]

Tanach **Examples of Gentile Salvation**

Once we know what to look for, we discover many examples of gentile salvation throughout the *Tanach*. Some might object to using the word "salvation" for what occurs in the Old Testament because it took place before the Cross. However Chapter 11 of the New Testament book of Hebrews states that there will be many Old Testament saints in heaven. Yeshua also refers to *Tanach* saints in His kingdom, *"And I say unto you, That many shall come from the east and west, and shall sit down with Abraham, and Isaac, and Jacob, in the kingdom of heaven"* (Matt 8:11; also see Luke 13:28). Their salvation rested on the same foundation as ours - faith/trust in the Word of God, made possible by God's grace in their lives.[16]

All the early faith heroes, Abel, Enoch, Noah, etc., were gentiles. Technically speaking, there were no Jews before Abraham had a great-grandson named Judah. Even Abraham and Sarah were gentiles. According to the Word, Abraham was the son of an idol worshipper. *"And Joshua said unto all the people, Thus saith the LORD God of Israel, Your fathers dwelt on the other side of the flood* [lit: river, i.e., the Euphrates] *in old time, even Terah, the father of Abraham, and the father of Nachor: and they served other gods"* (Josh 24:2).

Genesis 14:18b calls Melchizedek, who was a gentile, *"...priest of the most high God."* As King-Priest of Salem (later, Jerusalem) he blessed Abraham and accepted a tithe from him (14:19-20). That shows that God always had His people who declared His Name before men.

In the story of Moses, a Midianite priest named Jethro becomes Moses' father-in-law (Exo 3:1) as well as his counselor (Exo 18:19). Jethro was blessed when he blessed Israel in caring for the fugitive Moses (Exo 2:20-21). Jethro recognized the God of Israel as the only "capital-G" God. Not only did Jethro sacrifice to Him, but he also ate a covenant meal with Moses, Aaron, and the elders of Israel, indicating that he was now an integral part of the commonwealth of the house of Israel. *"And Jethro said, Blessed be the LORD, who hath delivered you out of the hand of the Egyptians, and out of the hand of Pharaoh, who hath delivered the people from under the hand of the Egyptians. Now I know that the LORD is greater than all gods* [lit.: mighty ones]: *for in the thing wherein they dealt proudly he was above them. And **Jethro**, Moses' father in law, took a burnt offering and sacrifices for God: and Aaron came, and all the elders of Israel, to eat bread with Moses' father in law before* [in the presence of] *God"* (Exo 18:10-12).[17]

Two gentile women, Rahab and Ruth, joined the household of Israel (Josh 6:25; Ruth 1:16-17; 2:12), and became ancestors of the promised Messiah (Matt 1:5).

God calls Job, a gentile of the land of Uz and probably contemporary with Abraham and Melchizedek, *"...my servant Job, that there is none like him in the earth, a perfect* [morally complete] *and an upright man, one that feareth God, and escheweth* [turns from] *evil..."* (Job 2:3b, see 1:1).

Balaam,[18] and Naaman the Syrian general, and Nebuchadnezzar[19] are a few well-known *Tanach* figures from among the nations who once had, or came to, a knowledge of the true and living God. These examples clarify that gentile salvation (in many cases without circumcision), did occur in the *Tanach*. Yet the fullness of gentile salvation comes only after our Lord Yeshua's death and resurrection.

God Speaks to Gentile Believers in the *Tanach*

The Lord speaks directly to the "nations," the gentiles, in the *Tanach*. Who are these gentiles to whom He gives vital marching orders? Consider which gentiles are the only ones reading and believing His Word today. They are those who have been grafted into Israel's Olive Tree; they are part of Messiah's Bride; they are servant believers in Messiah Yeshua. In His House, the "Commonwealth of Israel" (Eph 2:12), they have been given spiritual "permanent residency."[20]

The following verses indicate that when God speaks in the *Tanach* directly to His Body/Bride it is in reference to their response and responsibility to the restoration of the nation of Israel. In Isaiah 40:1-2a, the most familiar verse in this regard,

God is speaking to those of His people who are not of Israel. *"Comfort ye,* **comfort ye my people** [Israel[21]], **saith your God**. *Speak ye comfortably to* [lit: "Speak to the heart of"] *Jerusalem..."* God speaks to a people and calls Himself "your God." Besides Israel there has never been, nor will there ever be, any people God would declare His own other than gentile believers.

Isaiah 52:7 says, *"How beautiful* [feeling at home; comfortable] *upon the mountains are the feet of* **him that bringeth good tidings**, *that publisheth* [proclaims] *peace; that bringeth good tidings* [good news, gospel] *of good, that publisheth salvation; that* **saith unto Zion**, *Thy God reigneth!"* Who else could that be speaking of, other than the Body of Messiah, who are commissioned to bring good news and proclaim peace and salvation to the whole world, to the Jew first (Rom 1:16)?

The Lord is saying that His Church should proclaim to Israel, **"Your** *God reigns!"* [NKJV].[22] Our Lord, the God of all born-again believers, is still the God of Israel. Paul says that in Romans 11:24-29. We are not proclaiming to the Jewish people some strange god, but *their* God, and *their* promised Messiah. If the Gospel were presented to Jewish people in this way, the response might be different from the common, "Jesus may be for the gentiles, but I'm Jewish." Gentile believers, we urge you to proclaim to Jewish people the good news that *their* God reigns!

God speaks to the Body of Messiah in parts of Isaiah 62 also. In verses 6b-7, God wants the watchmen He has placed on Jerusalem's walls to be zealous in intercession for Israel, or as these verses state, *"...keep not silent, and give him* [God] *no rest til he establish, and til he make Jerusalem a praise in the earth."* Then in verses 10-11a, the Body is commanded to *"Go through, go through the gates; prepare ye the way of the people* [Israel]; *cast up, cast up* [build up] *the highway; gather out the stones; lift up a standard* [banner] *for the people. Behold, the LORD hath proclaimed unto* **the end** [farthest part] **of the world**, **Say** *ye to* the daughter of **Zion, Behold, thy salvation cometh...**"

Those stones on the highway causing Israel to stumble - what can they represent? Here are some strong possibilities:

~ the Church's past and present anti-Semitism and persecution of the Jews

~ replacement theology appropriating Israel's blessings for the Church while leaving God's curses for Israel

~ anti-Judaism insisting that a Jew who accepts Yeshua must become a gentile in lifestyle and commitments

~ resisting God's work of restoring Israel to her land

~ believers thinking that they must take an anti-Zionist stance in order to evangelize Moslems

~ interpreting the Bible by a humanistic world-view instead of by a Hebraic/*Tanach* perspective

Each one of these "stones" in the "highway" is a method used by the Adversary to weaken, deceive, and destroy God's people, both Jew and gentile, for gentiles who do these things come under God's curse (Gen 12:3).

Another area with which God commands the believer to be involved is *aliyah* (literally "going up"). In modern Hebrew *aliyah* means Jewish immigration to Israel - Jews returning to the land God has sworn to give them forever. A major goal of God's redemptive plan is to inspire, guide, and support *aliyah*. *"For, lo, the days come, saith the LORD, that I will bring again the captivity of my people Israel and Judah, saith the LORD: and I will cause them to return to the land that I gave to their fathers, and they shall possess it"* (Jer 30:3); *"Yea, I will rejoice over them to do them good, and I will plant* [establish] *them in this land assuredly with my whole heart and with my whole soul"* (Jer 32:41).

The Church is prophesied to facilitate this move of God. While reading the following scripture remember that God is speaking to Israel *about* the gentiles. *"Thus saith the Lord GOD, Behold, I will lift up mine hand to the Gentiles, and set up my standard* [signal; banner] *to the people: and they shall bring thy sons in their arms, and thy daughters shall be carried upon their shoulders"* (Isa 49:22).[23]

Is the Bride of Messiah carrying Zion's sons in her arms, Zion's daughters on her shoulders? Is she heeding the warning in Isaiah 60:12, *"For the nation* [gentile] *and kingdom that will not serve thee* [Israel] *shall perish; yea, those nations shall be utterly wasted."* We bless the Lord that He is revealing this to many believers throughout His kingdom. There are many individual Christians, as well as many Christian organizations who are standing in the gap now, helping to carry home Israel's children – for God's glory.[24]

There is an amazing prophecy in the *Tanach* that mentions Christians by name! In Jeremiah 30:24b God says *"...in the latter days ye shall consider it"* concerning what He has just declared in that chapter. The Hebrew for *"latter days"* is literally, "last days" and the very next verse (a new chapter) immediately continues with, *"At the same time..."* So during these last days, in 31:6, *"...there shall be a day, that the watchmen upon the mount Ephraim shall cry, Arise ye, and let us go up to Zion unto the LORD our God."* The biblical Hebrew word for "watchmen" is *notzrim,* which is the modern Hebrew word for "Christians"!

Obviously *notzrim* did not mean "Christians" in Jeremiah's day, but God, who knows the end from the beginning, used that specific word in this verse to leave no doubt that He is speaking to last days believers. (There are other Hebrew words for "watchmen" that He could have used.) And what does God then say to these believers? *"For thus saith the LORD; Sing with gladness for Jacob* [the Jewish people], *and shout among the chief of the nations:* **publish** [proclaim] **ye, praise ye, and say, O LORD, save thy people, the remnant of Israel**" (Jer 31:7). God is speaking to a people who are not Israel, but who will be able to hear His voice in the last days. He gives a command to *"Sing... shout... publish... praise... and say,"* which seems to mean sing/praise, educate, and intercede for the salvation of Israel.

In response to His Bride's obedience, especially in intercession, the Lord has brought and will continue to bring His people back to the land of Israel (31:8-9). Why is that? Because He has declared that the majority of Jewish people who will be saved, will be saved in the land of Israel. They will be brought back as unbelievers. Ezekiel 36:24-27 is one of the foremost examples of this sequence: *"For I will take you from among the heathen, and gather you out of all countries, and will bring you into your own land.* **Then** *will I sprinkle clean* [pure] *water upon you, and ye shall be clean* [pure]*: from all your filthiness, and from all your idols, will I cleanse* [purify] *you. A new heart also will I give you, and a new spirit will I put within you: and I will take away the stony heart out of your flesh, and I will give you an heart of flesh. And I will put my spirit within you, and cause you to walk in my statutes, and ye shall keep my judgments, and do them."*[25]

The Lord continues in Jeremiah 31:10, *"***Hear** *the word of the LORD, O* **ye nations**, [gentiles who are listening for His voice] **and declare** *it in the isles afar off, and say,* **He** *that scattered Israel* **will gather** *him,* **and keep** [guard] *him, as a shepherd doth his flock."* God desires His Bride to proclaim this to the world. In the midst of the news, views and confusion of the current situation in Israel, this is what our Father is doing. He wants the Church and the world to wake up to His mighty acts as He fulfills His Word before our eyes (Jer 1:12). Israel's national deliverance from both her enemies and her sins, has global consequences, and God desires the Church to take an active role in bringing it about. Paul sums up what is at stake in these verses.

> *"Now if the fall of them be the riches of the world,*
> *and the diminishing of them the riches of the Gentiles;*
> *how much more their fulness* [completeness]*?...*
> *For if the casting away* [rejection; repudiation]
> *of them be the reconciling* [restoration] *of the world,*
> *what shall the receiving of them be, but life from the dead?"*
> (Romans 11:12,15)

1   Paul is saying, with the Jews, not instead of the Jews. Replacement "theology" says instead of the Jews.

2   *Wycliffe Bible Encyclopedia,* Vol. 2, p.1164.

3   "Church" is in quotes because many people think of it as a gentile institution, even a physical building, as opposed to what it really denotes - the living community of believers, both Jew and gentile, in Messiah Yeshua.

4   The Hebrew word *"goyim"* and the Greek word *"ethnos"* can both be translated as "nations," or "peoples."

5   Ishmael (Gen 17:18-21; 21:12) and Esau (Gen 25:23; 28:3-4, 12-15) were not recipients of this specific covenant.

6   For proof that this verse refers to Messiah Yeshua and not the people Israel, see verses 5 and 6 of this passage in Isaiah 49.

7   For example, see Jer 33:7-9; Ezek 36:23; Rom 11:12,15.

8   Cp. Matt 2:1-2; 11:28-29; 12:17-21; Rom 15:9-12; Heb 4:9-11.

9   Cp. Luke 2:32; John 8:12; Acts 26:22-23.

10   Cp. John 10:16; Eph 2:11-22; 1 Thes 1:9-10.

11   God's economy seems to contain periods of overlap. Yeshua died but the sacrifices still went on in the Temple for 40 years. In June 1967, Jerusalem was no longer under gentile rule, and although Jews are receiving Messiah Yeshua in greater numbers than at any time since the first century, we are still in that overlap as the time of the gentiles comes to a close and before all Israel is saved.

12   Cp. I Thes 1:9-10; 1 Pet 1:18-19; Rev 7:9-10.

13   Some scholars see two fulfillments of this event, one here and one at the end of the Millennial reign of Messiah (see Rev 20:7-8).

14   Cp. Matt 28:19-20; Acts 15:16-17; Rev 11:15.

15   Deut 32:21; 1 Chr 16:31; Psa 65:2,5; 66:4; 68:32; 86:9; Isa 45:22-24; 49:1-7; 52:15; 55:4-5; Jer 3:17; Dan 7:13-14; Zech 8:20-23; 14:8-9,16.

16   See 2 Tim 3:14-15; Heb 11:39-40.

17   Covenant meals (also see Gen 26:26-30: 31:44-47) are the *Tanach* foundation for our covenant meal, Communion or the Lord's Supper. Read the following scripture about Aaron's and his sons' consecration to the priesthood and recognize that believers are now a kingdom of priests. *"And they shall eat those things wherewith the atonement was made, to consecrate and to sanctify them: but a stranger shall not eat thereof, because they are holy"* (Exo 29:33). Notice the parallels with the Bible's commands to us as found in 1 Corinthians 11:23-29.

18   Although there is no doubt that Balaam knew the true God, as he used God's covenant name *Yahweh* in addressing Him (Num 22:8-9,18,34-35; 23:3-5,8, etc.) we are not saying that Balaam was a *Tanach* saint (Num 24:1). The fruit of this particular prophet in facilitating Israel's apostasy (Rev 2:14), reminds us of Yeshua's warning against false prophets found in Matthew 7:15-23.

19   Naaman – 2 Kin 5:17; Nebuchadnezzar – Dan 4:34-37.

20   In the present day nation of Israel a non-Jew who has shown himself invaluable to the nation is often given what is termed "permanent residency," which includes almost all the rights of a citizen except voting in national elections.

21 In the *Tanach,* the expression "My people" of necessity refers to the descendants of Jacob.

22 It is regrettable that this scripture was altered when a song using it was written. To Jewish ears it sounds like replacement theory when gentile believers sing, "Our God reigns." Although technically correct, scripturally and especially in context, it borders on changing the Word of God.

23 See also Isaiah 60:1-16; 61:5; 66:18-23.

24 For practical ways to participate in fulfilling these prophecies, contact:

Christian Friends of Israel, (see contact information on the copyright page of this book).

Bridges For Peace (www.bridgesforpeace.com or write BFP, Box 1093, Jerusalem, Israel, or call 972-2-624-5004).

International Christian Embassy, Jerusalem (email <icej@icej.org.il> or write ICEJ, Box 1192, Jerusalem 91010, Israel or call 972-2-566-9823).

Ebenezer Emergency Fund (www.ebenezer-ef.org or write EEF, Ebenezer House, 5a Poole Road, Bournemouth BH2 5QJ, UK, or call 01202 294455 in UK, or in USA call 252-491-9201).

All these Christian organizations plus many more are actively involved in helping with the restoration of Israel.

25 Other examples include Jer 31:7-9; 32:37ff; Joel 2:18ff (in context this can only be Israel's salvation); Zech 12:10; Matt 23:37-39.

CHAPTER 19

Israel and Our Salvation

The last days restoration of the state of Israel is *essential* for believers' assurance of their eternal salvation. As extreme as this statement appears, it is a biblical fact.

Replacement Theory

A fundamental concept of our Biblical faith has been eaten away by centuries of anti-Semitism and replacement theology (better yet, "replacement theory" since there is no biblical basis for the idea). Replacement theory teaches that the Church has replaced Israel as the people of God and that Israel as a people and nation now have no special significance in the purposes and plan of God. The part of the Church which endorses replacement thinking claims all the *Tanach* promises of blessing while saying the Jewish people, because they rejected their Messiah, receive all the *Tanach* curses. But concerning this issue Paul, the apostle to the gentiles, cries by the Holy Spirit in Romans 11, *"God forbid!"*

Unfortunately, replacement thinking is still entrenched in the Church. Many Christians especially in the West give little credence to the 1948 rebirth of the nation of Israel as a miracle. Other believers see it only as a fulfillment of prophecy. Yet without the fulfillment of the promised miracle of Israel's resurrection in the last days, we would have little physical evidence, aside from archaeological interpretations, that the Bible is the word of the living, faithful, promise-keeping God. If we have doubts about God keeping His promises to Israel, how can we trust in what God says about the "foolishness" [1] of Yeshua's death on the Cross for our salvation? Let's follow this reasoning step by step.

Whose World?

The Scriptures state that God is the Lord of the earth. Therefore, any teaching that Satan gained dominion over this world at the Fall, is not based on the Word. Yes, he is the god of this world's man-made system, but only because man is a slave to sin. In spite of this, some teach that when Adam fell, he forfeited dominion of the world to Satan who then became the god of the earth. Such teachers imply that God had to figure out a legal way to come back into the world, so He decided to do this through a virgin's womb.

The Word tells us a different story. When Adam and Eve fell, God did not ask Satan's or anyone else's permission for what He was about to do. He cursed the serpent, then proclaimed the curses which the sin of Adam and Eve would bring, finally cursing the very ground. Both before and *after* the Fall, God is Lord of the world. Here are some post-Fall verses to verify this key doctrine.

*"And I will sever in that day the land of Goshen, in which my people dwell, that no swarms of flies shall be there; to the end thou mayest know that **I am the LORD in the midst of the earth**"* (Exo 8:22).

"And Moses said unto him [Pharaoh], *As soon as I am gone out of the city, I will spread abroad my hands unto the LORD; and the thunder shall cease, neither shall there be any more hail; that thou mayest know how that **the earth is the LORD's**"* (Exo 9:29; see 9:14-16).

*"**The earth is the LORD's**, and the fulness thereof; the world, and they that dwell therein"* (Psa 24:1).

*"Ye are my witnesses, saith the LORD, and my servant whom I have chosen: that ye may know and believe me, and understand that I am he: **before me there was no God formed, neither shall there be after me**"* (Isa 43:10).

Even Messiah Yeshua proclaims that His Father is God of the world. *"At that time Yeshua answered and said, I thank thee, O Father, Lord of heaven and earth..."* (Matt 11:25a).

God is still God, the only Lord of the earth, even after the Fall. Satan is not a god of anything except deception, embodied in the world system. The above scriptures indicating this are only a small sample of what the Bible says about God's sovereignty over His planet.

Whose Land?

Not only does God own the whole planet, but He has chosen a plot of ground in the Middle East which He calls *His* land and *His* inheritance, the land of Israel.

*"The land shall not be sold for ever: **for the land is mine**; for ye are strangers and sojourners with me"* (Lev 25:23). God could not be more precise about to whom the land of Israel belongs. Some confirming verses follow:

*"LORD, thou hast been favourable unto **thy land**: thou hast brought back the captivity of Jacob"* (Psa 85:1). The idiomatic term, *"the captivity of Jacob,"* refers to God's people, the Jews, living outside the Promised Land, in exile.[2]

*"And first I will recompense their iniquity and their sin double; because they have defiled **my land**, they have filled **mine inheritance** with the carcases of their detestable and abominable things"* (Jer 16:18). In that verse, the Lord calls the land of Israel His inheritance (see Exo 15:17).

He also calls the people of Israel His inheritance![3] *"In that day shall Israel be the third with Egypt and with Assyria, even a blessing in the midst of the land* [earth]*: Whom the LORD of hosts shall bless, saying, Blessed be Egypt my people, and Assyria the work of my hands, and **Israel mine inheritance** "* (Isa 19:24-25). Clearly land and people are inseparably linked in God's mind. Both are His inheritance and He uses them together to demonstrate to the world His sovereignty and faithfulness.

"Therefore thus saith the Lord GOD; Surely in the fire of my jealousy have I spoken against the residue of the heathen, and against all Idumea [Edom, Esau]*, which have appointed **my land** into their possession with the joy of all their heart, with despiteful minds, to cast it out for a prey"* (Ezek 36:5). All of Ezekiel 36 describes what the Lord has done and prophesies what He will do with the land and people of Israel. It is a chapter pinpointing God's acts in and through Israel today!

"For, behold, in those days, and in that time, when I shall bring again [return] *the captivity of Judah and Jerusalem* [after 1967]*, I will also gather all nations, and will bring them down into the valley of Jehoshaphat* [meaning "the LORD is judge"]*, and will plead with* [judge] *them there for my people and for my heritage Israel, whom they have scattered among the nations, and **parted*** [partitioned, divided] ***my land** "* (Joel 3:1-2). God declares that He will judge nations involved in carving up Israel, including in any "land for peace" process. The more nations try to push Israel to give away what ultimately is not hers to give, the more those nations will suffer judgments, either what insurance companies label "acts of God" (natural disasters of all kinds), or terror attacks, vicious crimes, lawlessness, immorality, and even war.[4] These will intensify if nations ignore these as warnings from God.

The Gospel To and Through the Jews

When God first called Abraham He promised him a land and blessings. *"Now the LORD had said unto Abram, Get thee out of thy country, and from thy kindred, and from thy father's house, unto a **land** that I will shew thee: And I will make of thee a great* *nation, and I will **bless** thee, and make thy name great; and thou shalt be a **blessing**: And I will **bless** them that **bless** thee, and curse him that curseth thee: **and in thee shall all families of the earth be blessed**"* (Gen 12:1-3).

Part of God's initial promise declared that through Abraham's seed all the "families," meaning nations or gentiles[5] of the earth would be blessed. Paul states that this was the Gospel preached to Abraham. *"And the scripture, foreseeing that God would justify the heathen through faith, preached before **the gospel** unto Abraham, saying, In thee shall all nations be blessed"* (Gal 3:8).

The promise of the gospel was confirmed to Abraham after he obeyed God in his willingness to sacrifice Isaac, the son of the promise. *"By myself have I sworn, saith the LORD, for because thou hast done this thing, and hast not withheld thy son, thine only son: That in blessing I will bless thee, and in multiplying I will multiply thy seed as the stars of the heaven, and as the sand which is upon the sea shore; and thy seed shall possess the gate of his enemies; **And in thy seed shall all the nations of the earth be blessed**; because thou hast obeyed my voice"* (Gen 22:16-18).

Then the promise was passed on through Isaac. *"And I will make thy seed to multiply as the stars of heaven, and will give unto thy seed all these countries; **and in thy seed shall all the nations of the earth be blessed**;"* (Gen 26:4). After Isaac the promise of the good news was confirmed to Jacob as he was fleeing from the wrath of Esau. *"And, behold, the LORD stood above it [the ladder], and said, I am the LORD God of Abraham thy father, and the God of Isaac: the land whereon thou liest, to thee will I give it, and to thy seed; And thy seed shall be as the dust of the earth, and thou shalt spread abroad to the west, and to the east, and to the north, and to the south: **and in thee and in thy seed shall all the families of the earth be blessed**"* (Gen 28:13-14).

We need to understand that what Messiah Yeshua said to the Samaritan woman applies to all unbelieving gentiles, *"Ye worship ye know not what: we know what we worship: for **salvation is of the Jews**"* (John 4:22). Remember why God says He created the Jewish people. *"...for I have created him for my glory, I have formed him; yea, I have made him...This people have I formed for myself; they shall shew forth my praise"* (Isa 43:7b,21).

And it was through the Jewish people[6] that Yeshua came as Abraham's greatest Seed, to make possible global salvation and the reality of God's indwelling Spirit in new hearts, thereby fulfilling the "blessing" part of God's promise. *"Now to Abraham and his seed were the promises made. He saith not, And to seeds, as of many; but as of one, And to thy **seed, which is Messiah**"* (Gal 3:16).

God's Land for God's People

Besides promising blessings for Abraham and his seed, as well as the Gospel blessing to the world, God also gave *His* land to Abraham, and to his seed through Jacob/Israel, as an inheritance. The following verses bring out the dual aspect of the children of Israel as God's inheritance, with the land of Israel as the inheritance of the children of Israel:

*"But the LORD hath taken you, and brought you forth out of the iron furnace, even out of Egypt, **to be unto him a people of inheritance**, as ye are this day. Furthermore the LORD was angry with me for your sakes, and sware that I should not go over Jordan, and that I should not go in unto **that good land, which the LORD thy God giveth thee for an inheritance**:"* (Deut 4:20-21).

This verse from Jeremiah is being fulfilled today: *"In those days the house of Judah shall walk with the house of Israel, and they shall come together out of the land of the north to **the land that I have given for an inheritance unto your fathers**"* (Jer 3:18).

As already mentioned previoiusly in "Whose Land?," Ezekiel 36 is a currently relevant chapter describing prophecies – past, present and future – in the Middle East. In verse 12, God speaks to the land of Israel itself, *"Yea, I will cause men to walk upon you, even my people Israel; and they shall possess thee, and **thou shalt be their inheritance**, and thou shalt no more henceforth bereave them of men"* (Ezek 36:12).[7]

How serious is God about giving the Land to the Jewish people? The Spirit of God speaks through King David, *"He hath remembered his covenant for ever, the word which he commanded to a thousand generations. Which covenant he made with Abraham, and his oath unto Isaac; And confirmed the same unto Jacob for a law, and to Israel for an everlasting covenant: Saying, Unto thee will I give the land of Canaan, the lot of your inheritance:"* (Psa 105:8-11).

God is stating something so important that He uses five different terms to describe it, *"...his **covenant for ever**, the **word**...he commanded to a thousand generations...his **oath**...**law**...**everlasting covenant**..."* And that whole section appears in the Word twice (see 1 Chr 16:15-18)![8] What is God stating in such strong terms? *"Unto thee **will I give the land of Canaan**, the lot of **your inheritance**."*

Why does God stress this so strongly? He knows that virtually no unbelievers, not even many believers, will want to believe that His relationship with the Jewish people and the unconditional promise of the land really do endure forever (Jer 31:35-37).

If understanding that passage in Psalms has not convinced you that God is serious about bringing the Jewish people back to the land of Israel, then read this: *"Yea, I will rejoice over them to do* *them good, and **I will plant them in this land assuredly with my whole heart and with my whole soul***" (Jer 32:41). Nowhere else in all of God's Word does He declare that He is going to do something with His whole heart and soul! Who will be able to resist His desire? Who in their right mind would want to resist what the Lord God Almighty is determined to do with all of His heart and soul? And yet a self-centered part of the Church ignores this God-centered part of His Word as if it has no importance. Can you imagine the spiritual condition of one who ignores God's heart and soul?

The Sanctification of God's Name

*"Therefore say unto the house of Israel, Thus saith the Lord GOD; I do not this for your sakes, O house of Israel, but **for mine holy name's sake**, which ye have profaned among the heathen, whither ye went. And **I will sanctify my great name**, which was profaned among the heathen, which ye have profaned in the midst of them; **and the heathen shall know that I am the LORD, saith the Lord GOD, when I shall be sanctified in you before their eyes**.*

*"For I will take you from among the heathen, and gather you out of all countries, and will bring you into **your own land**. Then will I sprinkle clean water upon you, and ye shall be clean: from all your filthiness, and from all your idols, will I cleanse you. A new heart also will I give you, and a new spirit will I put within you: and I will take away the stony heart out of your flesh, and I will give you an heart of flesh. And I will put my spirit within you, and cause you to walk in my statutes, and ye shall keep my judgments, and do them. **And ye shall dwell in the land that I gave to your fathers; and ye shall be my people, and I will be your God**"* (Ezek 36:22-28).

That crucial section reveals the reason God is determined to plant His people in His land. It is because He has chosen this way to sanctify His name. And sanctifying God's name is the first thing Yeshua told us to pray, *"After this manner therefore pray ye: Our Father which art in heaven, Hallowed [sanctified] be thy name"* (Matt 6:9).

What does "sanctifying" God's name mean? In Hebraic thinking, which is the mindset of the Scriptures, a person's name describes his essential character. God's Name represents who He is. Our God is holy, faithful, merciful, just, good, true, gracious, and long-suffering (Exo 34:5-7), etc. That is Who He is and there is nothing we can do to either add to or subtract from His nature.

We "sanctify His name" when we proclaim to the world and to the heavens that our God *is* indeed the Holy One, faithful in all His acts, merciful yet just, good and true, etc. And as we have just read in Ezekiel 36:23-24, we can use the restoration of Israel as the best last days example of the sanctification of God's name. God said that Israel's rebirth (as a nation and also spiritually when all Israel is saved) would sanctify His name among the nations. And God builds the fulfillment of His Word on the sure foundation of who He is! *"I will worship toward thy holy temple, and praise thy name for thy lovingkindness and for thy truth: for **thou hast magnified thy word** above* [not "over," but "**upon**"] ***all thy name***" (Psa 138:2).

Physical Land and Eternal Salvation

What then is the connection between Israel's end time physical restoration and our eternal salvation? It is simply that the promise of the land of Israel given as an everlasting covenant, sworn to by God, and the promise of eternal life given to those who trust in Yeshua, are *both* guaranteed by God's faithfulness and ability to keep His Word.

If God is fickle as opposed to faithful, or if He is a God who proclaims but cannot perform, then what assurance do we have of salvation? And if God, who made such remarkable promises to the Jewish people about their homecoming and inheritance, cannot or will not fulfill these promises, then what assurance do we have that He will fulfill His promises to us?

After a meeting someone asked if Yeshua's resurrection wasn't all the proof we needed for our assurance of salvation? Chuck responded, "How did Yeshua's resurrection prove He was the One whom God had sent? There were many Jews crucified during Yeshua's time, and there were others, like Lazarus, who were also raised from the dead. But the promised Messiah was prophesied to be crucified and raised from the dead on the third day. His death and resurrection are proof of Yeshua's Messiahship for only one reason - *they fulfill God's prophetic Word about Messiah.*"

Hiding His glorified body, Yeshua refused to focus on the miracle of His resurrection as proof of His Messiahship. Instead, He quoted prooftexts to two depressed disciples and reminded them that those *Tanach* prophecies of Messiah's life, death, and resurrection must be fulfilled. *"Then he said unto them, O fools, and slow of heart to believe all that the prophets have spoken: Ought not the Messiah to have suffered these things, and to enter into his glory? And beginning at Moses and all the prophets, he expounded unto them in all the scriptures* [the Old Testament] *the things concerning himself"* (Luke 24:25-27).

Even later, after revealing His identity to them, He repeated the point to make it unmistakable. *"And he said unto them, These are the words which I spake unto you, while I was yet with you, that all things must be fulfilled, which were written in the law of*

Moses, and in the prophets, and in the psalms, concerning me. Then opened he their understanding, that they might understand the scriptures [the Old Testament], *And said unto them, Thus it is written, and thus it behoved the Messiah to suffer, and to rise from the dead the third day:"* (Luke 24:44-46). If He so magnified the Scriptures, the *Tanach*, in the presence of the awesome miracle of His resurrection, can we do any less concerning the prophesied resurrection of Israel in the last days? May He open every disciple's understanding of the prophecies promising Israel's miraculous restoration today - for the sanctification of His Name!

Be encouraged! Trust God! God is fulfilling His Word right before our eyes! Israel has been resurrected from the dead; the Jewish people are returning to their ancient homeland; ancient cities are being rebuilt; Hebrew is being spoken and sung and prayed again, and all the world is so deceived that they are preparing to war against Jerusalem just as the prophet has spoken, *"Behold, I will make Jerusalem a cup of trembling unto all the people round about, when they shall be in the siege both against Judah and against Jerusalem. And in that day will I make Jerusalem a burdensome stone for all people: all that burden themselves with it shall be cut in pieces, though all the people of the earth be gathered together against it"* (Zech 12:2-3).

Conclusion

Where is all this in the New Testament? Romans 15:8 says, *"Now I say that Yeshua the Messiah was a minister* [servant] *of the circumcision* [the Jews] *for the truth of God, **to confirm the promises** made unto the fathers:"* As we have seen, those promises include *the inheritance of the land of Israel.* Yeshua's life, death, and resurrection confirm those promises.

The Word talks about having at least two witnesses testify to truth.[9] The Church testifies to Yeshua's resurrection, confirming the promises made to Israel, and Israel testifies by her resurrection, confirming the promises made to the Church.

> *"The grass withereth, the flower fadeth:*
> *but the word of our God shall stand for ever"* (Isa 40:8).

> *"Oh that the salvation of Israel were come out of Zion!*
> *when the LORD bringeth back the captivity of his people,*
> *Jacob shall rejoice, and Israel shall be glad"* (Psa 14:7).

---

1   See 1 Corinthians 1:18, 23, 25; 2:14.

2   Other examples of this usage are found in Ezra 6:21;8:35; Jeremiah 30:3,10; 33:7; 46:27; Ezekiel 39:25; Amos 7:17 and 9:14-15.

3   2 Kin 21:14, Isa 47:6.

4   Abortion, homosexuality, drugs, the occult, divorce, abuse - these things do not *bring* God's judgment; they ARE God's judgment!

5   In Hebrew, the word is *goyim,* which can be translated "nations," "gentiles," or "heathen" depending on the context and the theological bent of the translator.

6   Rom 1:3; 9:5.

7   See also Num 34:2; Deut 19:14; Josh 1:6; 1 Kin 8:36; Jer 12:14.

8   Matt 18:16; 2 Cor 13:1 .

9   Deut 17:16; 19:15; 2 Cor 13:1; 1 Tim 5:19.

CHAPTER 20

Your People Will Be My People - Part 1

We have already demonstrated that Israel and the Church have the same biblical roots – the *Tanach*. But there is something more, something that most of the Church has missed through the centuries, something usually missed also by those trying to restore "Jewish" roots to the modern Church – the intimate connection between the Jewish people and true Christians.

Shavuot

Shavuot, or literally in Hebrew - "Weeks," known in the Church as "Pentecost" or "Whitsunday," is one of the three pilgrim feasts when all Israeli males were to appear before God in Jerusalem (Exo 23:14-17; Deut 16:16). In the Church it is no longer observed according to the Hebrew lunar calendar and so usually no longer falls on the Hebrew calendar Feast of *Shavuot*. As early as the second century, gentile Church leaders made efforts to avoid celebrations on Jewish holy days and eventually created different holy days.

Many see Pentecost as the birthday of the Church. In Acts 2, on *Shavuot*, the risen and glorified Messiah poured out on the waiting disciples that Promise which was promised by His Father - the Holy Spirit (Luke 24:49; Acts 1:4-5; 2:32-33). At that moment the first "Messianic Jews" began to be empowered by one Spirit in one Body (1 Cor 12:13-14).

We can see that process in the symbolism of *Shavuot* and *Bikkurim*, first fruits of the barley harvest, which was the biblical feast on which Messiah rose from the dead (Lev 23:9-14). *Bikkurim* always occurs on the day after the *Shabbat* of Passover week (Lev 23:11). There are different opinions as to which *Shabbat* is meant – the weekly feast, or Passover itself, also called a *Shabbat*. If the weekly, then *Bikkurim* would always occur on the first day of the week, the day when Yeshua rose from the dead as the *Bikkurim,* the first fruits of the resurrection (1 Cor 15:20).

During *Bikkurim*, sheaves of individual grain stalks were offered in a wave-offering before God in the Temple. But the *Shavuot* offering, after 49 (7x7) days or seven "Weeks," on the fiftieth day (Greek: *pentecoste*), is a wave-offering of two loaves of bread.

Think of the ancient process of making bread. After cutting, the stalks are immediately assembled into bundles. Taken to a threshing floor, they are beaten to separate the grain, which is gathered into shallow baskets and repeatedly tossed into the air on a windy day - "winnowed," to blow out worthless bits. The cleaned grain is then thoroughly smashed to powder between stones to make flour. The flour is combined with oil and water, repeatedly pressed and squeezed - "kneaded," put in a hot oven and finally – bread, the staff of life.[1]

Isn't this what Yeshua does with us after we are harvested? We are saved as individuals, but immediately become part of a community, His Body. We also are transformed through the powerful processes of conviction and repentance resulting in sanctification, all of which is overseen by the Holy Spirit, so that we, like Yeshua, can be broken bread and poured out wine for others (thanks to Oswald Chambers for that analogy).

Yeshua's death and resurrection made possible the harvest of individual grains but it takes the infilling of the Holy Spirit's power to enable us to function according to His spiritual gifts as part of His Body. For that reason *Shavuot* is the birthday of the Church.

Rabbis say that after Israel left Egypt, Moses received the Ten Commandments on *Shavuot*.[2] Although Israel was given freedom on Passover, freedom without law leads to anarchy. So God gave the tablets of the Law and Israel became a nation. Because of that, Judaism recognizes *Shavuot* as the birthday of the people of Israel!

Although historically Israel and the Church have despised each other and felt they have little in common, is it coincidence that both have claimed *Shavuot* as their birthday?

Ruth and the Church

Jewish sages have assigned certain *Tanach* books to be read on the holy days. On *Shavuot*, *Ruth* is read, mainly because it occurs in the spring, like *Shavuot*, during barley harvest time (Ruth 1:22). Note that the book of *Ruth* is named for a gentile (1:4) who was willing to leave her country and family to stay with and minister to Naomi, her Jewish mother-in-law.

Naomi and her family had left Bethlehem because of a famine. She is about to return after losing her husband and both sons in Moab. Her two Moabite daughters-in-law want to go with her. One is convinced by Naomi to stay in Moab, but not Ruth. In one of the most touching declarations of faith and loyalty in the Bible, Ruth says, *"Intreat me not to leave thee, or to return from following after thee: for whither thou goest, I will go; and where thou lodgest, I will lodge: **thy people shall be my people, and thy God my God**: Where thou diest, will I die, and there will I be buried: the LORD do so to me, and more also, if ought but death part thee and me"* (Ruth 1:16-17).

In Israel Ruth finds a husband, Boaz, a wonderful foreshadow of Messiah Yeshua in the following points: he is a kinsman redeemer (2:1), a mighty man of wealth (2:1), a man of the law (3:12-13), the lord of the harvest (2:4,15-16), an advocate (4:1-6) and a bridegroom (4:13) with a gentile bride who becomes part of the household of Israel (4:11). Boaz not only mirrors Yeshua in all these things, but he and Ruth are blessed to become ancestors of the Davidic line (4:17) and of Yeshua Himself (Matt 1:5). Ruth's faithfulness to her Jewish mother-in-law birthed a desire to become grafted into Israel's Olive Tree, resulting in incredible blessing not just for her, but also for the world.

This poor gentile widow, who followed love and truth at whatever cost, becomes a matriarch in God's plan to bring salvation to the world. Ruth went the extra mile, not only leaving her country, but also seeking shelter under the wings of Naomi's God – the God of Israel, becoming part of Naomi's people – the people of Israel.

The Church has claimed the *"thy God shall be my God"* part of Ruth's confession. But down through the centuries the *"thy people shall be my people"* part has been ignored, rejected, and "replaced." As Psalm 102:13 says, the set time has come - the time to have mercy on Zion. The gentile Church is coming into a new revelation of themselves as the "other" part of the greater commonwealth of spiritual Israel, past, present, and future. Now is the time for the Church to proclaim its debt to the Jewish people (Rom 15:27) and stand with the Jews of today, the brethren of Yeshua and the Apostles.

The Church and Israel - Romans 11

Many believers today are excited about the truth they see in Romans 9-11. This convicting part of God's Word has historically been ignored or misinterpreted by the Church. The context is clear - Paul is proclaiming God's faithfulness to Israel despite the blindness of most of Israel to Yeshua as the promised Messiah.

But Romans 10:18-21 states that none of this took God by surprise. He knew Israel's response beforehand (see Acts 4:27-28).

"But to Israel he saith, All day long I have stretched forth my hands unto a disobedient [willfully, perversely disbelieving] *and gainsaying* [speaking against, contradicting, disobeying, refusing to relate] *people. I say then, Hath God cast away his people?* **God forbid**. *For I also am an Israelite, of the seed of Abraham, of the tribe of Benjamin. God hath not cast away his people which he foreknew"* (Rom 10:21-11:2a).

What is your answer to Paul's question, "Has God cast away His disbelieving and stubborn people?" The Church historically has answered, "Of course, and we have replaced Israel." The Holy Spirit's answer through Paul is, *"God forbid!"* Why? Because God will not contradict His Word, break His promises, or annul His everlasting covenant.

In Romans 11:7-10, Paul points to dire accusations and curses in the *Tanach* against disbelieving Israel. But even against such a background, he asks again, *"I say then, Have they stumbled* [erred, sinned] *that they should fall* [perish under judgment/condemnation]? **God forbid***: but rather through their fall* [sin, offense] *salvation is come unto the Gentiles, for to provoke them to jealousy"* (11:11). Why make the Jews jealous? To torment them? No! To cause them to recognize their Messiah!

Twice in that chapter God's Word gives a powerful *"God forbid"* to answer whether God has rejected or will reject Israel forever as His chosen nation. Yet the Church in many places continues to teach otherwise. What will you believe, the Word of God or traditional teachings that oppose His Word?

Paul twice points out the worldwide blessings that will result from Israel's national salvation (11:12,15), and finally he shares about the relationship between gentiles and Israel in God's plan.

The Olive Tree Connection

In the context of Romans 9-11, Paul talks about Israel as an ancient olive tree, some of whose natural branches have undergone heavy pruning because of the "disease" of unbelief. This cultivated olive tree (11:16-24) is the commonwealth - citizenship or community - of Israel (Eph 2:12). The healthy branches are living Jewish believers along with, as we shall see shortly, living gentile believers. The healthy roots are all the past *Tanach* saints, Messianic Jews, and gentile believers whose lives of faith in God and His promises have channeled nourishment for the growth of the tree.[3]

Yeshua, the greatest fulfillment and fulfiller of God's promises, came as the model for our faith, the DNA if you will, for this Tree of

Life - from taproot to branch. He is the first, the greatest, the strongest, the prophesied Root of Jesse and David, and He is God's Servant - called the Branch.[4] The olive tree under discussion is Rabbi Shaul's picture of the Commonwealth of the House of Israel.

What happens when gentiles trust in Yeshua? They are cut out of wild olive trees (Rom11:17) representing paganism and heathenism and grafted into Israel's cultivated tree nourished by faith in the God of Abraham, Isaac, and Jacob. Or as Paul states elsewhere, believers turn *"...from idols to serve the living and true God"* (1 Thes 1:9b). However, even though gentile believers are grafted into Israel's Olive Tree, much of the Church has acted, and still acts, as though it has been grafted into a Christmas tree – flashing its attractive lights and decorations, but unconcerned about its loss of roots and wondering why it is spiritually drying up and dying.

Saved gentiles are to share in *"the root and fatness of the olive tree"* (11:17). They do not take the Jews' place, but are *"among them, and with them."* Hear God's Spirit speaking through Paul to gentile believers, *"Boast not* [exult not] *against the branches* [natural branches that were cut off]. *But if thou boast, thou bearest* [support] *not the root, but the root thee"* (11:18).

After Paul warns Christians about pride against the Jews (Rom 11:20,24), and says a day will come when all Israel will be saved (11:26), he states, *"As concerning the gospel, they are enemies* [enemies of the Gospel - very strong in the original] *for your sakes: but as touching the election, they are beloved for the fathers' sakes. For the gifts and calling of God are without repentance"* (11:28-29). Jews - many still enemies of the Gospel, haters of Yeshua, despising and opposing Christians - are yet beloved by God. But that's not all. Turn it around and look at the other side of that coin – enemies of the Jews and haters of Israel are cursed by God (Gen 12:3; Num 24:9; Isa 49:25-26; Zech 12:9; Matt 25:40,45).

Saved gentiles have been supernaturally grafted against nature into a tree not their own, but saved Jews are natural branches. Yet when a Jew gets saved, gentile believers are often amazed. This shows how far the Church has strayed from a biblical perspective. Remember, the unbelievable miracle in Acts was that *gentiles* were being saved! But in regards to the Jewish people, Paul says that God is able to graft those natural branches in again, if they believe (11:23). They are more easily grafted back in because they belong there. Those branches need to hear this Good News.

Bride of Messiah, honor your spiritual forefathers through their physical descendants, just as you love your *physical* brothers and sisters even if they are unsaved. How? Paul completes this chapter using the word "mercy" four times (Rom 11:30-32). We can't imagine how different a situation we would be facing today if only the Church had obeyed God's Word and had mercy on Israel, provoking them to jealousy instead of forcing them to convert or die.

Not only do the Jewish people need the Good News, they need support and prayer covering as protection from the Adversary's attempts to destroy them. Church, wake up to the biblical truth that the existence of Israel is imperative to our very lives as believers! Israel's faith in the *Tanach* promises are the roots of Israel's Olive Tree. Remember, you do not bear the root but the root bears you (Rom 11:18b). If Israel is ever destroyed, the Word of God and His promises to Israel, His everlasting covenant, are proved to be lies and the Church's spiritual foundation crumbles.

The Enemy is prowling the corridors of churches, including Israel-loving churches, looking for a meal. Don't cut yourself off from your roots of faith! Stay in the Word of God and prayer; seek holiness; refuse the ways of the world; test every spirit.

No Longer Strangers

Another New Testament section that talks about the Jew/gentile relationship is Ephesians 2:11-3:12. Paul says that before salvation, gentiles were *"without Messiah, being aliens* [shut out from fellowship and intimacy] *from the commonwealth* [community, citizenship] *of Israel, and strangers from* [without knowledge of or a share in] *the covenants of promise, having no hope, and without God in the world:"* (Eph 2:12).

But Paul has good news for gentiles, *"...now in Messiah Yeshua ye who sometimes were far off are made nigh by the blood of Messiah. For he is our peace, who hath made both one..."* (Eph 2:13-14a; cp. 2:17 and Isa 57:19). Yeshua foresaw our being one when He said, *"And other sheep I have, which are not of this fold: them also I must bring* [lead], *and they shall hear my voice; and there shall be one fold, and one shepherd"* (John 10:16).

Paul says that gentiles in Messiah *"...are no more strangers and foreigners* [noncitizens], *but fellowcitizens with the saints* [who are Messianic Jews], *and of the household* [family] *of God;"* (Eph 2:19). Redeemed gentiles, even uncircumcised, could be saints along with redeemed Jews! This was news!

Finally, Paul shares concerning gentile believers and the *"mystery of Messiah"* which God has now revealed (Eph 3:1-5). The mystery is, *"That the Gentiles should be fellowheirs* [joint heirs], *and of the same body, and partakers of his promise in Messiah by the gospel:"* (Eph 3:6). To grasp this, remember Paul was a rabbi immersed in Hebraic culture.

Here is what we guess such a Pharisee might have thought when he first realized that gentiles could be saved without converting to Judaism. "The mystery of Messiah is that those gentiles, whom I used to look on as unclean dogs, should be joint heirs with God's people, my people - Israel, even a part of the same flock and able to partake of God's promises in the Jewish Messiah by this Good News!"

Or, as Paul says in another letter, *"Even the mystery which hath been hid from ages* [eternity] *and from generations, but now is made manifest to his saints: To whom God would make known what is the riches of the glory of this mystery among the Gentiles; which is Messiah in you, the hope of glory:"* (Col 1:26-27). Hear that! The Jewish Messiah in you gentiles is your hope of glory!

Church, could you be brought any closer to Israel and the Jewish people? You are saved because the God of Israel has placed the promised, prophesied Messiah of the Jews in you by His Spirit! Welcome to the family!!

"Behold, how good and how pleasant it is
for brethren to dwell together in unity!
It is like the precious ointment [anointing oil] *upon the head,*
that ran down upon the beard, even Aaron's beard:
that went down to the skirts of his garments;
As the dew of Hermon, and as the dew that descended upon
the mountains of Zion:
for there the LORD commanded the blessing, even life
for evermore" (Psa 133).

---

1 If one wants bread to seem more than it really is, be softer and easier to chew and swallow, and appear light and pure, the grain must have the life-germinating factor removed along with the protective seed cover. A rapidly reproducing fungus in an oil/liquid mixture is added which causes the dough to expand with gas and puff up to even twice normal size. The oven heat causes the outer layer to become rigid so that the bread remains fixedly puffed up. Once the outer layer is breached, the many air holes caused by the gas facilitate a rapid loss of moisture resulting in a dry unpalatability. The Bible compares false doctrine and hypocrisy to this rapidly reproducing fungus (Matt 16:12, Luke 12:1). The Bible also compares the grain seed to the Word of God (Luke 8:11-15, Matt 13:19-23).

2 Whether this was the actual day or not, is irrelevant to the point under consideration.

3 Romans 4:1-3,9-22; Gal 3:6-9; Heb 11:8-21.

4 See Isa 11:1,10; Jer 23:5-6; Zec 3:8; Rom 15:12; Rev 5:5; 22:16.

CHAPTER 21

Your People Will Be My People – Part 2

Gentiles Who Became Part of Israel in the *Tanach*

We have just discovered that the Church's relationship to the Jewish people should be in agreement with Ruth's commitment to Naomi, "...your people, my people, and your God, my God" (lit. translation, Ruth 1:16), and we have looked at some New Testament teachings which illustrate that relationship.[1] The *Tanach* also contains teachings on this subject. We barely touched on this relationship in a previous chapter,[2] so the emphasis here will explore beyond prophesied gentile salvation, and penetrate to that relationship between the Jewish people and redeemed gentiles as described in the *Tanach*.

The *Tanach* mentions by name two non-Jewish women, Rahab and Ruth, who by choice became part of the greater community of Israel. *"And Joshua saved Rahab the harlot alive, and her father's household, and all that she had; and she dwelleth* [settled, remained] *in Israel even unto this day..."* (Josh 6:25a). Rahab, like Ruth, is listed in Yeshua's genealogy (see Matt 1:5), and the New Testament cites her also as an example of faith proven by her works. *"By faith the harlot Rahab perished not with them that believed not, when she had received the spies with peace"* (Heb 11:31). *"Likewise also was not Rahab the harlot justified by works, when she had received the messengers, and had sent them out another way? For as the body without the spirit is dead, so faith without* [separated from] *works is dead also"* (James 2:25-26).

In Ruth's case, her faith in Israel's God made her eligible to marry Boaz. When Ruth questioned his kindness to her, a stranger, Boaz replied, *"It hath fully been shewed me, all that thou hast done unto thy mother in law...and how thou hast left* [to desert, leave behind]...*the land of thy nativity, and art come unto a people which thou knewest not heretofore. The LORD recompense thy work, and a full reward be given thee of **the LORD God of Israel, under whose wings thou art come to trust** [seek refuge, have hope in]"* (Ruth 2:11-12).

In using the phrase, *"**LORD** God of Israel" ("LORD,"* the tetragrammaton, God's personal name), Boaz indicates that Ruth knew Israel's God was different from her ancestors' gods. Ruth left her family and nation and joined herself to the Jewish people, putting her trust in their God, the only true God - the God of Israel.

The Law of Foreigners and Strangers

The *Torah,* God's teaching, instructs Israel to differentiate between gentiles who serve other gods, and gentiles who join themselves to Israel by trusting Israel's God. It seems this is not known or taught in today's Church, so there is much misunderstanding among believers concerning the relationship of the nation of Israel with the gentiles in her midst.

Many Christians say that Israel needs to accept and love the Moslems and that Moslems have an equal right to the Promised Land. We do believe Israel needs to treat all her citizens righteously, including her Moslem citizens. But *biblically,* there is a huge difference between Moslems, or any other people group who belong to another god, and Jews and Christians who belong to the God of Israel. This is misunderstood for two main reasons. The first reason is simply a lack of awareness that the Moslem god, *Allah* (the spirit principality behind Islam), has nothing in common with the Judeo-Christian God of Israel.[3] The second reason is more complex because most translations do not make a consistent difference between several Hebrew words.

The *Ger*

The Hebrew noun *ger* (Strong's #1616) comes from a root which means to live among a people who are not blood relatives. The *ger,*[4] without the protection of his homeborn "civil rights", was dependent on his host's hospitality, an important custom in the Middle East then and now. *Gerim* (plural) in Israel were for that reason considered a protected people.

The patriarchs and David, looking to God as their Protector, called themselves *gerim* in the promised land, *"By faith Abraham, when he was called to go out into a place which he should after receive for an inheritance, obeyed; and he went out, not knowing whither he went. By faith he sojourned* [resided as a foreigner] *in the land of promise, as in a strange* [foreign] *country, dwelling in tabernacles with Isaac and Jacob, the heirs with him of the same promise: For he looked for a* [lit: the] *city which hath foundations, whose builder and maker is God...These all died in faith, not having received the promises, but having seen* [known, perceived] *them afar off, and were persuaded of them, and embraced them, and* **confessed that they were strangers and pilgrims on the earth** *"* (Heb 11:8-10,13 referring to Gen 23:4).

King David is humbled that God would allow his and the people's offerings for the building of the Temple. He prays to the Lord, *"But who am I, and what is my people, that we should be able to offer so willingly after this sort? for all things come of thee, and of thine own* [lit: hand] *have we given thee"* (1 Chr 29:14). On what does he base his point of view? On the reality that all of God's people are strangers and sojourners. *"For we are strangers* [gerim - people in need of grace and hospitality] *before thee, and* **sojourners** *[toshavim – see below], as were all our fathers: our days on the earth are as a shadow, and there is none abiding* [remaining alive]*"* (Chr 29:15).

In Psalm 39:12, David pleads with God to hear his prayer based on the same theme, *"Hear my prayer, O LORD, and give ear unto my cry; hold not thy peace at my tears: for I am a* **stranger** *[ger]* **with thee, and a sojourner** *[toshav - see below], as all my fathers were."*

Concerning the land of Israel itself, God tells His people that they may not sell it because He is the owner and they are His protected guests. *"The land shall not be sold for ever: for the land is mine; for ye are strangers* [gerim] *and sojourners* [toshavim] *with me"* (Lev 25:23).

Likewise, the New Testament bears witness with the *Tanach's* point of view when it states that as believers, we need to see ourselves as in the world but not of it. *"If ye were of the world, the world would love his own: but because ye are not of the world, but I have chosen you out of the world, therefore the world hateth you"* (John 15:19; see 17:14-16). John goes on to warn the Church: *"Love not the world, neither the things that are in the world. If any man love the world, the love of the Father is not in him"* (1 John 2:15).

James, also writing to believers, declares in no uncertain terms: *"Ye adulterers and adulteresses* [fig: apostates]*, know ye not that the friendship of the world is enmity with God? whosoever therefore will be a friend of the world is the enemy of God"* (Jam 4:4).

The *Ger* in Israel

God told Israel to see *gerim* as proselytes, part of the community with most of the same rights as the native-born Israeli, yet not as children of Israel according to the flesh. In the following verses, the Hebrew for "stranger" is *ger*.

Shabbat laws applied to them. *"But the seventh day is the sabbath of the LORD thy God: in it thou shalt not do any work, thou, nor thy son, nor thy daughter, thy manservant, nor thy maidservant, nor thy cattle, nor **thy stranger** [ger] **that is within thy gates:"** (Exo 20:10; also 23:12).

If they were circumcised, *gerim* could celebrate Passover.[5] *"And when a **stranger shall sojourn with thee**, and will keep the passover to the LORD, let all his males be circumcised, and then let him come near and keep it; and he shall be as one that is born [a native] in the land: for no uncircumcised person shall eat thereof. **One law shall be to him that is homeborn, and unto the stranger** [ger] **that sojourneth among you"** (Exo 12:48-49; also Num 9:14).

Along with the congregation of Israel the *gerim* were obligated to observe other Feasts of the LORD as well. Unleavened Bread [*Hag haMatzot*] - *"Seven days shall there be no leaven found in your houses: for whosoever eateth that which is leavened, even that soul shall be cut off from the congregation of Israel, whether he be a **stranger**, or born in the land"* (Exo 12:19).

The Day of Atonement [*Yom Kippur*] - *"And this shall be a statute for ever unto you: that in the seventh month, on the tenth day of the month, ye shall afflict [or humble] your souls, and do no work at all, whether it be one of your own country, **or a stranger that sojourneth among you**: For on that day shall the priest make an atonement for you, to cleanse [purify] you, that ye may be clean from all your sins before the LORD"* (Lev 16:29-30). So we see that the blood atonement which purchased forgiveness for sins for all of the congregation of Israel included the *believing* strangers (*gerim*) who lived in the midst of her.

Tabernacles [*Succot*] - *"Thou shalt observe the feast of tabernacles seven days, after that thou hast gathered in thy corn and thy wine: And thou shalt rejoice in thy feast, thou, and thy son, and thy daughter, and thy manservant, and thy maidservant, and the Levite, **the stranger**, and the fatherless, and the widow, that are within thy gates"* (Deut 16:13-14).

The *ger* was to be present in the assembly when the Law was read and was also held accountable to its demands. *"When all Israel is come to appear before the LORD thy God in the place which he shall choose, thou shalt read this law before all Israel in their hearing. Gather the people together, men, and women, and children, **and thy stranger that is within thy gates**, that they may **hear**, and that they may **learn**, and **fear** the LORD your God, and **observe to do** all the words of this law:"* (Deut 31:11-12; see Lev 18:26).

Just like the children of Israel, the *ger* was condemned to death if he sacrificed to other gods. *"...Whosoever he be of the children of Israel,* **or of the strangers that sojourn in Israel**, *that giveth* [sacrifice] *any of his seed* [children] *unto Molech; he shall surely be put to death: the people of the land shall stone him with stones. And I will set my face against that man, and will cut him off from among his people; because he hath given of his seed unto Molech, to defile my sanctuary, and to profane* [defile, desecrate, pollute] *my holy name* [reputation]*"* (Lev 20:2b-3; see 17:8-9). In this verse, the Lord affirmed that the *ger's* behavior, just as much as the native Israelite's behavior, had an impact on Israel's witness to Himself.

The *ger* was also forbidden to eat blood, though unlike the Israelite, he could eat what had died by itself or was torn. *"And whatsoever man there be of the house of Israel,* **or of the strangers that sojourn among you**, *that eateth any manner of blood; I will even set my face against that soul that eateth blood, and will cut him off from among his people"* (Lev 17:10; but see Deut 14:21a).

Like the Israelite, he also underwent special cleansing, qualifying to be cleansed by the ritual of the red heifer. *"And he that gathereth the ashes of the heifer shall wash his clothes, and be unclean until the even: and it shall be unto the children of Israel, and* **unto the stranger that sojourneth among them**, *for a statute for ever"* (Num 19:10).

The *ger* enjoyed most of the same rights as the Israelite, and was not to be oppressed. *"Thou shalt* **neither vex** [maltreat] *a* **stranger, nor oppress him**: *for ye were* **strangers** *in the land of Egypt"* (Exo 22:21, see Jer 7:6).

He was to be treated righteously in judgment. *"And I charged your judges at that time, saying, Hear the causes between your brethren, and judge righteously between every man and his brother,* **and the stranger** *that is with him"* (Deut 1:16, see also 24:17; 27:19; Jer 22:3).

Even the cities of refuge were available to him. *"These six cities shall be a refuge, both for the children of Israel,* **and for the stranger, and for the sojourner among them**: *that every one that killeth any person unawares* [mistakenly] *may flee thither"* (Num 35:15).

Ultimately, he was expected to show the same honor and commitment to the LORD God as every Israelite. Moses sums up in Leviticus 24:22 by saying, *"Ye shall have one manner of law, as well* **for the stranger** [ger]*, as for one of your own country: for I am the LORD your God."*

Finally, God specifically states that He loves the *gerim*, and then commands Israel to love them as well. *"For the LORD your God is God of gods, and Lord of lords, a great God, a mighty, and a terrible, which regardeth not persons, nor taketh reward: He doth execute the judgment of the fatherless and widow, and* **loveth** *the stranger, in giving him food and raiment. **Love ye therefore the stranger**: for ye were **strangers** in the land of Egypt"* (Deut 10:17-19; also Lev 19:34).

The *Ger* – a Type of the Christian

The *ger* is a wonderful foreshadow of the gentile believer grafted into Israel's Olive Tree. He became an actual part of the Commonwealth of Israel with most of the same obligations toward God as the Israelite. Because he had made a deep commitment to the God of Israel *and* the people of Israel, there can be no comparing the *ger* with the native Canaanites, demonized idol worshippers practicing human sacrifice, whom God commanded Israel to destroy.[6]

There are instructions concerning the lifestyle of the *ger* that Christians should consider. Have you ever celebrated Passover? Have you ever fasted on Yom Kippur? As we have already noted,[7] the Feasts of the Lord are specific times of the year when God wants to meet with His people – and the true Christian has certainly become an integral part of His people. Other instructions to *gerim* are also mentioned, but the point is that the *ger* was to accept the descendants of Jacob as his community, and the God of Jacob as his God. He stood with Israel. And we believe that the God of Israel desires the same attitude from His Church.

The Toshav

There are other Hebrew words which are also translated "strangers," "sojourners" or "aliens" [foreigners]. *Toshav* (*Strong's* #8453) is often paralleled with *ger*. In the following verses, *ger* is translated "stranger," while *toshav* is translated "sojourner."

When buying the burial plot in Hebron for Sarah, Abraham uses both terms to describe himself. *"I am a **stranger** and a **sojourner** with you: give me a possession of a buryingplace with you..."* (Gen 23:4a). God uses both terms in describing Israel's relationship to the Land. *"The land shall not be sold for ever: for the land is mine; for ye are **strangers** and **sojourners** with me"* (Lev 25:23).

Israel was commanded to have compassion on the *ger* and the *toshav* when they were in distress. *"And if thy brother be waxen poor, and fallen in decay with thee; then thou shalt relieve [strengthen] him: yea, though he be a **stranger**, or a **sojourner**; that he may live with thee"* (Lev 25:35). The *ger* and *toshav* were to be dealt with just as the Israelis would deal with their flesh and blood brothers.

Both could flee to the cities of refuge for protection. *"These six cities shall be a refuge, both for the children of Israel, and for the **stranger**, and for the **sojourner** among them: that every one that killeth any person unawares may flee thither"* (Num 35:15).

King David describes his people's position before God with these same terms, *"For we are **strangers** before thee, and **sojourners**, as were all our fathers: our days on the earth are as a shadow, and there is none abiding"* (1 Chr 29:15); *"Hear my prayer, O LORD, and give ear unto my cry; hold not thy peace at my tears: for I am a **stranger** with thee, and a **sojourner**, as all my fathers were"* (Psa 39:12).

But there are differences from the *ger*. The *toshav* could not participate in Passover. *"A **foreigner** [toshav] and an hired servant shall not eat thereof"* (Exo 12:45). He could also be bought as a slave. *"Moreover of the children of the **strangers** [toshavim] that do sojourn among you, of them shall ye buy, and of their families that are with you, which they begat in your land: and they shall be your possession. And ye shall take them as an inheritance for your children after you, to inherit them for a possession; they shall be your bondmen for ever..."* (Lev 25:45-46a).

The Nekar

Another word sometimes translated "stranger" is *nekar* (# 5236). We have the words translated from *nekar* bolded in the following verses.

The *nekar* was to be circumcised after he was bought and then became part of an Israeli's household. *"And he that is eight days old shall be circumcised among you, every man child in your generations, he that is born in the house, or bought with money of any **stranger**, which is not of thy seed"* (Gen 17:12). But whether circumcised or not, he could not celebrate Passover. *"And the LORD said unto Moses and Aaron, This is the ordinance of the passover: There shall no **stranger** eat thereof:"* (Exo 12:43).

Israel was forbidden to lend among themselves based on usury, or interest, but they could do so with the *nekar*. *"Unto a **stranger** thou mayest lend upon usury; but unto thy brother thou shalt not lend upon usury: that the LORD thy God may bless thee in all that thou settest thine hand to in the land whither thou goest to possess it"* (Deut 23:20). Also, the *nekar* could never be king over Israel. *"Thou shalt in any wise set him king over thee, whom the LORD thy God shall choose: one from among thy brethren shalt thou set king over thee: thou mayest not* [do not have the authority or right to] *set a **stranger** over thee, which is not thy brother"* (Deut 17:15).

One of God's accusations against rebellious Israel was that they brought *"into my sanctuary **strangers*** [lit. sons of *nekarim*], *uncircumcised in heart, and uncircumcised in flesh...to pollute* [defile, desecrate] *it..."* (Ezek 44:7a). Obviously, those *nekarim* **should** have been circumcised in flesh according to Gen 17:12 quoted before. This was Israel's neglected responsibility. Not only that, the Levites had allowed unbelievers among these uncircumcised *nekarim* into God's sanctuary to do the work they should have done themselves, as recorded in the same passage (Ezekiel 44:8), *"And ye have not kept the charge of mine holy things: but ye have set keepers of my charge in my sanctuary for yourselves."*

*"Thus saith the Lord GOD; No **stranger**, uncircumcised in heart, nor uncircumcised in flesh, shall enter into my sanctuary, of any **stranger** that is among the children of Israel"* (Ezek 44:9). Here God implies that the *nekarim* who become circumcised in both heart *and* flesh *would* have access to His house. Unlike the caste system of India, God's regulations provide for "upward mobility." *Nekarim* could rise above their spiritual lot in life by submitting themselves to the God of Israel. This foreshadows the "stranger" of today who, having been circumcised in heart, becomes a living stone in God's Holy Spirit temple.

All of the following verses can also be seen as foreshadows of the Christian. For example, look at what Isaiah 56:3a, 6-8 states, *"Neither let the son of the **stranger** [nekar], that hath joined himself to the LORD, speak, saying, The LORD hath utterly separated me from his people...Also the sons of the **stranger** [nekar], that join themselves to the LORD, to serve him, and to love the name of the LORD, to be his servants* [includes worshippers], *every one that keepeth the sabbath from polluting it, and taketh hold of* [with determination, courage and strength] *my covenant; Even them will I bring to my holy mountain, and make them joyful in my house of prayer: their burnt offerings and their sacrifices shall be accepted* [approved] *upon mine altar; for mine house shall be called an house of prayer for all people. The Lord GOD which gathereth the outcasts of Israel saith, Yet will I gather others to him, beside those that are gathered unto him."* Here again we see the joining, or "grafting in," of the stranger/gentile to the commonwealth of the house of Israel *because of the stranger's commitment to Israel's God.*

Solomon prayed for the *nekarim* who would come to pray in Jerusalem to find favor with God because of His great name, *"Moreover concerning a **stranger**, that is not of thy people Israel, but cometh out of a far country for thy name's sake; (For they shall hear of thy great name, and of thy strong hand, and of thy stretched out arm;) when he shall come and pray* [or intercede] *toward this house; Hear thou in heaven thy dwelling place, and do according to all that the **stranger** calleth to thee for: that all people of the earth may know thy name, to fear thee, as do thy people Israel; and that they may know that this house, which I have builded, is called by thy name"* (1 Kings 8:41-43). So come!

Finally, Isaiah prophesies that *nekarim* will minister to Israel, helping in her end time restoration, *"And the sons of strangers* [nekarim] *shall build up thy walls...And strangers* [zarim – see below] *shall stand and feed your flocks, and the sons of the alien* [nekar] *shall be your plowmen and your vinedressers"* (Isa 60:10a; 61:5).

The *Zar*

One final word translated as "stranger" is *zar* (#2114), which means neither an acquaintance nor one related to the community in any way. The following verses show the distinction between the *zar* and the *ger, toshav* and even the *nekar*.

A *zar* was not to eat any of the holy sacrifices. In a foreshadow of Communion,[8] *"And Aaron and his sons shall eat the flesh of the ram, and the bread that is in the basket, by the door of the tabernacle of the congregation. And they shall eat those things wherewith the atonement was made, to consecrate and to sanctify them: but a stranger* [zar] *shall not eat thereof, because they are holy"* (Exo 29:32-33). In Leviticus, the same thought is continued but with added parameters, *"There shall no stranger* [zar] eat *of the holy thing: a sojourner of the priest, or an hired servant, shall not eat of the holy thing. But if the priest buy any soul with his money, he shall eat of it, and he that is born in his house: they shall eat of his meat. If the priest's daughter also be married unto a stranger* [zar], *she may not eat of an offering of the holy things"* (Lev 22:10-12). There is a rich parallel here between a priest buying a soul who is then able to eat of the holy things and God purchasing us with His own blood (Acts 20:28), called redemption, and our freedom to then take communion.

The *zar* was forbidden to be anointed with the holy oil (see Exo 30:33). They were not allowed to help with the tabernacle or priesthood. Their presence defiled God's House. *"And when the tabernacle setteth forward, the Levites shall take it down: and when the tabernacle is to be pitched, the Levites shall set it up: and the stranger that cometh nigh shall be put to death"* (Num 1:51); *"And thou shalt appoint Aaron and his sons, and they shall wait on* [protect or attend to] *their priest's office: and the stranger that cometh nigh shall be put to death"* (Num 3:10; see also 16:40).

David says that the *zar* does not believe in the God of Israel. *"For strangers are risen up against me, and oppressors seek after my soul: they have not set God before them. Selah"* (Psa 54:3). God is angry with Israel for being corrupted by *zarim*. *"Only acknowledge thine iniquity, that thou hast transgressed* [rebelled] *against the LORD thy God, and hast scattered thy ways to the strangers under every green tree, and ye have not obeyed my voice, saith the LORD"* (Jer 3:13).

Accordingly He uses them as an instrument of judgment on His people. *"...Like as ye have forsaken me, and served strange gods in your land, so shall ye serve **strangers** in a land that is not yours"* (Jer 5:19b); *"And I will...deliver you into the hands of **strangers**, and will execute judgments among you"* (Ezek 11:9; also 7:21; 28:10). When Jerusalem was finally destroyed, Israel experienced the fulfillment of God's threatened judgments. *"Our inheritance is turned* [turned over] *to **strangers** [zarim], our houses to aliens [nekarim]"* (Lam 5:2).

However, when God saves Israel, she will no more be in bondage to *zarim*. *"For it shall come to pass in that day, saith the LORD of hosts, that I will break his yoke from off thy neck, and will burst thy bonds, and **strangers** shall no more serve themselves of him* [Israel]*: But they* [Israel] *shall serve the LORD their God, and David their king* [metaphor for Messiah]*, whom I will raise up unto them"* (Jer 30:8-9).

Isaiah praises God because of His judgment on the *zarim* (25:2,5), but he also foresees a time when God will use even the *zarim* to help with Israel's final restoration. Today we see many gentile *non-believers* helping to restore the nation. *"And **strangers** [zarim] shall stand and feed your flocks, and the sons of the alien shall be your plowmen and your vinedressers"* (Isa 61:5). Could this also foresee Israel's population of Moslem Arabs, descendants of thousands who flooded in from surrounding nations in the 20th century to find work? It must include the unbelievers among the imported Eastern European and Far East laborers in Israel today.

After our Lord's return, His city of Jerusalem, will allow no unbelievers, no *zarim*. *"So shall ye know that I am the LORD your God dwelling in Zion, my holy mountain: then shall Jerusalem be holy, and there shall no **strangers** pass through her any more"* (Joel 3:17). Was Paul thinking of this when he said to gentile believers, *"Now therefore **ye are no more** [no longer] **strangers and foreigners, but fellowcitizens** with the saints* [in context: believing Jews]*, and of the household of God;"* (Eph 2:19).

The Stranger in the Land

So who has a biblical right to live in Israel peacefully with the children of Israel? Anyone law-abiding, including the heathen, the *zarim* (Isa 61:5). Who has a right to the land itself? The sojourners, the *gerim*, who trust in the God of the land of Israel and obey His laws, settling down as part of the people of Israel. *"And it shall come to pass, that ye shall divide it by lot for an inheritance unto you, and to the **strangers** [gerim] **that sojourn among you**, which shall beget children among you: and they shall* *be unto you as born in the country among the children of Israel; they shall have inheritance with you among the tribes of Israel. And it shall come to pass, that in what tribe the **stranger sojourneth**, there shall ye give him his inheritance, saith the Lord GOD"* (Ezek 47:22-23).

Biblically, a believer who recognizes Israel's covenant stewardship in this Land and considers himself part of the people of Israel could have an inheritance here. But *biblically*, a Moslem or any other kind of heathen does not have an inheritance here. How God deals with this today politically is up to Him, but that is the scriptural principle. God is not happy with people who bring strange gods into His land or with Israel's accepting them (see Jer 3:13 above; also see Jer 12:14-17). In many nations politics and religion are kept separate. In Israel they cannot be separated. The God of Creation has chosen this Land for His physical home, and He is coming soon to take up residency once more.

Conclusion

Queen Esther can be seen as a portrait of the last days Church. She is chosen to become the bride of the world's most powerful king, yet she hides her Hebrew roots! At a time when the existence of her people is threatened, Esther reveals her true family connection and intercedes for her people.

Bride of Messiah, Israel is being threatened with extinction through satanic attacks in every area right now - spiritual, socio-cultural, and political – and you have access to the King's throne. Plead for grace and mercy for Israel. As Mordecai says to Esther (4:13), *"Think not with thyself* [lit: in your soul] *that thou shalt escape in the king's house, more than all the Jews. For if thou altogether holdest thy peace at this time, then shall there enlargement* [relief] *and deliverance arise to the Jews from another place; but thou and thy father's house shall be destroyed..."* (Est 4:13-14a). The Hebrew word translated "destroyed" means just that: to perish, vanish, or go astray. Yes, precious Bride of Christ, your spiritual life is at stake. Israel's roots support you, not the other way around (Rom 11:18). If you think Israel's existence does not matter to you – you are walking in deception!

God will save Israel because of His covenant promises, and because He is the faithful God who has acted, and will act, not for Israel's sake, but for His holy name's sake (Ezek 36:22-23). But He wants His Bride's help.[9]

The encouragement Mordecai speaks to Esther applies to the Church today, *"...and who knoweth whether thou art come to the kingdom for such a time as this?"*

May He give us all grace for the courage to do what He calls us to do. *"Your kingdom come - Your will be done on earth as it is in heaven,"* in the name of our Messiah and Lord, Yeshua. Amen!

---

1   Rom 11 and Eph 2:11-3:10.

2   Chapt. 18, The Bride in the *Tanach*.

3   See the following for more information on this subject: *Inside Islam* by Reza F. Safa (Creation House, 1996); *Who is this Allah?* by G.J.O. Moshay (Dorchester House Pub., 1995) *The Islamic Invasion* by Robert A. Morey (Harvest House Pub., 1992).

4   See *The Theological Wordbook of the Old Testament*, Editors Harris, Archer and Waltke, Moody Press, Chicago, Vol. I, pp.155-156.

5   Believers in Yeshua have their harts circumcised. Foreskin circumcision, according to Paul, "avails nothing" for them, although Jewish believers are still to circumcise their sons as a sign of God's eternal covenant with Israel (Gen 17:9-14). But gentile believers can get so caught up in their "Jewish" roots that they forget that it is a spiritual and social connection, not a fleshly one. We personally know of one young man who circumcised himself with dire results! (Rom 10:2).

6   Do not extrapolate this fact into a modern day command to destroy pagans - something the church has wrongly condoned off and on down through the ages. Yeshua's disciples are commanded to love and pray for enemies, although nations still have every right to defend themselves.

    God's command to Israel to cleanse the Promised Land from pagan influence can be seen from two perspectives. One, it was necessary to protect Israel from the corruption effect of paganism in their new life as a nation separated to God (Num 23:9; Deut 7:1-6,16). Secondly, Israel was God's instrument of judgment on those nations who were given adequate time to repent, but chose not to serve God (Gen 15:16; Deut 9:1-6).

7   See Chapter 3, Endnote 1.

8   See Chapter 11, sec. "After the Resurrection," commentary on Psa 22:26.

9   Whatever your general prayer burden for your community - whether concerning salvation, government, media, pollution, youth, crime, abortion, the elderly, whatever it is - if it applies - pray it for Israel first, and be prepared for spiritual warfare as well as blessings.

Epilogue

In Psalm 1 the person who delights in God's teaching and meditates on it day and night is likened to a tree planted by a river. Such a tree never dries up and its fruit never fails. It is nourished when the water from the river penetrates the soil of the riverbank and picks up nutrients from the soil. The tree is not immersed in the river or it would drown. The water or the soil, separately, cannot sustain life. The river represents the Spirit of God. The tree must be planted in the soil of Truth - the Word of God. The Word of God is said to be "alive" because it is saturated with the Spirit of God, just as cells are always in contact with blood vessels, and just as riverbanks never lack moisture.

If you want to grow spiritually, you cannot separate the Spirit of God from the Word of God. They are a unity, a channel of spiritual power and life. Yeshua said, *"It is the Spirit who gives life...**The words that I speak to you are spirit** and they are life"* (John 6:63 NKJV), and again, *"If you abide in Me and **My words** abide in you, you will ask what you desire, and it shall be done for you. By this My Father is glorified, that you bear much fruit; so you will be My disciples"* (John 15:7-8 NKJV).

Yeshua said that those who believe in Him would receive spiritual power, that *"rivers of living water"* would flow from them. However, there is a requirement for receiving this power (John 7:38-39). Yeshua stated this requirement when He *"...cried out, saying, 'If anyone thirsts, let him come to Me, and let him who believes in Me drink'"* (John 7:37b NKJV). In Proverbs 1 Wisdom personified cries out, *"Turn* [repent] *you at my reproof: behold, I will pour out my spirit unto you, **I will make known my words** unto you"* (v 23). Spiritual power filters through the Word of God, bringing the nourishing Truth into the roots of our faith. The roots of our faith transport that power upward through

Israel's Olive Tree, into the branches which turn that power, that "living water", into spiritual fruit.

In order to bring Yeshua's life to the world, believers need to "eat, drink and breathe" the Word of God, to immerse themselves and be refreshed in God's Word and to dialog with Yeshua while doing so. This is communion with God, helped by the Holy Spirit. *"God is faithful, by whom you were called into the fellowship of His Son.."* (I Cor 1:9 NKJV). There is no other "formula" for receiving daily spiritual power from God.

We desire to see Yeshua's Body, rooted in truth and ripening spiritual fruit while standing strong against temptations and the storms of false teaching. Pray that the Lord raises up pastors, teachers, and other workers to edify His Body. The night is coming when no one can work. Do you desire to be fully equipped for the end of the age? *"Study to shew thyself approved unto God, a workman that needeth not to be ashamed, rightly dividing the word of truth"* (2 Tim 2:15).

"And he showed me a pure river of water of life, clear as crystal, proceeding from the throne of God and of the Lamb. In the middle of its street and on either side of the river, was the tree of life, which bore twelve fruits, each tree yielding its fruit every month. And the leaves of the tree were for the healing of the nations. And there shall be no more curse, but the throne of God and of the Lamb shall be in it, and His servants shall serve Him." (Rev 22:1-3, NKJV).

Roots of Our Faith was created from articles originally written for *Christian Friends of Israel* and sent out regularly in their mailings as well as in our own newsletter, *Watchmen from Jerusalem*. In 1995 the first twelve articles were published by *CFI* as a book, which has since sold out.

After twelve more articles of the *Roots of Our Faith* series were written, we and *CFI* decided that all of the articles should be combined in one book. This required expansion and extensive revision, reformatting, plus a new cover - in other words, a new book. The revised and expanded *Roots of Our Faith* is an excellent resource for personal study, as a Bible study guide, as a reference for sermon preparation, or as a class textbook.

Chuck, a gifted speaker, travels world-wide giving up-to-date *Roots of Our Faith* and *Israel and the Church* seminars. To schedule Chuck for a teaching seminar, conference, or to subscribe to our bi-monthly newsletter, *Watchmen from Jerusalem*, please contact:

Chuck & Karen Cohen, PO Box 427, Jerusalem 91003, Israel
e-mail: watchmenfromjerusalem@yahoo.com

To arrange a CFI Conference or to order *Roots of Our Faith* books
please contact:

Christian Friends of Israel
P.O. Box 1813 Jerusalem 91015, ISRAEL
Tel: 972-2-6264172 • Fax: 972-2-6264955
e-mail: cfi@cfijerusalem.org • website: www.cfijerusalem.org

Scripture Index

Topic Index